T0369877

Book Supplement Series to the
Journal of Chinese Philosophy
Editor: Chung-ying Cheng

CHINESE PHILOSOPHY IN EXCAVATED EARLY TEXTS

Edited by

Chung-ying Cheng and

Franklin Perkins

This edition first published 2010
© 2010 Journal of Chinese Philosophy

Registered Office
John Wiley & Sons Ltd, The Atrium, Southern Gate, Chichester, West Sussex, PO19 8SQ, United Kingdom

Editorial Offices
350 Main Street, Malden, MA 02148-5020, USA
9600 Garsington Road, Oxford, OX4 2DQ, UK
The Atrium, Southern Gate, Chichester, West Sussex, PO19 8SQ, UK

For details of our global editorial offices, for customer services, and for information about how to apply for permission to reuse the copyright material in this book please see our website at www.wiley.com/wiley-blackwell.

The right of Chung-ying Cheng to be identified as the author of the editorial material in this work has been asserted in accordance with the Copyright, Designs and Patents Act 1988.

All rights reserved. No part of this publication may be reproduced, stored in a retrieval system, or transmitted, in any form or by any means, electronic, mechanical, photocopying, recording or otherwise, except as permitted by the UK Copyright, Designs and Patents Act 1988, without the prior permission of the publisher.

Wiley also publishes its books in a variety of electronic formats. Some content that appears in print may not be available in electronic books.

Designations used by companies to distinguish their products are often claimed as trademarks. All brand names and product names used in this book are trade names, service marks, trademarks or registered trademarks of their respective owners. The publisher is not associated with any product or vendor mentioned in this book. This publication is designed to provide accurate and authoritative information in regard to the subject matter covered. It is sold on the understanding that the publisher is not engaged in rendering professional services. If professional advice or other expert assistance is required, the services of a competent professional should be sought.

Library of Congress Cataloging-in-Publication Data

Chinese philosophy in excavated early texts / edited by Chung-ying Cheng and Franklin Perkins.
    p. cm. — (Book supplement series to the Journal of Chinese philosophy)
    ISBN 978-1-4443-4989-4
  1. Philosophy, Chinese—221 B.C.–960 A.D.   2. Manuscripts, Chinese.   I. Cheng, Zhongying, 1935– II. Perkins, Franklin.
    B126.C495 2010
    181'.11—dc22

                                                                    2010050379

Set in 11.25 on 13.25pt Times Ten by Toppan Best-set Premedia Limited

01—2010

Book Supplement Series to the

Journal of Chinese Philosophy

Editor: Chung-ying Cheng

CHINESE PHILOSOPHY IN EXCAVATED EARLY TEXTS

Edited by
Chung-ying Cheng and Franklin Perkins

CHUNG-YING CHENG

INTRODUCTION:
CHINESE PHILOSOPHY IN EXCAVATED
EARLY TEXTS

In 1973, *Boshu Yijing yu Laozi*《帛書易經與老子》were excavated in Mawangdui. In 1993, *Zhushu Zaoqi Rujia Zhuzuo*
《竹書早期儒家著作》were unearthed in Guodian. Recently, more
zhushu 竹書 were discovered, which are known as *Qinghuajian*
《清華簡》. In 1997, a group of excavated texts in bamboo inscriptions
were bought by the Shanghai Metropolitan Museum and thus has
become known as《上海竹书》. These newly discovered texts aroused a
great deal of enthusiasm among many Chinese and Western scholars in
pursuing information, knowledge and wisdom from ancient Chinese
tradition of Confucianism and Daoism as if those philosophers of
ancient time have come back to life all at a sudden from the underground to enlighten us. For myself I started early with my intense
interest in the Boshu Yijing and then gradually turned to the Guodian
and Shanbo 上博 manuscripts of Daoism and Confucianism. What I
have been interested are the philosophical significances of those texts
in regard to issues of Chinese concepts of cosmic being and becoming,
human self-being and human self-transformation, knowing, understanding, moral thinking and moral action. Specifically, the way those
concepts are formed and developed suggested to me a methodology of
growing and transformation from some notion of origin, source and
root to a full-bodied concretized or concrete reality in a process of
interaction, differentiation and integration, which I come to describes
as "onto-genetic" or "onto-generative" (***ben-ti***). This no doubt is
related to early my onto-hermeneutical thinking. In a period from 2004
to 2009 I have explored intermittently questions of onto-hermeneutic
interpretation in early and contemporary Chinese Philosophy In light
of excavated texts such as "***taiyi sheng shui*** 太一生水," philosophical
reasons why Xunzi objects to and criticizes Wu Xing theory attributed
to Zisi and Mencius, and whether we may understand the theory of
nature-emotion (***xing-qing***) as implying an onto-generative integration of Zisi, Mencius and Xunzi.

CHUNG-YING CHENG, Professor, Department of Philosophy, University of Hawaii
at Manoa. Specialties: Confucianism and Neo-Confucianism, hermeneutics/onto-
hermeneutics, philosophy of language. E-mail: ccheng@hawaii.edu

Journal of Chinese Philosophy, Supplement to Volume 37 (2010) 1–5
© 2010 Journal of Chinese Philosophy

The above anticipations motivated my goal of developing a special theme on the philosophical studies of these excavated materials. I cordially invited Professor Franklin Perkins of DePaul University, who shared the common thoughts and enthusiasm, to coedit the present Supplement issue.

What are the broad significance and value of these underground texts dated back to 300–350 BCE? Obviously, these underground texts are tremendously significant and valuable, because they represent and indicate a genuine part of ancient history with the mark of intelligence and insight of human being, and this should make us wonder how we are related to them and in what way they have actually contributed to what we know today. Hence to know the texts from the past is to know humanity at the present. In this sense we could be informed about the times and sometimes events under which these ancient texts were formed.

For instance, the discovery of *Qinghuajian*, which deals with questions of transferring or succeeding political rule as recorded in the Chinese Classic *Shangshu*《尚書》or *Shiji*《史記》(Book of History), could indicate or add weight to the belief that the Xia 夏 Dynasty was not just a historical legend but a culture with legitimate rule in a time earlier than either Shang 商 or Zhou 周. However, the significance and value of these excavated texts are far beyond historical and cultural considerations.

Such canonic materials present themselves as human thoughts composing of analytical distinctions and empirical observations with well-considered evaluations in either explicit arguments or hidden ones. In this sense they address to us as philosophical dialogues and dialectical explorations, showing a process of inquiry and a way of thinking. As we have examples of philosophical thinking and definitions in major classics of Daoism and Confucianism, we have come to a vivid representation and detailed delineation of meaning and use of words and terms, often ending in highly insightful propositions that explain and sometimes illuminate texts we know in our received tradition. They show versions or texts of differences and variations because of local innovations or renovations.

It is always intriguing to raise question as to whether there is a standard text in the beginning or how a plurality comes to exist after a paradigm left a cluster of expositions. In the case of the *Yijing* 《易經》(the *Book of Changes*) there could be a standard proto-type text in use for thousand years, but the same system of symbols could be arranged in different ways because of multiple orderings of numbers. But for the Confucian tradition the teaching of Confucius could result in division of schools and excavated texts such as "*Wu Xing*" 〈五行〉and "*Xing Zi Ming Chu*" 〈性自命出〉(XZMC henceforth) could represent ontological and analytical explorations that end in the formation of other classical texts such as *Zhong Yong* 《中庸》 and *Daxue*《大學》. This type of similar variations in method or representation may apply to the case of excavated Daoist texts like *Daodejing*《道德經》 A and B as well, but we witness here far more accord and unison of representation than in Confucian texts. By and large, these texts Daoist or Confucian disclose how disciples of Confucius or believers of Laozi are truly inspired followers of the *dao*. They together make ancient Chinese indisputably a people of philosophy par excellence. Philosophy here means wisdom of care as well as love of wisdom.

One singularly important issue concerns how we come to have virtuous actions (*de zhi xing* 德之行) as exemplified in actions of *ren*, *yi*, *li*, *zhi*, or *xin* as taught by Confucius. The acumen of this question lies in that we can describe these actions of virtue as simply actions not necessarily having anything to do with virtue. The question therefore reduces to where virtues come from, from an internal process of impulse in mind or from compliance with an external standard? It is in fact a question derived from the inner tension between *li* and *ren* in the Confucius' thinking. As Confucius speaks of unity of the *dao* of his thought, what would be a Confucian answer?

The *Boshu* and *Guodian* texts on *Wu Xing* or five virtues lead us to think that virtues must bear a mark of their own as derived from human mind or human nature. It leads us to think that those moral principles must be shared by all men so that our actions based on them will not only be called good but morally virtuous. The question of internal ontogenesis of virtues is the first query into moral psychology that would have to lead to the question of the ultimate origin of human nature or humanity.

How does question of an internal origination of virtues lead to a theory of human nature is extremely interesting as it marks a great difference of Chinese or Confucian philosophy from Greek philosophy. Whereas Socrates and Plato could take human minds as taking copies from Platonic ideas and thus satisfying the question of origin, the Chinese or Chinese seekers have to reflect and speculate on how human beings become human beings as a whole body, not just as minds. This is, the Confucian has to take feelings and emotions of humanity seriously and observes them to be constituents of virtues that are eventually shared by all people. Hence they come to take the common way of wisdom and virtue in human interactions as derived from and reflected in human feelings. This is the statement of "*Dao sheng yu qing* 道生於情" in the excavated text of XZMC. What is to be taken in mind is the vividness of the lived-through quality of deep experience of the thinker, and it is not a state of pure speculation but an articulation of vision and embodiment of the vision in the individual philosophical thought of the author(s) as the thinker(s).

There are two more instances as to how these excavated texts appeal to our own observations and reflections on things of history and nature. On the history side the excavated texts of *Rongchengshi* 容成氏 and *Tangyuzhidao* 唐虞之道 seem to indicate a utopia in the imagined past of antiquity, reflecting a state of both criticism and aspiration of the times during the Warring States Period. However, the authors of these texts who present the case of succession of sagely yielding (*shan rang* 禪讓) need not to be simply treated as utopian dreamers of the early Daoists, rather, they can be seen as suggesting a different way of conceiving the rise of human society and political government.

For we could well imagine that in an early ecology of abundance of life supplies, people needs a ruler who would volunteer to organize people for resisting common foes or for solving problems because of natural disasters. The political leadership of a ruler is taxing but the ruler has to use it without selfish desires in order to be worthy of respect given to him by the people supporting him, and he must start as a talented person in the first place. This volunteer sage-king origin of government needs not to be a sheer figment of imagination, for we can see still selfless people today who did just the same and they did that because they can also enjoy doing it. This is different from and even in stark contrast with theories of origins of government as we find in Hobbes, Lock, and Rousseau.

Furthermore, I want to point out the text titled "*Taiyi Sheng Shui* 《太一生水》" as a sophiscated illustration of the Chinese cosmological and cosmogonic way of thinking. It is clear that *taiyi* is not the same as *taiji* that in the *Yizhuan*《易傳》gives rise to a sequence of symbolic states of *yin* and *yang* combinations, which would stand for changes and transformations of both nature and human affairs. To speak of giving birth to water is highly Daoistic and *Yijing*-oriented. Why so? For the Daoists water is always a symbol of formless and abundance, and for the *Yijing* thinkers water would represent the states of change that spans the invisible vapor or *qi* 氣 and the life that is nourished by water. The deeper aspect of this text is in the idea of "*fanbu* 反哺" feedback or "reverse nourishing."

That is, the very spirits of heaven and earth is with all life and human beings in a nourishing and "return nourishing" cycle. This is a cycle of life that would continue and sustain by itself. There is the implication that the universe is indeed a cosmos or a living harmony in the process of ceaseless generation, for what return nourishing has made possible is that there is no separation of the present from the past and the upper from the lower, all of which are mutually supported in an interdependent network. This image of the world at large is a world that Daoists and *Yijing* thinkers and diviners could embrace without disparagement, even though we may not have to use *yin-yang* symbols for showing how interactions have taken place. They have taken place in the simplest way, the nourishing and return nourishing way of water and things nourished by water. We may need this cosmic image for our environmental consciousness and our survival may depend on raising this consciousness.

It is clear that among the nine articles there are many highly significant topics presented and discussed by well-established specialists, philosophers and historians, of the fields. The formation of this volume is an arduous process because diverse approaches have to be introduced and appreciated to reconsider these fundamental issues of the *Boshu* and *Zhujian* in a philosophical manner. The multiple styles of writing have to be made in uniform and the quotations of the inscriptions have to be made congruous. This means that both writers and editors have to go through a tedious process of inquiring into the excavated texts many times and carefully weighing evidence and interpretation in balance. It is indeed a test of the method of onto-hermeneutical methodology, which is a theory I have been advocating. To a large extent, it is in fact presupposed by many contributors in presenting their results in coherent and relevant reference.

But all these difficulties, linguistic, technical, or ideological, have to be overcome by our supporting team. First of all, Professor Franklin Perkins not only took part in the editorship, but more than that, he has been devoted to many painstaking labors of corresponding, translating/retranslating, revising, and copy-editing. I thank Frank for joining me in time and relieving me in need. Our Managing Editor Linyu Gu went over each paper many times and made sure each detail as perfect as possible. I thank her for her diligence, patience, and suggestions on behalf of all contributors. I was much boosted in spirit because of these colleagues in pushing the publication to reality, for without them I doubt whether we would have the present result at hand. As always, I thank On-cho Ng, our Associate Editor, for taking care of rights matters and other issues on my behalf in the final stage. We also would like to express our warm gratitude to Wiley-Blackwell's editors whose hard work made it possible to meet the tight publication schedule. Most of all, on behalf of the *Journal*, I deeply thank our contributors from both Mainland China and America. They took two solid years to make these fruitions, and their public spirits made their expertise available to our readers and other scholars, who are involved in a noble enterprise of envisioning and articulating the formation of early Chinese philosophy, whether Daoist, Confucian, or *Yijing*-ist.

UNVERSITY OF HAWAII AT MANOA
Honolulu, Hawaii

LI XUEQIN AND LIU GUOZHONG

THE TSINGHUA BAMBOO STRIPS AND ANCIENT CHINESE CIVILIZATION[1]

In July 1925, Wang Guowei 王國維 gave a famous lecture at Tsinghua University, entitled "Scholarly Knowledge of New Discoveries in China in the Past Twenty to Thirty Years."[2] Professor Wang pointed out at the start that in China, "from ancient times, most new scholarly knowledge has arisen from new discoveries," emphasizing how in history, newly discovered materials have given great impetus to the development of scholarship in China. Moreover, he said that two of the greatest discoveries in Chinese scholarship from the Han on were the Kongzi wall documents and the Ji Tomb (*jizhong* 汲塚) documents. Both of these discoveries relate to the recently excavated Warring States bamboo texts.

The Kong wall documents were bamboo texts discovered in a wall in the ancient residence of Kongzi in Qufu, Shandong Province, in the early period of the Western Han. Their content centers on the *Shang Shu* 《尚書》. Among them were sixteen chapters that were not included in the "New Text" *Shang Shu* transmitted from the early Han by Fu Sheng 伏生. Because the *Shang Shu* then discovered used characters written in the early period of the Warring States, with character forms quite different from the Han Dynasty *li* 隸 writing style, people have called them the "Old Text" *Shang Shu*. The "Old Text" and "New Text" versions of the *Shang Shu* have obvious differences in chapter divisions, character forms, content, and other aspects. Because of these differences, this discovery led to what is known as the conflict between old and new texts, which became a great issue in the history of Chinese scholarship and whose influence still remains down to the present. The Ji Tomb documents were a collection of bamboo texts from the state of Wei 魏 in the Warring States Period, which were discovered inside a tomb in Ji Prefecture, Henan Province, at the beginning of the Western Jin 晉. The excavated texts had

LI XUEQIN, Professor and Director, Institute for Chinese Thought and Culture, Tsinghua University. Specialties: ancient Chinese history and culture, archaeological materials, philology. E-mail: xqli@mail.tsinghua.edu.cn
LIU GUOZHONG, Professor, College of Humanities, Tsinghua University. Specialties: ancient Chinese history and culture, excavated texts. Email: lgzh6@yahoo.com.cn

Journal of Chinese Philosophy, Supplement to Volume 37 (2010) 6–15
© 2010 Journal of Chinese Philosophy

more than seventy chapters, the most important of which was a historical text in the form of annals, known as the *Bamboo Annals* (*Zhushu Jinian*《竹書紀年》). This had an important effect in correcting the chronology of Chinese history and other historical facts, and it has received great attention from scholars, many of whom have over the ages used the "Bamboo Annals" to correct the errors of the *Shi Ji* 《史記》.

For these reasons, the discoveries of the Kong wall documents and the Ji Tomb bamboo texts have had a great influence in the history of scholarship. Unfortunately, the materials originally discovered were all later lost in transmission. The "Old Text" *Shang Shu* that we now see has lost the original appearance of the Kong wall documents and was forged by people in the Wei-Jin Period. There is thus no way to rely on them in researching the early history of Chinese culture. The *Bamboo Annals* was lost early and no longer exists, so scholars can only compile a few lost passages by relying on quotations in other ancient texts. This content is limited, though, leaving behind endless regrets for those researching ancient Chinese civilization.

Since the twentieth century, an immense number of bamboo strips have been excavated from various places around China, dating from the Warring States down to the Wei-Jin Period. These already altogether approach 300,000 strips. In addition, there are excavated silk manuscript materials, such as the Zidanku 子彈庫 Chu silk manuscripts, the Mawangdui 馬王堆 Han tomb silk manuscripts, and so on. It is as if these bamboo and silk manuscripts have opened up for us an underground library of truly immense value. As Qiu Xigui 裘錫圭 puts it:

> These materials can help us solve problems that were originally unsolvable or even fundamentally undiscovered in the ancient texts that were transmitted over generations. They can also help us examine the achievements of those who previously corrected and annotated the ancient books, and determine what is correct in some unresolved controversies.[3]

If we categorize the newly discovered bamboo and silk manuscripts according to content, they can generally be divided into the categories of "books" (*shuji* 書籍) and "documents" (*wenshu* 文書). Because the manuscripts include every kind of classic text that people of the time were accustomed to reading, they have important significance for researching the history of Chinese culture and the development of scholarship. Many of the important bamboo and silk manuscripts, like the Yinqiaoshan 銀雀山 Han bamboos, the Mawangdui silk manuscripts, the Guodian 郭店 Chu bamboos strips, the Shanghai Musuem Chu bamboos strips, and so on, have led to lengthy and heated discussions in the scholarly world both in and out of China, and to a large degree have transformed our knowledge of the thought and culture of China's early period. Research on the bamboo and silk manuscripts has already been recognized as a prominent area of study that is vitally developing.

The types of texts that have already been excavated are truly plentiful. The newly excavated bamboo and silk manuscripts already cover all of the categories used in the "Treatise on Literature" (*Yiwen Zhi* 〈藝文志〉) chapter of the *Han Shu*《漢書》 to categorize the texts of the Han Dynasty imperial library, such as the six classics, master's works, odes and rhapsodies, military texts, numerology, divination techniques, and so on. But what has been most regrettable for scholars is that, among these, they have so far not been able to discover materials like the *Shang Shu* or *Bamboo Annals*, materials that would be important for researching the history of the early period of Chinese civilization.[4] This had undeniably been a great gap.

To our delight, the opportunity to fill this gap has finally appeared. In July 2008, through the donation of an alumnus, Tsinghua University rescued and received into its collection a mass of Warring States bamboo strips that had been smuggled out of China. This collection has become commonly known as the precious documents of the Tsinghua Bamboo Strips. They belong in age to the late middle of the Warring States Period, and they should have come from within the boundaries of what was then the state of Chu. The quantity of these bamboo strips has been arranged and calculated, and altogether they number 2,388 strips (including broken pieces). The form and structure of the strips vary greatly. Regarding length, the longest are 46 cm (corresponding to two *chi* 尺 in the Warring States Period), and the shortest are just 10 cm. The longer strips all were bound with three lines of string, so that the regular grooves and even traces of some of the binding strings can be clearly seen. Most of the character forms are written in a refined and neat way, and the majority have come down to the present still exceptionally clear. A smaller number of bamboo strips still have red marking lines, the so-called "Columns of Vermilion Thread" (*Zhusilan* 朱絲欄), which are truly beautiful to see.

On October 14, 2008, Tsinghua University invited eleven scholars and specialists (from Peking University, Fudan University, Jilin University, Wuhan University, Sun Yat-sen University, Chinese University of Hong Kong, the National Bureau for Cultural Relics, the National Institute for Cultural Heritage, the Shanghai Museum, and the Jingzhou Museum) to open a "Conference to Authenticate the Bamboo Strips of the Tsinghua University Collection." At that conference, Li Xueqin introduced the process of acquiring the Tsinghua bamboo strips and the general condition of the strips at that time. Moreover,

he asked the eleven authoritative scholars and specialists to undertake a detailed examination and authentication of the strips in the
collection. The specialists together affirmed:

> The content of this mass of bamboo strips is rich and plentiful. On
> initial examination, most of them are written books (*shuji* 書籍),
> among which are some in the categories of "classics" (*jing* 經) and
> "histories" (*shi* 史), which are extremely important for investigating
> Chinese history and traditional culture. Most of these have not pre-
> viously been seen in pre-Qin bamboo manuscripts, and they hold the
> highest scholarly value. They also have great value for researching
> the form and structure of texts constructed from bamboo, ancient
> Chinese characters, and so on. . . . From looking at the form and
> structure of the bamboo strips and the characters, they should be
> Warring States era bamboo texts excavated from the area of Chu.
> They are truly precious historical artifacts that get to the core of
> traditional Chinese culture. They are a discovery of rarely seen great-
> ness and will surely receive the attention of national and interna-
> tional scholars. For the study of history, archeology, ancient philology,
> textual studies, and many other areas, they will produce an influence
> that is both broad and deep.

In December 2008, Peking University's accelerator mass spectrom-
etry laboratory and the laboratory specializing in fourth-century
archaeology were entrusted by Tsinghua University to perform AMS
carbon-14 dating on a blank fragment of the Tsinghua bamboo strips.
Their results, following correction based on comparisons with tree
rings, put the pieces to be from around 305 ± 30 BCE, fully matching
the dates estimated by the aforementioned authentication specialists.

The content of the Tsinghua bamboo strips is rich and plentiful.
Based on our initial understanding, there are ritual texts similar to the
Yi Li《儀禮》, divination texts related to the *Zhou Yi*《周易》, historical
texts close to the *Guo Yu*《國語》, and so on. Although at present we
still cannot determine altogether how many kinds of texts there are,
based on our present understanding, it can be said that they thrill the
heart. The most stimulating discovery in the Tsinghua bamboo strips
is the reappearance of the *Shang Shu*. The *Shang Shu* is a collection of
important historical documents from the three dynasties of the Xia,
Shang, and Zhou. It is one of the most important foundations for
researching ancient history. Most of the *Shang Shu* was destroyed in
the Qin Dynasty through Qin Shihuang's "burning of books and
burial of scholars," but now many chapters of the *Shang Shu* have
been discovered in the Tsinghua bamboo strips, all of which are
written manuscripts from before Qin Shihuang's burning of the
books. Some of the chapters have transmitted versions, such as the
"Metal-bound Coffer" (*Jin Teng* 〈金縢〉), "Announcement to Kang"
(Kang Gao 〈康誥〉), and so on, but their sentence structures often
differ from the transmitted versions and even some of the chapter

titles are not the same. Even more are lost chapters that have never been seen, either not appearing in the transmitted editions of the *Shang Shu* at all, or else appearing only as "Old Text" forgeries. For example, the "Command to Fu Yue" (*Fu Yue zhi Ming* 〈傅説之命〉) discovered in the Tsinghua bamboo strips and the "Command to Yue" (*Yue Ming* 〈説命〉) quoted in many pre-Qin documents is a different thing from the "Old Text" forgery of the "Command to Yue" transmitted to the present. There are also a few lost chapters never seen before, whose significance for researching the history of high antiquity is difficult to estimate and must await further arrangement and research.

Another important part of the content of the Tsinghua bamboo strips are historical documents in the form of annals. The historical events they record start from the beginning of the Western Zhou and extend down to the early period of the Warring States. In comparison with the *Spring and Autumn Annals* and the *Shi Ji*, they include much new material and historical events that previous documents had not recorded. Based on its structure and some of the sentences that have already been seen, the genre of these annals is very similar to that of the *Bamboo Annals*. Its publication could well open up a new dimension of research into cultural history from the Western Zhou to the Spring and Autumn and Warring States periods.

Everyone interested in Chinese history and culture knows the significance of the *Shang Shu* and historical documents like the *Bamboo Annals* for historical research. If in the Tsinghua bamboo strips one now sees the actual original version of the "Old Text" *Shang Shu* and historical documents close to the *Bamboo Annals*, it would give new hope for researching ancient Chinese culture and would certainly produce a deep and long lasting effect in the scholarly world. Some unresolved questions regarding the *Shang Shu* and *Bamboo Annals* might very well be solved by these new discoveries.

Work on the Tsinghua bamboo strips is proceeding smoothly. Tsinghua University has founded a special "Center for Excavated Texts Research and Protection" (CETRP) (*Qinghua Daxue Chutu Wenxian Yanjiu yu Baohu Zhongxin* 清華大學出土文獻研究與保護中心) to organize and coordinate the work of arranging, researching, and preserving the Tsinghua bamboo strips and other important excavated texts. This research center was jointly established by the Department of History, the library, and the Department of Chemistry. Li Xueqin holds the position of director. At present, CETRP is intensely engaged in arranging and preserving the Tsinghua bamboo strips and has already attained some initial results in transcribing and explaining the strips.

On April 13, 2009, scholars affiliated with CETRP introduced the earliest arranged bamboo strip text, the "*Bao Xun*"〈保訓〉, in a collection of articles in the *Guangming Daily*《光明日報》.[5] Of those, Li Xueqin's "Last Words of King Wen of Zhou" gives a relatively complete introduction to the condition of the "*Bao Xun*" bamboo strips. The full text of the "*Bao Xun*" altogether has eleven bamboo strips; their length is 28.5 cm and each strip has twenty-two to twenty-four characters. Of these, the top half of the second strip is broken off and has not yet been found, but the rest of the content has on the whole already been fully matched together. Presently, photographs and an initial transcription of the "*Bao Xun*" strips have already been formally published in 2009 in volume six of *Wen Wu*《文物》.[6]

The "*Bao Xun*" bamboo strips contain the last words of King Wen of Zhou, issued to the royal heir (who became King Wu) when facing the end of his life. The "Announcement of King Kang" ("*Kang Wang zhi Gao*"〈康王之誥〉) chapter of the *Shang Shu* records "do not harm the rare command of our high ancestor."[7] Previous people have already pointed out that the "remote ancestor" (*gaozu* 高祖) here refers to King Wen, and that *guaming* 寡命, is just *guming* 顧命, and thus refers to the last words of King Wen, given while facing the end of his life. Yet these last words have never been discovered. The "*Bao Xun*" text now discovered allows us to understand the content of King Wen's last words, and so naturally is of greatest importance. The "Bao Xun" text fits the genre of the *Shang Shu* perfectly. In the very beginning, the text announces that these events happened "in the fiftieth year of King Wen," which fits with the phrase, "enjoyed the state for fifty years," recorded in the "Against Indulgence" (*Wu Yi* 〈無逸〉) chapter of the *Shang Shu*, thus proving that King Wen of Zhou really was in position for fifty years.[8] In addition, from the expression "in the fiftieth year of King Wen," we can see that King Wen may have already been called "king," *wang* 王, while he was still alive, which could have important meaning for researching the relationship between Shang and Zhou at that time. In the "*Bao Xun*" text, King Wen talks to the royal heir about two historical traditions: one is in relation to Shun and the other is the Shang Dynasty remote ancestor Shang Jia-Wei. What King Wen wants to discuss in using both is "*zhong* 中 [middle, center, balance]," a concept rich in philosophical meaning. While the meaning of *zhong* in the text is difficult to fully grasp, it must relate to an idea or way of thought 思想觀念. This thought of "*zhong*" or "the way of the middle [*zhongdao* 中道]," is the heart of the whole "*Bao Xun*" text. This without doubt will have important meaning for researching the origins and transmission of Ru thought.

Soon after, CETRP began to arrange and put together a text of
music odes from the time of King Wu of Zhou. The connection and
ordering of the strips of the text is now already complete, and
although there are still individual additions and subtractions to be
made, its features are more or less apparent.[9] The text altogether has
fourteen strips and each strip varies in having twenty-five to twenty-
nine characters. A title is written on the back of the last strip: "*Qi Ye*,"
〈郘夜〉. Based on the writing system of the bamboo slips, Qi is the
name of a state, the same state of Qi 耆 or Li 黎 found in received
texts. The bamboo text begins by saying: "In the eighth year of King
Wu, there was a punitive attack on Qi, and Qi was greatly defeated.
When they returned, there was an '*Yin Zhi*' 飲至 ceremony in the
great hall of King Wen." This relates to one of the great events of the
final years of the Shang Dynasty. The "Documents of Shang" section
of the *Shang Shu* has a related chapter called "The Chief of the West
Defeats Qi" (*Xibo Kanli* 〈西伯戡黎〉). Based on the records in the text
of the bamboo manuscript, in the eighth year of King Wu, after the
Zhou generals returned from success in their punitive attack on the
state of Qi, they held an "*Yin Zhi*" ceremony in the ancestral temple
of King Wen. Among those participating were King Wu, the Duke of
Zhou 周公, the Duke of Bi 畢, the duke of Zhao 召, Xin Jia 辛甲, Zuo
Ce Yi 作冊逸, Shi Shang Fu 師尚父, and others. In the ritual, they
drank liquor and composed odes. Among these are the contents of the
odes of King Wu and the Duke of Zhou for the Duke of Bi, which
have never before been known. Surprisingly, one stanza of the ode
composed by the Duke of Zhou relates to the "*Xi Shuai*" 〈蟋蟀〉, ode
in the "Airs of Tang" section of the *Shi Jing* 《詩經》. This was really
outside anyone's expectations. This bamboo text has both historical
value and literary significance, and is without doubt an exceptionally
great discovery.

From the current point of view, the discovery of the "*Qi Ye*"
bamboo slips is significant in many different ways. The most important
are the following five points:

1. To correct our knowledge of the "Chief of the West Conquers
   Qi" chapter of the *Shang Shu*, which provides important docu-
   mentation relating to the Zhou attack on the state of Qi. During
   the Han Dynasty, sources like the *Great Commentary on the
   Shang Shu* (*Shangshu Dazhuan* 《尚書大傳》) or the "Annals of
   Zhou" chapter of the *Shi Ji* all considered the "Chief of the
   West" to be King Wen of Zhou. But that feudal state was too
   close to the capital of Shang, so for King Wen to use troops to go
   there did not fit the historical circumstances. Thus from the Song
   Dynasty on, many scholars have suspected that the "Chief of the

West" referred to King Wu of Zhou, but they were unable to raise any proof. Now the "*Qi Ye*" bamboo text clearly records that "King Wu in the eighth year" attacked Qi, thus verifying this suspicion. For this reason, the "Chief of the West Conquers Qi" chapter of the *Shang Shu* should be taken as a document reflecting the relationships between Shang and Zhou at the time of King Wu.

2. To clarify the specific time at which the people of Zhou eliminated the state of Qi. According to the "Annals of Zhou" in the *Shi Ji* and other documents, the people of Zhou attacked Qi in the time of King Wen, but based on this bamboo text, we can know that the attack did not happen until the eighth year of King Wu. This clarifies the specific time of the Zhou destruction of Qi. Furthermore, this date fits the circumstances more reasonably than the claim that Qi was attacked during the reign of King Wen.

3. To vividly represent the ancient "*Yin Zhi*" ceremony. Based on what is recorded in the *Zuo Zhuan* and other classical texts, in ancient times, after a triumphant return from a group attack or hunting expedition, they would hold an activity to celebrate success, sharing drinks in the ancestral temple, which was called the "*Yin Zhi*," "Libation to Celebrate Success." For example, in the fifth year of Duke Yin, the *Zuo Zhuan* says: "Every three years the troops are marshaled and sent out; when they return there is the libation to celebrate success [*yin zhi*], to count the troops and supplies."[10] Du Yu 杜預 notes that the libation in the temple was to count the chariots, soldiers, equipment, and what was attained.[11] Also, in the second year of Duke Huan, it says: "Any public expedition was announced in the ancestral temple. Upon return, there was a libation of successful completion, residing in ranks, and meritorious deeds were recorded."[12] The historical documents, though, do not explain the detailed circumstances of the *Yin Zhi* ceremony from pre-Qin times. This recently discovered chapter of odes vividly represents this ceremony. After King Wu, the Duke of Zhou, and others return from victory, they hold the *Yin Zhi* ceremony in the ancestral temple of King Wen of Zhou, together drinking liquor and composing odes that praise those people and officers who have attained hard-earned merit. Two thousand years later, when we read these lively odes again, it is as if the scene were reenacted before our eyes.

4. To discover the odes and songs composed by King Wu, the Duke of Zhou, and others, which have never appeared in the historical records. Because these odes are lyrics of music sung

in the *Yin Zhi* ceremonies of that time, they are vivid images reflecting the intimate relationship between music and the odes.

5. To reveal the surprising relation between the "*Xi Shuai*" ode and the Duke of Zhou. According to the *Minor Preface* 《小序》, the "*Xi Shuai*" ode in the "Airs of Tang" section of the *Shi Jing*: "Criticizes Duke Xi of Jin, who was stingy to the point of not fitting ritual. Thus one made this ode in concern for the people." From this newly discovered text, we can now know that the "*Xi Shuai*" ode surprisingly is connected to the Duke of Zhou. This point can be said to be a new thread unknown for thousands of years. It awakens us to the need to newly reexamine the background and content of the "*Xi Shuai*" ode. In reading the text carefully, we can see that the Duke of Zhou composed this "*Xi Shuai*" to hold a profound meaning, directed toward warning everyone not to indulge in pleasures and forget future difficulties. The Shanghai Museum Warring States bamboo text called "Discussing the Odes" (*Shi Lun* 〈詩論〉) fits this exactly, saying "the '*Xi Shuai*' knows difficulty."[13]

Added together, the "*Bao Xun*" and "*Qi Ye*" bamboo texts altogether have twenty-five strips, occupying only around one percent of the total number of Tsinghua bamboo strips, which reach to 2,388. Yet the currently published materials have already drawn a great reaction in the scholarly world and have already had a deep effect on research in ancient Chinese civilization. What precious and rare materials will be found in other parts of the Tsinghua bamboo strips, what pleasant surprises and discoveries they will bring for the scholarly world, what kind of stimulation they will have for research on ancient Chinese civilization—all these are eagerly awaited.

The work of arranging and preserving the Tsinghua bamboo strips is presently proceeding in good order. Because of their immense quantity, the difficulty of explaining the characters, and the obscurity of their ancient content, it will be a long-term and difficult duty to connect, arrange, and publish these thousands of bamboo strips one by one in orderly reports. Perhaps only after the Tsinghua bamboo strips have been completely arranged and published will their great scholarly value then be fully realized. Following a deeper entry into the work of arranging and researching the Tsinghua bamboo strips, many ancient Chinese mysteries will gradually be understood and known.[14]

TSINGHUA UNIVERSITY
Beijing, China

ENDNOTES

An early version of this article was published in Chinese shown in the following reference: *"Qinghua Jian yu Zhonguo Gudai Wenming Yanjiu"* "清华简与中国古代文明研究" (*Qinghua* Bamboo Strips and Study on Ancient Chinese Culture), *Guoxue Xuekan*《國學學刊》(Journal of Chinese Classics Studies) 4 (2009). For the current publication, we deeply thank Professor Franklin Perkins for translating, revising, and editing on behalf of us. We also thank Professor Chung-ying Cheng for inviting our contribution and providing remarks.

1. Translated from Chinese by Franklin Perkins.
2. The lecture was published in *Tsinghua Zhougan*《清華周刊》and later collected in *Jingan Wenji Xubian*《靜庵文集續編》, edited by Zhao Wanli 趙萬裡. See *Wang Guowei Yishu*《王國維遺書》(Shanghai: Shanghai Shudian Publisher, 1998), volume 3, 699–708.
3. *"Kaogu Faxian de Qin Han Wenzi Ziliao dui yu Jiaodu Guji de Zhongyaoxing"* "考古發現的秦漢文字資料對於校讀古籍的重要性" in *Qiu Xigui Zixuanji*《裘錫圭自選集》(Zhengzhou: Daxiang Publisher, 1998), 171.
4. The famous scholar Zhang Zhenglang 張政烺 when he was alive always said that when we excavate the *Shang Shu*, that will be truly great. See Li Xueqin, *Zouchu Yigu Shidai*《走出疑古時代》(Shenyang: Liaoning University Press, 1994), 5.
5. Li Xueqin, "Last Words of Zhou Wen Wang" "周文王遺言": Zhao Pingan 趙平安, "'*Bao Xun*' de Xingzhi he Jiegou" "《保訓》的性質和結構" in *Guangming Ribao*《光明日報》, April 13, 2009.
6. Tsinghua University Center for Excavated Texts Research and Protection, "*Qinghua Daxue Cang Zhanguo Zhujian 'Baoxun' Shiwen*" "清華大學藏戰國竹簡《保訓》釋文," *Wen Wu*《文物》6, 2009.
7. *Shisan Jing Zhushu*《十三經注疏》(Taipei: Yiwen Yinshuguan Publisher, 1955), 289.
8. Ibid., 242.
9. Li Xueqin, "*Qinghua Jian 'Qi Ye*'" "清华简《耆夜》," *Guangming Ribao*《光明日報》, August 3, 2009.
10. Yang Bojun 楊伯峻, *Chunqiu Zuozhuan Zhu*《春秋左傳注》(Beijing: Zhonghua Shuju, 1995), 42–43.
11. *Shisan Jing Zhushu*《十三經注疏》, 1727.
12. Ibid., 91.
13. "*Kongzi Shi Lun*" 〈孔子詩論〉, strip 27 下, in *Shanghai Bowuguanzang Zhanguo Chuzhujian I Duben*《上海博物館藏戰國楚竹簡（Ⅰ）讀本》, ed. Ji Xusheng (Taipei: Wanjuanlou Tushu Fufen Publisher, 2004).
14. In response to Professor Chung-ying Cheng's inquiry, the Tsinghua bamboos strips contain much material concerning the Xia 夏 Dynasty, which we are currently in the midst of arranging. A volume of arranged reports to be published at the end of this year collects the "*Yin Zhi*" 〈尹至〉 and "*Yin Gao*" 〈尹誥〉, two chapters of materials similar to the *Shang Shu*. Both are historical materials whose content concerns the destruction of the Xia by Shang Tang 商湯 and Yi Yin 伊尹. Other materials will have to be arranged and published in the near future.

FRANKLIN PERKINS

RECONTEXTUALIZING *XING*:
SELF-CULTIVATION AND HUMAN NATURE IN
THE GUODIAN TEXTS

Our understanding of classical Ru ("Confucian") thought is structured around its three great figures—Kongzi, Mengzi, and Xunzi. This understanding generally begins by positing tensions among the earliest Ru, perhaps Kongzi himself, which then culminate around the great question dividing Mengzi and Xunzi—is the *xing* 性 (characteristic tendencies or nature) of human beings good or bad? Into this familiar story now comes a tangle of short and difficult excavated texts buried at the end of the fourth century BCE. Facing the unfamiliarity of these texts and the immense hurdles in understanding them, it is natural to begin by determining how they fit into our general schema of the early Ru. Thus the most emphasized question has been—what is their position on the goodness or badness of human nature? Seeking an answer from the Guodian texts, though, obscures what is probably most significant about them—they have no concern for the question! Ultimately, the greatest light the excavated texts shed on Mengzi's claim that human *xing* is good may be in showing that this claim turned the discussion of *xing* in a new direction, a direction which came to overshadow the debates from which it originally emerged.[1]

These recently discovered texts also force us to reconsider another common story about the development of early Ru thought—A.C. Graham's claim that philosophical debates about *xing* did not originate from the Ru but were taken up in response to the philosophy of the "Individualists," represented by Yang Zhu.[2] Graham puts the story succinctly:

> Down to the fourth century BC *hsing* [*xing*] is not a philosophical term; it belongs to the ordinary language of everyone who worries about his health and hopes to live out his natural span. It enters philosophy with the advocates of *yang sheng* 養生 'Nurture of Life,' the individualists who first urge the advantages of private against

FRANKLIN PERKINS, Associate Professor, Department of Philosophy, Chair, Chinese Studies Committee, DePaul University. Specialties: early Chinese philosophy, early modern European philosophy, comparative philosophy. E-mail: franklinperkins@hotmail.com

Journal of Chinese Philosophy, Supplement to Volume 37 (2010) 16–32
© *2010 Journal of Chinese Philosophy*

public life, and refuse to sacrifice a hair of their bodies for power, possessions or any other external benefit which involves the risk of injury to health and life.[3]

According to Graham, Yang Zhu used *xing* normatively: the purpose of life is to fulfill or follow one's *xing*, which justifies certain kinds of activities and excludes others. In taking Yang Zhu as one of his main philosophical opponents, Mengzi inherits this normative use of *xing* while redescribing its content so as to justify different norms. Mengzi does this by introducing spontaneous tendencies toward virtue, his famous four "sprouts" (*duan* 端). As Graham puts it, "The only final satisfactory solution for Confucians is therefore a demonstration that it is when he is acting morally, not when he is pursuing his own longevity, that man fulfills his nature."[4]

While Mengzi clearly opposes Yang Zhu's elevation of life as the highest good, Graham's evidence for the link between Yang Zhu and debates about *xing* is remarkably slim.[5] The *Mengzi* never associates *xing* with Yang Zhu and never appeals to *xing* in opposing him; Mengzi's arguments for the goodness of *xing* are directed only at Gaozi, who can now be identified as a rival Ru. This suggests that at the time of Mengzi, philosophical debates about *xing* were a Ru issue, and it is significant that *xing* does not appear as a central term in the *Mozi*, the *Dao De Jing*, or the" inner chapters" of the *Zhuangzi*. It would go too far to say that the excavated texts *disprove* Graham's story, but they place it in deep doubt. One problem is simply chronological: the Chu bamboo texts were likely written too close to the time of Yang Zhu to have incorporated his views, yet they comfortably use *xing* as a philosophical concept. The strongest evidence against Graham's history, though, is that the Chu bamboo texts show no sign of reacting against or responding to the "individualist" position.

This article is meant as a step toward reconstructing the original set of concerns in which *xing* became a locus of philosophical debate, arguing that this context did not involve the question of the goodness of *xing* nor the use use of *xing* to establish certain norms. The argument draws on a number of excavated texts buried in what was the state of Chu around 300 BCE, but centers on the "*Xing Zi Ming Chu* 〈性自命出〉" (XZMC hereafter).[6] Before turning more specifically to the role of *xing* in that text, we must first sketch out its basic model of human psychology. We can begin with the first lines:

> In general, though people have *xing*, the heart [*xin* 心] lacks stable commitment [*zhi* 志]. It awaits things and then moves, awaits being pleased and then acts, and awaits practice and then is stable. The *qi* 氣 of pleasure, anger, grief, and sorrow is *xing*. Its appearing on the outside is because things stimulate it.[7]

Human beings have a nature that consists of dispositions and tendencies to react in certain ways, their *xing*. When stimulated by things, this *xing* stirs, forming specific reactions that can be labeled as *qing* 情, natural or genuine feelings. Concrete psychological states thus involve three elements—our dispositions, external things, and concrete emotions, desires, and so on. The list of emotions in this passage should not be taken too narrowly—if we examine how terms are paired in the text, then the list would include joy (*le* 樂), anxious concern (*you* 憂), anger (*wen* 慍), and even reverence (*jing* 敬).[8] These emotions are examples of *qing*, which are said to come out from (*chu* 出) or be born from (*sheng* 生) *xing*. Two other types of reactions are explained through *xing*:

> Loving and hating are *xing*. What is loved and what is hated are things. Affirming as good or [not good is *xing*]. What is affirmed as good or not good are circumstances.[9]

Loving and hating (*haowu* 好惡) refer to desires in general, as another line emphasizes that the natural power of the desires (*hao*) of the eyes and ears easily leads us to our deaths.[10] While loving and hating follow from our nature, they only take form in relation to particular things, what is loved and what is hated. The following line is more difficult to interpret, and some commentators have taken it as staking a position within debates about the goodness of *xing*, basically as claiming that *xing* can be good or bad and what makes *xing* good or bad are circumstances.[11] Such a reading, though, fits neither the immediate context of the sentence, which is about the dependence of the activities (rather than the quality) of *xing* on external stimulants, nor the broader context of the article, which shows no further concern with the question of whether or not *xing* is good. Given the parallel with the first line on loving and hating, "good (*shan* 善)" should be an action of our *xing* which only happens in relation to an object, with "circumstances" or "conditions" (*shi* 勢) as its object. Grammatically, the use of *shan* as a transitive verb indicates that it should be read putatively, so that "good" would mean to "affirm as good" or "judge as good."[12] The meaning, then, is that the tendency or ability to judge as good or bad is natural for us, but these judgments actually arise only in response to particular circumstances. This tendency to judge would be close to the "heart of affirming and negating" (*shifeizhixin* 是非之心) which Mengzi names as the sprout of wisdom.[13] It might also explain the claim in the "*Yu Cong* II 〈語叢二〉" that, "wisdom is born from *xing*."[14] The use of *shan* in the XZMC, though, specifically emphasizes that we naturally make ethical evaluations.[15]

The relationship between *xing* and *qing* is articulated through *qi*, vital force or energy. *Xing* has a certain dynamic force which is moved or directed by things; this movement of *qi* forms particular desires and emotions (pleasure, anger, grief, sorrow, etc.). On this view, *xing* and *qing* would be two sides or states of the same thing, what the *Zhong Yong*《中庸》distinguishes as the emotions before and after they have issued forth (*fa* 發), and the "Classic of Music (*Yue Ji* 〈樂記〉)" contrasts as the stillness (*jing* 静) of *xing* and its movement (*dong* 動) when stimulated (*gan* 感) by things.[16] The distinction between *xing* and *qing* addresses the status of dispositions, explaining how we can have certain characteristics even when those are not being acted upon or stimulated. Coming from the context of Western philosophy, it is difficult not to see the relationship between *xing* and *qing* as one between potentiality and actuality, but precisely because of this similarity, the use of Aristotelian terms could be misleading. On an ontological level, this movement is not shifting something from potential into actual being but rather channeling an actually existing force into various directions. Some of the reactions of our *xing* are good and some are bad; there is no sense that good reactions actualize our *xing* in ways that bad reactions do not and thus no sense that actions are justified because they actualize our *xing*.[17] Thus *xing* does not offer a teleology, and a discourse of "actualization," "realization," or "fulfillment," would be out of place. As we will see, this also means that what defines the good must involve external factors.

We can now turn to the function of *xing* in the XZMC. The use of "although" (*sui* 雖) in the opening line suggests the text enters an existing context by opposing or qualifying some claim about *xing*. While it is difficult to project what that claim may have been, these lines make two related points. First, *xing* is underdetermining. Although we share the same *xing*, we vary both because we experience different things and because different practices (*xi* 習) set our commitments in different ways. This emphasis on limiting the determining role of *xing* appears elsewhere in the text: "Within the four seas, their *xing* is one. It is in using their hearts that each becomes different. Education (*jiao* 教) is what makes them so."[18] Second, as long as we remain at the level of our nature, we react erratically to whatever we happen to encounter. It is only through practice that we can develop a settled intention and thus some level of self-control. These two points come together in justifying self-cultivation, the first showing that it is possible and the second that it is necessary in order to have any self-control.[19]

These opening lines indicate the main concern of the text: how to move from our natural state of reacting to whatever happens to come along to a state in which we have a stable intention or commitment to what is right. The progression from natural reactions to what is right is outlined following the opening lines:

> *Xing* comes out from conditions [*ming* 命] and conditions come down from heaven [*tian* 天]. The way begins from *qing* [natural feelings] and *qing* are born from *xing*. The beginning is close to *qing*; the ending is close to rightness [*yi* 義].[20]

The derivation of *xing* from heaven is not unusual: Mengzi emphasizes the connection, Xunzi defines *xing* as what "is given by heaven," and the *Zhong Yong* says that "what is conditioned from heaven (*tianming* 天命) is called *xing*."[21] As the example of Xunzi illustrates, though, this linkage cannot be taken as implying anything about the moral quality of our *xing*. While the progression from heaven to *qing* can be taken as a natural and spontaneous chain, the movement from *qing* to rightness differs by depending on *dao*, which is not a cosmic "Dao" but rather the human way practiced by the Ru.[22] Only in the end, after dedicated practice, are we close to what is right. This means that our natural feelings themselves are not fully correct; at the same time, the rooting of the way in *qing* suggests that correct actions cannot disengage from our natural feelings.

The process of self-cultivation is one of taking our internally grounded reactions and modifying them so as to make them correct. This is explained in terms of modify *xing* itself:

> In general, for *xing*, some things move it, some entice it, some restrain it, some hone it, some draw it out, some nourish it, and some grow it. What moves *xing* are things. What entices *xing* is being pleased. What restrains *xing* are deliberate reasons [*gu* 故]. What hones *xing* is rightness. What draws out *xing* are circumstances [*shi* 勢]. What nourishes *xing* is practice. What grows *xing* is dao.[23]

This passage describes a progression which starts with the immediate reactions stirred by things, moves to "restraining" or "honing" *xing*, and then progresses to "nourishing" and "growing." However one takes the details of the passage, it shows that *xing* itself is modified through self-cultivation.[24] Thus there is an ambiguity in the term *xing*, which can refer either to our dispositions at any given time or the dispositions with which we are born.[25]

We can examine this process of self-cultivation in three steps: the role of *qing* in the origination of the way (the internal), the importance of the way as leading to right actions (the external), and the process of internalizing rightness (uniting external and internal). The claim that "the way begins from *qing*" can be taken on several levels. It is partly a historical claim:

> Rituals are made from *qing*. Some made them arise, suiting affairs and relying on rules [*fang* 方] to regulate them. The order of what was first and last then were appropriate to the way. From this order they made them restrained, so they were refined.[26]

Rituals first arose from natural human feelings but were then modified to fit things and to have due measure, ending with restrained moderation (*jie* 節) and cultured refinement (*wen* 文). A similar point is made a few lines earlier with the claim that the *Odes*, *Documents*, *Rituals*, and *Music*, were all born from human beings and then formed through the deliberate work of sages.[27]

The claim that the way is born from *qing* also describes the relationship between teacher and student. One passage says: "Any sound, if it comes from *qing*, is sincere, and then it enters and moves people's hearts deeply."[28] The stimulation of correct feelings through music is the main method of self-cultivation emphasized in the text.[29] This effect is only possible, though, if the music expresses *qing*, not only in its historical origins but also in its immediate performance. In this sense, the way begins in the genuine feelings of the performer, which stimulate the feelings of the listener. Music points to a third sense in which the way can be said to start from *qing*, which is on the level of the individual, whose path toward virtue begins by having certain *qing* stimulated. The repeated and practiced eliciting of correct feelings leads those feelings to become regulated and easier, more fixed on what is appropriate.

The way remains in continual interplay with *qing*. The music and rituals that constitute the way were created by the sages based on their *qing*, they are then performed to express the *qing* of the performers, and these performances then move the *qing* of other people. The process is reciprocal: "If its sound changes then [the heart follows it]; if its heart changes then the sound also is so."[30] This circular or reciprocal progression offers a response to what becomes a troubling question once *xing* is discussed as "good" or "bad": the origin and value of culture. If *xing* is simply good, one does not need the culture developed by the sages; if *xing* is simply bad, it impossible that this culture would ever arise. In the XZMC, cultural forms emerge from natural feelings but are then refined so as to turn back and shape those original feelings. This process is progressively cyclical, so that these refined feelings lead to further refinements of cultural forms, which further refine feelings, and so on. The tradition (the human way) expresses millennia of such gradual development and refinement.

The fact that *qing* must be transformed requires that cultivation be guided by something other than our natural reactions, by something external. The break from *qing* appears in an emphasis on deliberate action, as in the passage on the ways *xing* is affected, which says, "what restrains *xing* are reasons [*gu* 故]" and then explains "reasons" as deliberateness, literally "having actions [*youwei* 有爲]."[31] The latter is not a standard phrase, but its negation is familiar from the *Dao De Jing*: *wuwei* 無爲, "not having actions" or more commonly "non-action." Liu Xinlan, Chen Wei, and Chen Linqing all take *youwei* as action directed toward a purpose.[32] Li Tianhong says it is actions based on reasons.[33] Liu Zhao translates it as "acting deliberately [*guyi zuode* 故意做的]."[34] This "having actions" appears close to the *wei* (偽) used by Xunzi to refer to deliberate or forced actions in contrast to the spontaneous responses of our *xing*. Thus one stage in the cultivation of our *xing* requires that we act deliberately, according to reasons.[35] This deliberateness was also required for the formation of the way, as the origin and compilation of the four classics was said to arise from deliberate action, *youwei*.[36]

The role of deliberateness in creating the way and in modifying our nature points toward rightness, which is what the way is said to bring us closer to. The phrase "what restrains *xing* are reasons" is directly followed by, "what hones *xing* is rightness."[37] The use of *li* 厲, to sharpen or hone, a term also used by Xunzi, suggests the role of rightness as resisting and shaping our natural tendencies.[38] The relationship between rightness and our natural reactions can be clarified by contrast with benevolence, which is connected explicitly to *xing* through care *ai* 愛: "There are seven kinds of care; only care from *xing* is near to benevolence."[39] The care from our *xing* most likely refers to the care that emerges spontaneously and naturally within family relations.

This connection appears in several Guodian texts, as the "*Yu Cong* II" says: "Care is born from *xing*, familial affection [*qin* 親] is born from care, loyalty is born from familial affection."[40] The XZMC contrasts rightness and benevolence in two passages. The first says: "Disliking him but not able to fault him—this is one who has reached rightness. Faulting him but not able to dislike him—this is one who is earnest in benevolence. Enacting it without errors—this is one who knows the way."[41] The contrast with benevolence is easily explained as between correctness of actions and a caring intention, which could err but would be difficult to hate. Rightness and the way both center on correct actions, on avoiding errors.[42] The second passage in the XZMC says that within the family, kindness (*en* 恩) outweighs judgments about rightness, while outside of the family, one insists on rightness.[43] This aligns with a contrast between benevolence as originating from familial feelings, and rightness as based on objective standards of correctness.[44]

On one level, the XZMC uses discussions of *xing* to distinguish those aspects of morality that follow from our natural spontaneous reactions and those that must be learned and deliberately developed. In this context, the contrast between benevolence as internal and rightness as external refers to the *origins* of those virtues in relation to *xing*. At the same time, rightness does not remain external: otherwise, self-cultivation would require a transformation in our *actions* but not a transformation of our *qing*. Thus on another level, *xing* serves as what can and must be transformed and worked at. We can approach this through concerns about the limits of deliberate action:

> Generally, in learning, it is seeking the heart that is difficult. Following what is to be done [*cong qi suowei* 從其所為] is close to attaining it, but that is not like using the speed of music. Although one can do the work, if one cannot attain its heart, it is not worthy of honor. Seeking the heart and having deliberate action, one cannot attain it. People's not being able to use deliberate action thus can be known.[45]

The emphasis on the limits of deliberate actions (again literally, "having actions," *youwei*) does not necessarily contradict their importance elsewhere.[46] The formulation of the classics and what counts as right must go beyond feelings to deliberate considerations, and self-cultivation too must have a deliberate element. Deliberate actions, though, do not suffice, because being good is not just doing the right thing. If one's heart is not in the actions, the actions are not honorable. Deliberately doing the right thing surely is necessary sometimes and will indeed bring one closer to being good, but its effectiveness is limited, because it does not directly engage our feelings. Much more effective is music, whose sounds immediately stimulate appropriate reactions.

While rightness is grounded more in the external and benevolence in the internal, the ultimate goal is for all of the virtues to be internally motivated. This goal appears in other Guodian texts, although differing in its details. For example, the "*Wu Xing*" makes this distinction as between good actions (*xing* 行) and the good action of *de* 德, virtuous power.[47] In that text, all good actions can and should become internally motivated. This link between *de* and the internal is echoed in the XZMC as well: "Education is that by which *de* is born in the center."[48] Education (*jiao*) involves external guidance, but giving birth to *de* in the center is an *internal* change. Similarly, music is a form of education whose entering and exiting is the beginning of *de*.[49] The process of giving birth to *de* in the center, of cultivating our feelings so that our *qing* align with what is appropriate, is the process of taking the external and making it enter. This relationship between benevolence and rightness, the internal and external, also fits the "*Yu Cong* I": "Of the human way, some go out from the inside and some enter in from the outside. Those which go out from the inside are benevolence, loyalty, and sincerity. [Those which enter] from [the outside are rightness, ritual, and (?)]."[50] This passage helps clarify a vague line early in the XZMC: "One who knows *qing* can externalize it; one who knows rightness can internalize it."[51] Knowing *qing* entails knowing how to express feelings outwardly in proper form, while knowing rightness means being able to internalize it to align our genuine feelings.

This need to connect the internal and the external is generated by one of the central concerns of the XZMC: sincerity.[52] This concern appears already in the claim above that if good actions are performed without the right heart, they are not valuable.[53] Another passage says simply:

> Every person's deliberate[54] actions can be hated. If deliberate then [concealing?],[55] if concealing then calculating, if calculating then no one will engage with them.... Every person's actions from genuine feeling [qing] can be pleasing. If using genuine feelings, even if there are errors they are not hated. If not using genuine feelings, then even if difficult it is not worthy of honor.[56]

The role of the heart in deliberate actions comes out both because they lead to calculative thinking (lü 慮) and because the text uses a form of *wei* that includes the heart radical (忄爲). The use of the heart radical in both the Guodian and Shanghai versions of the text shows it is a deliberate choice, pointing toward a kind of action involving presence of mind.[57] The passage plays on the ambiguity of its two key terms, *qing* and *wei*. The core meaning of *qing* is the genuine reactions of our *xing*, with emotions as the prime example, so the sense of the term encompasses both emotion and genuineness. Similarly, I have been taking *wei* as deliberate actions, but because deliberate actions do not follow from our *qing*, they have a sense of artificiality and even deception. Thus this passage can be read as contrasting deliberate action with spontaneous emotion *or* as contrasting the fake with the genuine.[58] In fact, the passage implies both contrasts, warning that deliberate actions tend toward scheming and then to deception.

To conclude, we can consider a passage that contrasts the key virtues of benevolence, rightness, and sincerity (*xin* 信):

> Reciprocity is the orientation [*fang* 方] of rightness. Rightness is the orientation of respect. Respect is the regulator of things. Earnestness is the orientation of benevolence. Benevolence is the orientation of *xing*, *xing* then gives birth to it. Loyalty is the orientation of sincerity. Sincerity is the orientation of *qing*, and *qing* comes from *xing*.[59]

There is disagreement on aspects of this passage, but each line describes a progression toward the basis of one of the virtues.[60] Benevolence directly connects to the natural tendencies, *xing*, which we have by birth. In contrast, the root of rightness is in the order or regulation (*jie* 節) of things/events (*wu* 物). This emphasis on the order of things connects back to the formation of ritual and the classics, both of which refer to rightness and to ordering, restraining, or regulating (*jie* 節). Sincerity (*xin* 信) bridges between the two virtues. Although both benevolence and sincerity link to *xing*, they relate differently. Benevolence belongs directly to *xing* and what is born with us. Sincerity links immediately to *qing*, to our true feelings, which are activities of our dispositions already brought out by events in the world. Sincere people are reliable, loyal, and trustworthy because their actions express their genuine feelings. They unite the internal and the external. This sincerity applies to both benevolence and rightness: whether moving from the inside or from the outside, ultimately all must be sincere expressions of our *qing* and *xing* in action.

In sum, the human way can be said to begin and end in *qing*, genuine feelings. It begins from the spontaneous reactions of our natural tendencies and ends with feelings and desires that are correct and appropriate. What mediates this transition is the way, particularly the classic collections of odes, documents, rituals, and music, all of which initially emerged from spontaneous human feelings but then underwent a gradual and deliberate process of development guided by the demands of living harmoniously in the world. The main difficulty and thus main focus of self-cultivation is not in acting according to what is appropriate but rather in cultivating our nature so that appropriate actions genuinely emerge from it. The ultimate goal is common to all early Ru texts, what Kongzi famously described as his highest stage of achievement: "at seventy I could follow what my heart desired without overstepping proper measure."[61]

Given the development of Warring States Ru thought into Mengzi and Xunzi, we can of course ask if the XZMC takes human nature, *xing*, as good or bad, both or neither. The text does not provide a clear answer.[62] Our natural tendencies can be considered good, in that goodness is initiated by them and develops in continuity with them, but they also must be transformed to be closer to rightness, which at the very least means they are not good enough. Elements such as natural care for family point to Mengzi, but the emphasis on deliberate action points more toward Xunzi. The long list of what happens to our *xing* reflects this ambiguity: "honing" echoes the language of Xunzi, but "nurturing" and "growing" sound more like Mengzi. What is most significant, though, is that the XZMC appears not to have been written in the context of a debate around the goodness or badness of human nature. If it were, we would expect a clear statement locating it in that debate, or at least explicitly rejecting it.

More profoundly, such a debate would not be directly relevant to the main concerns of the text. The central predicament in the XZMC lies in the tension between two positions: that virtuous actions must be sincere and so internally rooted in our *xing*, and that correct behavior involves conformity to rules developed with regard to the needs and orders of the world around us. The combination of these two commitments precludes two relatively simple ethical positions:

taking ethics either as a development of our natural tendencies or as simply doing the right thing. In the XZMC, ethics can neither be purely internal nor purely external. As a result, *xing* becomes the most precious aspect of actions but also something that must be modified, honed, and nourished.

How does this context help to clarify early Ru debates around *xing*? We can here suggest three points for further consideration. First, debates about whether *xing* is good or bad emerged from an earlier concern about the virtues as internal or external, which was itself rooted in questions of self-cultivation. It makes sense that one might enter such a dispute by arguing that our natural tendencies are good (making the virtues internal) or bad (making them external), and we see the two debates linked by both Gaozi and Mengzi. For example, in claiming that "benevolence, rightness, ritual propriety, and wisdom are not welded onto us from outside," Mengzi uses his theory of the goodness of *xing* to reject the position of "*Yu Cong* I," that some virtues comes in from the outside.[63]

The Guodian texts do not resolve questions about the precise nature of the dispute between Mengzi and Gaozi, but if we assume maximum continuity with the XZMC, then the dispute should be grounded in differences of emphasis in the process of cultivation. Gaozi holds on to the XZMC's language of both nourishing and restraining our *xing*. Mengzi would be opposing the latter aspect, focusing only on nourishing and extending. This would go along with his claim that aside from familial concern, human beings naturally have other dispositions, like feelings of shame or deference, which can be mobilized in the process of self-cultivation. We can consider two other possibilities. We might take Gaozi as defending the XZMC's position that the rules of rightness and ritual were developed through the deliberate actions of sages, and then take Mengzi as making a radical (and implausible) claim that these rules emerged spontaneously from our nature. Alternately, we could take Mengzi as defending the XZMC's claim that externally derived rules must be enacted with genuine feelings, in which case Gaozi would be making the radical claim (for a Ru) that rightness only entails deliberate action without any genuine feeling. Both interpretations seem unlikely in the context of the Guodian texts, although we cannot be sure how far the *Mengzi* breaks from that context.[64]

Second, Ru debates on whether *xing* is good or bad were probably not concerned, at least initially, with normative theory but rather with disagreements about the process of self-cultivation. That is, they were not concerned with *why* the way of the Ru is good but rather with *how* one follows that way. Human *xing* is not irrelevant to the content of the way, which is born from natural feelings and would be limited by what it was possible for human beings to genuinely feel. Nonetheless, the focus of the XZMC is on modifying *xing* to align with the way. There is no sense that modifying *xing* might be wrong or only justified because it better expresses *xing*. In other words, the XZMC recognizes no imperative toward developing, actualizing, or realizing our *xing*, not even as an option to be rejected. In this context, Graham's claim that Ru debates around *xing* originated from the attempt to *justify* the Ru way against Yang Zhu appears very unlikely. This context further suggests that Mengzi's claim that *xing* is good is directed toward methods of self-cultivation, not toward justifying the Ru way. Of course, Mengzi may represent a break from the position of the XZMC, using *xing* in a new manner to justify the way, but then we would expect signs that his position is innovative in this way, particular in polemical debates about *xing*, with Gaozi or with Xunzi. The fact that those debates do not contain explicit concerns about *justifying* the way strongly suggests that the relevance of *xing* for Mengzi is the same as for the XZMC and Xunzi: the characteristics of our nature are simply the most important facts to be considered in self-cultivation and developing any functional social order.

Third, because the XZMC encompasses elements emphasized by both Xunzi and Mengzi, it allows us to see the commonality in early Ru views of *xing*. First, all three texts take *xing* to consist of dispositions which, when uncultivated, simply respond spontaneously to whatever happens to be perceived. For Mengzi these reactions include things like King Xuan of Qi's spontaneous concern when he happens to see an ox going to slaughter, while Xunzi emphasizes reactions of desire for things in the world.[65] Second, all three take self-cultivation as modifying these spontaneous reactions. For Mengzi, this is a matter of strengthening, refining, and extending certain *qing* (the four sprouts) and of giving those reactions dominance over others (the desires of the senses). For Xunzi, it is a matter of extending and refining certain desires (like those involved in the appreciation of music) while giving them consistent dominance over other more disruptive desires. Third, all three see some role for deliberate thought in this process of cultivation. The XZMC and Xunzi use similar terms and place more importance on this aspect of self-cultivation, but Mengzi also gives a key role to thinking or concentrating (*si* 思), which prevents us from being "pulled along" by things in the world.[66] Finally, all three project the same ideal: a condition in which all our spontaneous reactions to the world are exactly and effortlessly appropriate. The difference between the three, then, is not in how they think of *xing* itself but rather in the content they attribute to it. This difference has widespread consequences for how they approach the process of self-cultivation, which is precisely what was at issue in early Ru discussions of *xing*.

DEPAUL UNIVERSITY
Chicago, Illinois

Endnotes

This article benefitted from feedback at the Midwest Conference on Chinese Thought, particularly later discussions with Ted Slingerland and Dan Robins. I am also grateful for suggestions from Chung-ying Cheng and the editorial work of Linyu Gu. My understanding of the XZMC was helped by discussions with Ding Sixin and Sang Jingyu at Wuhan University while on a Fulbright Research Grant.

1. This turn probably did not begin with Mengzi himself, since *Mengzi* 6A6 lists a variety of positions on the goodness of *xing*; the only specific person mentioned is Gaozi, who was an older contemporary (Jiao Xun 焦旬, *Mengzi Zhengyi*《孟子正義》[Beijing: Zhonghua Shuju Publisher, 1987]). Wang Chong 王充 pushes a concern with the goodness of *xing* back to Shi Shuo 世碩, although it is difficult to know how reliable his account is, coming so much later (for example, it is unlikely that Shi Shuo had a theory of *xing* that appealed to *yin* and *yang*, which is how Wang Chong explains it) (Huang Hui 黃暉, *Lun Heng Jiaoshi*《論衡校釋》[Beijing: Zhonghua Shuju Publisher, 1996], chap. 13, 132–33). Czikszentmihalyi suggests that Wang Chong's discussion of Shi Shuo may be an "invented history" (Mark Czikszentmihalyi, *Material Virtue: Ethics and the Body in Early China* [Leiden: Brill, 2004], 216).
2. For Graham's position, see "The Background of the Mencian (Mengzian) Theory of Human Nature," reprinted in *Essays on the Moral Philosophy of Mengzi*, ed. Xiusheng Liu and Philip J. Ivanhoe (Indianapolis: Hackett Publishing, 2002), 1–63. Graham's account has been widely accepted, for example, followed explicitly by Bryan Van Norden, *Virtue Ethics and Consequentialism in Classical Chinese Philosophy* (Cambridge: Cambridge University Press, 2007), 200–211, Aaron Stalnaker, *Overcoming Our Evil: Human Nature and Spiritual Exercises in Augustine and Xunzi* (Washington, DC: Georgetown University Press, 2006), 39, and more tentatively by Kwong-loi Shun, *Mencius and Early Chinese Thought* (Stanford: Stanford University Press, 1997), 35–47. Robert Eno has questioned Graham's account (*The Confucian Creation of Heaven: Philosophy and the Defense of Ritual Mastery* [Albany: State University of New York Press, 1990], 257, n 58).
3. Graham, "Background," 6.
4. Ibid., 13.
5. Ibid., 12. The only direct evidence linking Yang Zhu to the term *xing* is the *Huainanzi's* comment that what Yang Zhu promoted was to "keep *xing* whole [全性], protect genuineness, and not let things exhaust one's form" (Xiong Lihui 熊禮匯, *Xinyi Huainanzi*《新譯淮南子》[Taipei: Sanmin Shuju, 2002], 670). While this probably represents Yang Zhu's basic position, it does not necessarily represent Yang Zhu's own vocabulary or way of conceptualizing that position. The other evidence is Graham's use of passages from the *Zhuangzi* and *Lüshi Chunqiu* as representative of the position of Yang Zhu. While such passages show a concern for nourishing life, such concerns were widespread and the attribution of such passages to a single "school" tracing back to Yang Zhu is very unlikely. Even if those passages were written by "followers" of Yang Zhu, we cannot assume their philosophical vocabulary was the same as his, just as Mengzi's use of *xing* does not prove that Kongzi used *xing* as a central concept.
6. Quotations from the *Xing Zi Ming Chu*〈性自命出〉(XZMC hereafter) and other Guodian texts are based primarily on Liu Zhao, *Guodian Chujian Jiaoshi*《郭店楚簡校釋》(Fuzhou: Fujian Renmin Publisher, 2003) and are cited by strip

number. I have also consulted the reconstructions of the text in Li Tianhong, *"Xing Zi Ming Chu" Yanjiu*《〈性自命出〉研究》(Wuhan: Hubei Jiaoyu Publisher, 2003); Ding Yuanzhi, *Guodian Chujian: Rujia Yiji Sizhong Shizhe*《郭店楚簡儒家佚籍四种釋析》(Taipei: Taiwan Guji Publisher, 2000); and Chen Wei, *Guodian Zhushu Bieshi*《郭店竹書別釋》(Wuhan: Hubei Jiaoyu Publisher, 2002), as well as the Shanghai museum version of the text, known as the "Xing Qing Lun〈性情論〉," ed. Ji Xusheng and Chen Linqing in *Shanghai Bowuguanzang Zhanguo Chuzhujian I Duben*《上海博物館藏戰國楚竹簡（I）讀本》, ed. Ji Xusheng (Taipei: Wanjuanlou Tushu Fufen Publisher, 2004). All translations are my own, but I have consulted passages translated in Attilio Andreini, "The Meaning of *qing* 情 in the Texts of Guodian Tomb no. 1," in *Love, Hatred, and Other Passions: Questions and Themes on Emotions in Chinese Civilization*, ed. Paolo Santangelo and Donatello Guida (Leiden: Brill, 2006), 149–65; Erica Brindley, "Music and Cosmos in the Development of 'Psychology' in Early China," *T'oung Pao* 92, nos. 1–3 (2006): 1–49; Shirley Chan, "Human Nature and Moral Cultivation in the Guodian 郭店 Text of the Xing Zi Ming Chu 性自命出 (Nature Derives from Mandate)," *Dao: A Journal of Comparative Philosophy* 8, no. 4 (2009): 361–82. Chen Ning, "The Ideological Background of the Mencian Discussion of Human Nature: A Reexamination," in *Mencius: Contexts and Interpretations*, ed. Alan Chan (Honolulu: University of Hawai'i Press, 2002), 17–41; Paul Goldin, *After Confucius* (Honolulu: University of Hawai'i Press, 2005); Michael Puett, "The Ethics of Responding Properly: The Notion of *qing* 情 in Early Chinese Thought," in *Love and Emotions in Traditional Chinese Literature*, ed. Halvor Eifring (Leiden: Brill, 2004), 37–68; and James Behuniak, *Mencius on Becoming Human* (Albany: State University of New York Press, 2005).

7. XZMC, 1–2.
8. Ibid., 29, 43 (joy), 31–32 (anxious concern), 34–35 (anger), 66–67 (reverence).
9. Ibid., 4–5.
10. Ibid., 43–44.
11. Behuniak, *Mencius on Becoming Human*, 81, and Chan, "Human Nature and Moral Cultivation," 365, both translate the line roughly this way. See also Guo Yi (Li Tianhong, 139); Ding Yuanzhi, *Guodian Chujian*, 27–28; Andreini, "Meaning of *qing*," 157; Ding Sixin, *Guodian Chumu Zhujian Sixiang Yanjiu*《郭店楚墓竹簡思想研究》(Beijing: Dongfang Publisher, 2000), 177; and Liang Tao, *Guodian Zhujian yu Si-Meng Xuepai*《郭店竹簡與思孟學派》(Beijing: Zhongguo Renmin Daxue Press, 2008), 145–46.
12. Li Tianhong, Liu Xinlan, and Zhao Jianwei read the line in basically this way (Li Tianhong, 138–39); Chen Wei, *Guodian Zhushu Bieshi*, 179, explains it as "consider good," and Puett, "Ethics of Responding Properly," 47, translates *shan* as "deeming things good." There is precedence for this use of *shan* in the Chu bamboo strips. In the "*Kongzi Shi Lun*〈孔子詩論〉" Kongzi says of the "*Wan Qiu*〈宛丘〉" ode: "I affirm it as good," literally "I *shan* it (*wu shan zhi* 吾善之)" (Ji Xusheng, *Shanghai Bowuguanzang I*, 69, slips 21–22). *Shan* is probably used in the same way in the phrase "affirm its refinement (*shan qi jie* 善其節)" (XZMC, 21).
13. *Mengzi*, 2A6, 6A6.
14. "*Yu Cong* II," 21.
15. I am grateful to Professor Chung-ying Cheng for pointing this out.
16. Zhu Xi 朱熹 explains the line from the *Zhong Yong* in just these terms, saying that pleasure, anger, sorrow, and joy are *qing* and that the condition of their not having yet issued forth is *xing* (*Sishu Zhangju Jizhu*《四書章句集注》[Beijing: Zhonghua Shuju Publisher, 2003], 18). For the "Classic of Music," see Sun Xidan 孫希旦, *Li Ji Jijie*《禮記集解》(Beijing: Zhonghua Shuju Publisher), 984. Similar passages are given in Ding Yuanzhi, *Guodian Chujian*, 22, and Li Tianhong, 135. Andreini, "Meaning of *qing*," 155–56, has a nice account of this relationship with emphasis on the external and internal.
17. Dan Robins provides ample evidence from a wide range of received texts showing that *xing* refers to actual current characteristics rather than a potentiality or proper course of development ("The Warring States Conception of *Xing* 性," *Dao: A Journal of Chinese Philosophy*, forthcoming). Coming from an analysis of *qi*, Behuniak also

argues that *xing* should be understood in terms of configurations of actual force rather than in terms of potentiality or teleology.

18. XZMC, 9.
19. My analysis leaves out the central role of the heart in the XZMC. For a discussion of this issue, see Franklin Perkins, "Human Motivation and the Heart in the *Xing Zi Ming Chu*," *Dao: A Journal of Comparative Philosophy* 8, no. 2 (2009): 117–31, which fills out aspects of the text not considered here.
20. XZMC, 2–3.
21. *Mengzi*, 6A7, 6A15, 7A1, 7A38; *Xunzi*, chap. 22, "*Zhengming*〈正名〉," (Li Disheng 李滌生, *Xunzi Jishi*《荀子集釋》 [Taipei: Xuesheng Shuju Publisher, 1979], 529); *Zhong Yong*, Zhu, 17. For an excellent discussion of this connection between *tian* and *xing*, see Liang, *Guodian Zhujian yu Si-Meng Xuepai*, 143–45.
22. XZMC, 15, 40–41.
23. Ibid., 9–12.
24. There is some uncertainty around almost every phrase in the passage, but the most important disagreements are around the character taken here as *ni* 逆 and translated as "entice," and the character taken as *jie* 節, translated as "restrain." Using *ni* seems to be the majority position (Liu Zhao, *Guodian Chujian Jiaoshi*, 94; Li Tianhong, "*Xing Zi Ming Chu*" *Yanjiu*, 144–45; Chen Linqing [Ji Xusheng, 160–62]; Ding Yuanzhi, *Guodian Chujian*, 38; Chen Wei, *Guodian Zhushu Bieshi*, 183) but its meaning is uncertain. I have followed Puett in translating it as "entice." There is no consensus on the second, and I have followed Chen Linqing (who follows Qiu Xigui) in taking it as *jie* 節, restrain, regulate, or refine (Ji Xusheng, 162). Chen Ning, "A Reexamination," 24–26, makes an interesting case that it should be *jiao* 矯, which means to straighten and is a term Xunzi uses for modifying *xing*. That would pair nicely with hone (*li*), another term that Xunzi uses.
25. The one other passage (XZMC, 51–53) that associates *xing* and goodness should be read in the context, not as a claim about what *xing* naturally *is* but what *xing* can *become*.
26. XZMC, 18–20. While the point that rituals began with human *qing* and were modified to be appropriate is clear, there are disagreements on the details. I have followed Li Tianhong, "*Xing Zi Ming Chu*" *Yanjiu*, 155. Liu Zhao, *Guodian Chujian Jiaoshi*, 95–96 is similar. For other views, see Ji Xusheng, 165, 171–73, and Li Tianhong, 151–55.
27. XZMC, 15–18.
28. Ibid., 23.
29. On the role of music, see Brindley, "Music and Cosmos"; Brindley, "Music and 'Seeking One's Heart-Mind' in the 'Xing Zi Ming Chu,' " *Dao: A Journal of Comparative Philosophy* 5, no. 2 (2006): 247–55; and Edward Slingerland, "The Problem of Moral Spontaneity in the Guodian Corpus," *Dao: A Journal of Comparative Philosophy* 7, no. 3 (2008): 250–51.
30. XZMC, 32–33.
31. Ibid., 11; 13.
32. Li Tianhong, 146; Chen Wei, *Guodian Zhushu Bieshi*, 184; Ji Xusheng, 161–62.
33. Li Tianhong, 146.
34. Liu Zhao, 95.
35. Puett, "Ethics of Responding Properly," 48, translates *gu* as "intention" and *youwei* as "activity." Chan, "Human Nature and Moral Cultivation," 367, similarly takes *gu* as "purposeful activities," and *youwei* as "what is done through effort." I think it is slightly more plausible to take *youwei* itself as intentional activity and then *gu* as the reasons for that activity. Goldin, *After Confucius*, 41, takes *gu* as "causes" but *youwei* as "efficacious." A few commentators take *gu* as referring to the classics or the past, as Behuniak, *Mencius on Becoming Human*, 82, translates it as "things already brought about." For other views, see Li Tianhong, 146, Ji Xusheng, 161–62, and Chan, "Human Nature and Moral Cultivation," 367 n. 17.
36. XZMC, 15–18.
37. Ibid., 11.
38. Xunzi, "*Xing E*"〈性惡〉, 743.
39. XZMC, 40.

40. "*Yu Cong* II," 8–9. See also "*Wu Xing*" 〈五行〉, 32–33, and "*Yu Tang Zhi Dao*" 〈唐虞之道〉, 7–10.
41. XZMC, 54–55.
42. Similar associations appear in other Guodian texts. For example, the "*Yu Cong* III," 35–37, explicitly associates rightness with appropriateness (*yi* 宜) and benevolence with care (*ai* 愛). A line from the "*Yu Cong* I," 22–23, says, "Benevolence is born from people; rightness is born from the way."
43. XZMC, 58–59. This appears in clearer form in "*Liu De*" 〈六德〉, 30–31.
44. See also "*Wu Xing*," 33–42. Czikszentmihalyi, *Material Virtue*, 113–27, nicely discusses these passages in the broader context of tensions between familial loyalty and public good.
45. XZMC, 36–38. Chen Linqing (Ji Xusheng, 204–5); Liu Zhao, *Guodian Chujian Jiaoshi*, 100; and Chen Wei, *Guodian Zhushu Bieshi*, 202, all take the passage as indicating the limits of deliberate action. Similarly, Slingerland, "Problem of Moral Spontaneity," 249, takes *youwei* as "trying/striving," and Brindley, "Music and Cosmos," 31, as "with purpose." Li Tianhong, "*Xing Zi Ming Chu*" *Yanjiu*, 176, though, takes *wei* here as "insincere," and Chan, "Human Nature and Moral Cultivation," 371, translates it as "artifice/hypocrisy." It should be noted that in the Shanghai Museum text (but not the Guodian), the form of *wei* 爲 includes an image of the heart *xin* 心. The Shanghai text is also slightly shorter: "In any study, if one seeks the heart with deliberate actions, it cannot be attained. People's not being able to use deliberate action thus can be known" (Ji Xusheng, 203).
46. Slingerland nicely shows that the Guodian texts reflect an explicit debate about deliberate action.
47. E.g., "*Wu Xing*," 1–2.
48. XZMC, 18.
49. Ibid., 27–28.
50. "*Yu Cong* I," 18–21. The last clause is reconstructed based on the parallel. Commentators agree that rightness and ritual are among those which enter from outside, but there is disagreement on the third term. Ding Sixin, *Guodian Chumu Zhujian Sixiang Yanjiu*, 230, takes it as wisdom.
51. XZMC, 3–4.
52. There is some consensus on sincerity as one of the central concerns of the Guodian texts. Czikszentmihalyi, *Material Virtue*, 51–52, takes this concern as emerging in response to accusations of hypocrisy against the Ru. Slingerland takes up a similar concern but in relation to spontaneity. Brindley, "Music and 'Seeking One's Heart-Mind,' " discusses sincerity in relation to music.
53. XZMC, 36–38; cf. 44–47.
54. *Wei* here and at the start of the next sentence is written with a heart radical in both Guodian and Shanghai Museum versions of the text (Liu Zhao, 102; Ji Xusheng, 209).
55. There is no agreement on the character I follow Chen Linqing (Ji Xusheng, 218) in taking as *yin* 隱, "concealing." For other options, see Li Tianhong, 183.
56. XZMC, 48–51.
57. I take this point from Pang Pu, "*Ying Yan Shu Shuo: Guodian Chujian Ji Zhongshan Sanqi Xin Pang Wenzi Shishuo*" 〈郢燕書說—郭店楚簡及中山三器心旁文子試說〉, in *Wenhua Yi Ou* 《文化一隅》 (Zhengzhou: Zhongzhou Guji Chubanshe Publisher, 2005), 39–41. For discussions of this, see Slingerland, "Problem of Moral Spontaneity," 248–49, and Edward Shaughnessy, *Rewriting Early Chinese Texts* (Albany: State University of New York Press, 2006), 26–28.
58. Chen Linqing takes *wei* here as deliberate action (Ji Xusheng, 217–18), and Pang Pu argues that this is the meaning of *wei* with the heart radical (Pang, "*Ying Yan Shu Shuo*," 39–40). Most, though, take *wei* as deceptive and *qing* as genuine (e.g., Liu Zhao, *Guodian Chujian Jiaoshi*, 102–3; Li Tianhong, "*Xing Zi Ming Chu*" *Yanjiu*, 182–84; Chen Wei, *Guodian Zhushu Bieshi*, 197; Ding Yuanzhi, *Guodian Chujian*, 99–100).
59. XZMC, 38–40.
60. There is little agreement on the first character, which I have followed Liu Zhao, *Guodian Chujian Jiaoshi*, 100–101; Chen Linqing (Ji Xusheng, 206); and Liang,

Guodian Zhujian yu Si-Meng Xuepai, 146, in taking it as *shu* 恕, reciprocity. Chung-ying Cheng suggests it might be *cha* 察, discernment. The other main disagreement is on how to interpret *fang* 方. I follow Chen Ning, "A Reexamination," 26, who translates it as "orientation." Liang, *Guodian Zhujian yu Si-Meng Xuepai*, 146–47, is similar, taking it as a way or principle. Li Tianhong, *"Xing Zi Ming Chu" Yanjiu*, 178, and Liu Zhao, *Guodian Chujian Jiaoshi*, 100–101, take it as expression or manifestation. Chen Linqing explains *fang* as "of the same kind" (Ji Xusheng, 203–4; also Chen Wei, *Guodian Zhushu Bieshi*, 203).

61. *Lun Yu* 2.4 (Yang Bojun, *Lunyu Yizhu* [Beijing: Zhonghua Shuju Publisher, 2002]).
62. On this point, see Brindley, "Music and 'Seeking One's Heart-Mind,' " 248, Slinger-land, "Problem of Moral Spontaneity," 251–54, Liang, *Guodian Zhujian yu Si-Meng Xuepai*, 154–57, and Chan, "Human Nature and Moral Cultivation," 380–81.
63. *Mengzi*, 6A6; *"Yu Cong* I," 18–21.
64. The three positions outlined here roughly correspond to the three alternatives discussed by Shun, *Mencius and early Chinese thought*, 94–112, and taken up by Van Norden, *Virtue Ethics and Consequentialism*, 287–301. Both have excellent analyses of the various possibilities. Shun takes the dispute as about the source of knowledge of rightness, roughly the second alternative described here. Van Norden takes it about whether or not rightness requires any proper feelings, roughly the third alternative.
65. *Mengzi*, 1A7; *Xunzi*, "Xing E," 544.
66. *Mengzi*, 6A15.

CHEN LAI

THE GUODIAN BAMBOO SLIPS AND CONFUCIAN THEORIES OF HUMAN NATURE[1]

Based on general clues remaining from the pre-Qin Confucian School, Kongzi claimed that "by nature human beings are similar but by habits they become differentiated," Mengzi who lived during the middle of the Warring States Period, advocated that human nature is good, while Xunzi, from the latter part of the Warring States Period, claimed that human nature is bad. These became the three standard models for Confucian theories of human nature as we know them today. However, in contrast to the theories of Mengzi and Xunzi, Kongzi in the *Lun Yu* did not clearly present his thoughts on human nature. Without material close to the period when Kongzi lived for additional support, how should "being similar by nature" be interpreted? Furthermore, in addition to Mengzi and Xunzi, from the pre-Qin and Han all the way to the Sui and the Tang Dynasties, there continuously were Confucian theories intermingling the "good" and "bad" in human nature. These were gradually forgotten after the Song Dynasty.

Following the publication of the *Guodian Chu Slips* (*GDCS* hereafter), I used a selection of articles to point out that the *GDCS* prove that mainstream perspective of the pre-Qin early Confucian theories of human nature was not that human nature was good, or at least they had not yet formed the concept of the goodness of human nature. This is one of the most important contributions of the *GDCS*. Within the *GDCS*, the "*Xing Zi Ming Chu* 〈性自命出〉" (*XZMC* hereafter) and other texts used a logical structure linking heaven (*tian* 天)-destiny (*ming* 命)-human nature (*xing* 性)-emotion (*qing* 情)-the way (*dao* 道), to discuss the basic quality and actual functioning of human nature. It emphasized that *ming* descends from heaven, *xing* comes from *ming*, *qing* is derived from *xing*, and *dao* is derived from *qing*. What is bestowed by heaven is *xing*, which is our natural or heavenly born (*tiansheng* 天生) likes and dislikes, which also is the internal *qi* (vital energy) of human joy, anger, sadness, and happiness. When this

CHEN LAI, Professor, Department of Philosophy, Dean of Academy of Chinese Learning, Tsinghua University. Specialties: Confucian philosophy, Neo-Confucianism, contemporary Confucian philosophy. E-mail: chenlai@mail.tsinghua.edu.cn

Journal of Chinese Philosophy, Supplement to Volume 37 (2010) 33–50
© *2010 Journal of Chinese Philosophy*

qi is expressed externally, it becomes *qing* (emotions), and when *qing* fits with moderation and restraint (*zhongjie* 中節), it is *Dao*.

This type of interpretation in terms of natural life or growth resembles naturalistic theories of human nature. Its philosophical basis is "using *qi* to discuss *xing*" rather than using *li* 理, integral patterns or "principle," as the ground upon which the theory of human nature was developed. As it is likely that the *XZMC* is the product of the direct disciples of Kongzi, this point of view should be closest to Kongzi's own view of human nature, continuing and developing it. What is striking is that this kind of view is similar to most of the theories of human nature that we know from the pre-Qin and Han periods, which shows that this point of view on human nature was actually the mainstream early Confucian view. Mengzi's theory that human nature is good and Xunzi's claim that human nature is bad both were rather rare and exceptional during the early development of Confucian thought. The excavation of *GDCS* presents important documents that contribute to the reintroduction of the ancient Confucian theories on human nature. At the same time, the publication of *GDCS* gave us a new opportunity to rethink the continuity and changeability of the "Confucian Tradition."[2]

I. Reanalysis of the Views of Human Nature in the *GDCS*

The *XZMC* within *GDCS* concentrates on the topic of human nature, and its perspective holds many noteworthy points. The following discussion is separated into different topics.

1. "Human Nature" and "Likes and Dislikes"

The *XZMC* says: "Likes and dislikes are human nature; what is liked and disliked are things."[3] The direct meaning of this statement is that likes and dislikes are our basic nature, while things (*wu* 物) are the objects of like and dislike. Here the relation between things and our nature, *xing*, clearly has a sense of the internal and the external. As I have previously pointed out, "likes and dislikes" (*haowu* 好惡) could be explained in two ways. First, "likes and dislikes" could point to the activities of emotion and desire, so that "likes and dislikes is human nature" would say that the feelings of liking and disliking are manifestations of internal nature. Second, "likes and dislikes" could point to the internal tendencies and needs of human beings. If A sees beauty and likes it, this is emotion (*qing* 情), but it is not that A sees beauty today and likes it and then tomorrow sees beauty again and dislikes it. Whenever A sees beauty she or he will like it. Therefore, each action of A liking or disliking beauty will reflect and express A's internal "likes." These internal "likes" are exactly human nature. Having clarified these two possible explanations, the key to what is most reasonable is to decide if "likes and dislikes" refers to *qing* (emotion) or to *xing* (nature).

If the likes and dislikes belong to *qing*, why does it say that "likes and dislikes are *xing*?" When such a question is raised, we must remind ourselves that the distinction between *xing* and *qing* was not generally recognized during the pre-Qin period, so we must take care not to impose a clear distinction that only came later. Looking at the context, "liking and disliking" in the phrase, "liking and disliking is *xing*, what is liked and disliked are things," points at the activities of awareness and emotions. Therefore, the "likes and dislikes" that are human nature should point toward the activities of emotion—*qing*. Thus "likes and dislikes are *xing*" emphasizes that the feelings of liking and disliking are actually rooted within human nature. At the same time, the end of the passage emphasizes that "*qing* are generated from *xing*," thus making an effort to distinguish *xing* and *qing*. In this way, "liking and disliking are *xing*" can be understood in relation to "*qing* are generated from *xing*," that feelings of liking and disliking are derived from our basic nature. From a philosophical point of view, the likes and dislikes are on the phenomenal level of conscious activities, not on the ontological level. Further, the likes and dislikes here refer to the likes and dislikes of emotion and desire, which are not the same as the likes and dislikes of virtue, mentioned by Mengzi.

In pre-Qin thought, using likes and dislikes or emotions (*qing*) to discuss *xing* was very common. For example, the "Book of Music" says, "When likes and dislikes do not have internal constraints, then external things entice them."[4] This also is an example of speaking according to the distinctions of human nature and things (*xing* and *wu*), as well as internal and external. The pre-Qin and Han periods have another special characteristic which is the joined naming of "*qingxing*" together. The *Xunzi* also often uses likes and dislikes to discuss *qingxing*, and pre-Qin intellectuals often did not distinguish between *qing* and *xing*. For example the *Xunzi* says, "the likes and dislikes, joy, anger, sadness and happiness of *xing* is *qing*," and, "if the people have the *qing* of likes and dislikes while they do not have the appropriate standards to respond to joy and anger, there will be disorder."[5] Such statements tend to use *qing* to discuss *xing*, which in effect makes our emotional activities, desires, and needs our basic nature. Although using "*qing* are generated from *xing*" to explain and interpret "liking and disliking is *xing*" could be considered a bit forced, this explanation shows that the *XZMC* passage had already made an abstract distinction between *qing* and *xing*. This improves on the earlier theory that did not distinguish the two.

This analysis shows that of the two types of explanations mentioned, the *XZMC* should be taken as categorizing likes and dislikes as *qing*, rooting these *qing* in our basic nature, *xing*. From this we can deduce that the earliest theories of human nature in the classical period did not separate *xing* and *qing* but took the feelings of liking and disliking or of joy, anger, sadness, and happiness, as *xing*. They took the phenomena of desires and emotions directly as the nature with which human beings are born. This conception of human nature takes *xing* as special qualities had from birth. The next development then took the feelings (*qing*) of liking and disliking as rooted in *xing*, taking the *qi* 氣 of joy, anger, sadness, and happiness as *xing*. They thus distinguish the internal nature from the external projection of emotions.

2. *"Xing" and the "Qi of Joy and Anger"*

Another important passage in the *XZMC* is: "The *qi* of joy, anger, sadness and sorrow is *xing*; its appearing externally is because things attract it."[6] This "*xing*" should not be explained as "rooted in *xing*" or "the manifestation of *xing*," because the following phrase, "when it appears externally," already presupposes that the "*qi* of joy, anger, sadness and sorrow is *xing*" indicates the "internal." Thus this sentence explains that the *qi* (vital energy) of joy, anger, sadness, and sorrow is *xing*, and that when this *qi* appears externally it is because of the attraction of external things. "Appearing externally" should indicate the *qing* (emotions) of joy, anger, sadness, and sorrow. Therefore, the *qi* of joy, anger, sadness, and sorrow is not the same as the *qing* of these sentiments; the former has not appeared externally whilst the latter has appeared.

Using *qi* to discuss *xing* is not commonly seen in extant pre-Qin materials. This passage from the *XZMC* takes the philosophical standpoint of "using *qi* to discuss *xing*." *Xing* is the "internal" *qi* of joy, anger, sadness, and sorrow which has not yet "appeared externally"; that which appears is *qing*. The distinction between the internal and the external expresses the distinction between *xing* and *qing*, which is an advance over using *qing* as *xing*. This mode of thought can be seen in some pre-Qin materials, as in the "*Wen Wang Guan Ren* 〈文王官人〉" chapter of the *Da Dai Li Ji*《大戴禮記》:

> The people have five *xing*: joy, anger, desire, anxiety and fear. When *qi* of joy is internally accumulated, even if one wants to hide it, exposed [*yang* 陽] joy will appear (externally). When the *qi* of anger

is internally accumulated, even if one wants to hide it, exposed anger will appear. When the *qi* of desire is internally accumulated, even if one wants to hide it, exposed desire will appear. When the *qi* of anxiety is internally accumulated, even if one wants to hide it, exposed anxiety will appear. When the *qi* of sorrow is internally accumulated, even if one wants to hide it, exposed sorrow will appear. When the five *qi* are genuinely established inside, they take form on the outside. The people's *qing* cannot be hidden.[7]

This passage also appears in the "*Guan Ren Jie*〈官人解〉" chapter of the *Yi Zhou Shu*《逸周書》, but with slight differences in wording, as in the first phrase, which says the "five *qi*" instead of "five *xing*." This shows that humans have five *xing*, which are the *qi* of joy, anger, desire, anxiety, and sorrow. The "five *qi*" belongs to the internal or what is in the center, while "*yang*," exposed, expresses the *qing* that appear. The accumulation of joyous *qi* internally will certainly issue joyous *qing* externally. This kind of thinking is congruent with this section of the *XZMC*. From a philosophical perspective, this type of exposition uses concrete material to express the originally abstract concept of *xing*. A similar move from abstract to concrete is often seen in ancient Greek philosophy.

Another section of the "Book of Music" contains a similar view:

Thus the first kings rooted it in *qing* and *xing*, examined it with measure and number, and regulated it with ritual and rightness. They fit with the harmony of living *qi* and they led the actions of the five constancies, making them *yang* but not dispersed and *yin* but not blocked, their hard *qi* not angry and their soft *qi* not timid, the four mixed smoothly in the center and issued to act on the outside.[8]

"The four mixed smoothly in the center and issued to act on the outside" explains "rooted it in *qing* and *xing*," which is the same as "when the five *qi* are genuinely established inside, they take form on the outside" from the "*Wen Wang Guan Ren*" chapter cited above. The "four" should indicate the four *qi* of *yin* 陰, *yang* 陽, *gang* 剛 (hard), and *rou* 柔 (soft), and "mixing in the center" refers to the internal, showing that the four *qi* are actually *xing*. Accordingly, the manifested *qi* of joy is the *qing* of joy, the manifested *qi* of anger is the *qing* of anger, and so on. Each type of emotion that is seen externally will be based in a matching kind of *qi* that is internal. This *qi* is *xing*. The concept of *xing*, based on its whole developed meaning, should indicate basic and distinctive characteristics. However, the philosophical abstraction of early Chinese philosophy still could not completely depart from the concrete, so it took *qi* as the substance of the *xing* from which *qing* are derived.

3. "Xing" and "Qing"

The above indicates that when joyous *qi* is gathered inside, feelings of joy issue on the outside, so that joyous *qi* is the origin or basis of joyous *qing*. Thus it says: "*Qing* are generated from *xing*." This type of theory of *qing* coming from *xing* based on *qi* as foundation differs from the way in which the Confucians of the Song Dynasty based their theory of *xing* on pattern or principle (*li* 理). For example the Cheng-Zhu "School of Principle" (*Li Xue* 理學) claimed that *xing* is *li*, and that *xing* is expressed as *qing*. The "School of Principle," though, also had the idea that "the seven *qing* are expressions of *qi*," which is closer to the theory of the *XZMC*.

"*Qing* are generated from *xing*" appears twice in the *XZMC*, so this proposition was highly regarded by the author. The same proposition also appears in the "Yu Cong," but with further development:

> Love [*ai* 愛] is born from *xing*, endearment [*qin* 親] is born from love, loyalty is born from endearment.
>
> Desires are born from *xing*, considerations are born from desires.
>
> Knowing is born from *xing*, *mao* 卯 [smoothly following] is born from knowing.
>
> Charity is born from *xing*, *yi* 易 [ease] is born from charity.
>
> Disliking is born from *xing*, anger is born from disliking.
>
> Joy is born from *xing*, happiness is born from joy, sorrow is born from happiness.
>
> Irritation is born from *xing*, worry is born from irritation, grief is born from worry.
>
> Fear is born from *xing*, *jian* 監 [greed] is born from fear.
>
> Strength is born from *xing*, taking a stand is born from strength.
>
> Weakness is born from *xing*, doubts are born from weakness.[9]

When it is said that "*qing* are generated from *xing*," what does *qing* refer to? It should include love, desire, knowing, endearment, dislikes, joy, irritation, fear, and others. Based on this passage, all of these emotions are derived from nature (*xing*). These emotions can be the most primary emotions. When it says that happiness is born from joy, worry is born from anger, anger is born from dislikes, and endearment is derived from love, although all are emotions, the former are the foundations for the latter, which develop and strengthen them, as "when there is irritation there is worry" thus says "worry is derived from irritation." We can establish two levels of feelings: the primary level and the derivative level, both of which are *qing*. The "*Yu Cong*" does not mention that "likes" are born from *xing*, but it mentions that dislikes are; logically this should encompass "Likes and dislikes is generated from *xing*." It is notable that the *XZMC* says "the *qi* of joy, anger, sorrow and sadness are xing," while within the "*Yu Cong*," only "joy" is derived from *xing* and the other three emotions are derivative. This shows that the concrete explanations of the emotions in the "*Yu Cong*" have some differences from the *XZMC*.

The *GDCS* reveals that the early Confucian conception of human nature was not meant to explain the basis of the virtues but to explain the basis for emotions and likes and dislikes. The discussion of *xing* in terms of *qi* should be understood from this side.

4. Human Nature—Xing 性 and Heart/Mind—Xin 心

The *XZMC* says: "Within the four seas, their natures are the same, but the use of the heart/mind is different for each. Teaching makes it so."[10] Kongzi said "by nature human beings are similar but by habits they become differentiated." This passage from the *XZMC* clearly inherits this idea from Kongzi. Humans all have a nature of joy, anger, likes, and dislikes, so one can say their natures are alike, or that, "by nature they are close." However, the heart/mind of humans are not the same. Here, the heart/mind refers to the level of ethical consciousness, which is the result of education. Therefore, it is said that "the use of the heart/mind is different for each; teaching makes it so," because "teaching is what gives birth to virtue (*de* 德) in the center." From this expression, we can see that the author does not have a view of *xing* as basically good or basically bad.

Of course, even if human nature were "good," one might still say that the use of the heart/mind is different because of teaching, but this passage does not explicitly put forth this idea. If we say that this theory of human nature is similar to and a further development of Kongzi's own theory, then it could be said that Kongzi's theory that humans by nature are similar would be based on taking human nature in terms of joy, anger, likes, and dislikes. It is worth noting that the author of the *XZMC* thinks that human nature and the heart/mind are different. The basic nature of human beings can be the same while their heart/minds differ. This emphasis on the separation of *xin* and *xing* shows that human nature belongs to the level of innate characteristics (*benzhi* 本質), while the heart/mind is on the level of conscious phenomena (*yishi xianxiang* 意識現象). The text says further, "The heart/mind has no set intention; it waits on things and then moves, waits on being pleased and then acts, waits on practice and then is set."[11] This shows that the author's concept of the heart/mind points to ordinary knowing and originally does not have a set direction.

Aside from this, the "*Cheng Zhi Wen Zhi* 〈成之聞之〉" (*CZWZ*) also mentions: "The common people all have *xing* [*min jie you xing*

民皆有性].” The idea is that the sages and the common people have a similar nature. The *CZWZ* further says:

> The task is in winning the trust of the people. The "Yue Ming 《説命》" says: "Get trust from the masses and accomplish one's virtue [*yun shi qi de* 允师淒德]." This refers to the fact that winning the trust of the people can accomplish one's virtue. The nature of sagely people and the nature of common people will grow and be established. The moral integrity of these is still the same [*weiyou feizhi* 未有非之]. Restrained in this, then they still are so. Even if the people affirm the dao, there is still nothing much to select. Reaching their length and breadth, thickness and greatness, then sagely people cannot hesitate in fear. This is because people all have *xing* but sagely people cannot be imitated.[12]

This passage starts from the importance of being trusted by the masses, but it is very difficult to understand. The general meaning seems to be, the nature of the sages and the nature of the people is had by both without much difference. Average people and those lower are all like this. The liking people have for the *dao* is not born from heaven (*tiansheng* 天生) but made so by continuous practice and cultivation. When practice and cultivation accumulate depth and breadth, one becomes a sage. Therefore, although the common people have *xing*, it is difficult to reach the realm of the sage (precisely because the practice and cultivation of the common people is not sufficient). This perspective also can be considered a manifestation of the theory differentiating *xing* and *xin*, if it is the latter that enables sages to become different.

5. "Xing" (Nature) and "Wu" (Material Things)

While formed from different pieces of writing, the thought in the "Book of Music" is basically consistent. Consider the following examples:

> The movement of the human heart/mind is caused by things.[13]

> Being stimulated by things and moving is the desires of *xing*. When knowing reaches to things, then likes and dislikes take form.[14]

> Since the stimulation by things is boundless, then the likes and dislikes of human beings are without regulation.[15]

> Therefore, the common people have the nature of blood-and-*qi* and knowing of the heart, but they do not have constancy in joy, anger, sadness and happiness. They are stimulated by things and move, and the way of the heart takes form.[16]

In these explanations, there is always the juxtaposition of internal heart/mind and external things, recognizing that the movement of the heart/mind, the movement of desire, and the formation of likes and dislikes are all evoked by "things." These conscious or "subjective" activities, emotions, and desires all originate by being stirred by external things. The *XZMC* and the "Book of Music" have similar perspectives, that "what moves *xing* are things," or, "its appearing externally is because things attract it."[17] Here the "it" indicates *xing* while *xing* seen on the outside is *qing*; appearing externally is the "likes and dislikes taking form." The *XZMC* differs from the "Book of Music" in that it not only discusses the moving of the heart/mind but also discusses the moving of human nature itself. This line of thought advocates that although human beings have a *xing* of liking and disliking, it is only through the enticement of things (that which is liked and disliked) that the likes and dislikes are expressed or externalized. Actually, things stimulating our nature into movement often appear in the "School of Principle" in the Song and Ming Dynasties, although of course this was influenced by the "Book of Music" rather than the *XZMC*.

If likes and dislikes are manifestations of human nature, what is the content of human nature? The "Book of Music" says, "people have the nature of blood-and-*qi* and knowing of the heart (*xueqi xinzhi zhi xing* 血气心知之性), but they do not have constancy in joy, anger, sadness and happiness." This stipulates that the root of human nature comes from the blood-and-*qi* and knowing of the heart. This "blood-and-*qi*" defines desire, while the "knowing of the heart" sets the ability to understand. Therefore the theory of human nature within the "Book of Music" definitely does not conceptualize *xing* as ethical. The *XZMC's* discussion of *xing* in terms of the *qi* of joy, anger, likes, and dislikes, should be similar to this blood-and-*qi* of human nature. Furthermore, if things are able to stimulate and evoke the manifestations of human nature, this nature stimulated obviously does not point to an innate ethical quality but rather to the basic character of living and surviving.

6. "Xing" Human Nature and "Xi" Practice

The *XZMC* has this notion of the cultivation of human nature:

> What moves *xing* are things. What entices *xing* is being pleased. What models *xing* are deliberate reasons. What hones *xing* is rightness. What draws out *xing* are circumstances. What nourishes *xing* is practice. What grows *xing* is *dao*. . . . Practicing is having that by which to practice their nature.[18]

The *Lunyu* and *Mengzi* only mention practice, *xi* 習, a few times, and never explicitly link practice to the topic of human nature, *xing*. However, a quotation from Kongzi in the "*Bao Fu*〈保傅〉" chapter of the *Da Dai Li Ji* specifically discusses the relationship between "practice" and "human nature": "Kongzi said, 'Few are completed as if by heavenly nature; practice [*xi*] makes it constant.' Thus the Yin and Zhou Dynasties lasted long because they had the dao."[19] "Practice" in *GDCS* seems to have two meanings. "What nourishes human nature is practice" speaks broadly of customary habits which could be neutral, while practice in "practice is having that by which to practice one's nature," seems to refer to the positive work of cultivating our nature. Based on this, it would mean "cultivation."

The idea of cultivating *xing* is also mentioned by Mengzi, as in "Retaining the heart/mind and nourishing *xing*, one serves Heaven."[20] Here Mengzi emphasizes "retaining one's heart/mind" as a form of cultivating one's nature. While not using the term *xi*, practice, Mengzi certainly takes the idea of cultivating or nourishing, *yang* 養, very seriously, as we see in his description of barley, which is the same in kind and varies in growth only by how it is cultivated.[21] The cultivation here is certainly cultivation added after what is natural or from heaven (*houtian* 後天). Thus he adds, "So if it attains its nourishment, nothing will not grow; if it loses its nourishment, nothing will not die."[22] This relates to the nourishing of *xing*. As a concept, though, *yang* (cultivate), is not necessarily positive. Shizi 世子 thought, "If one raises up the goodness in our nature, nourishing and perfecting it, then goodness grows. If one raises up the badness in our nature, nourishing and perfecting it, then badness grows."[23] Here, the meaning of *yang*, to nourish or cultivate, has the neutral sense of practice in general.

One problem should be mentioned here—does "the differentiation of the heart/mind" through cultivation also create a "differentiation of human nature?" If so, then how is the idea of "their natures being one" maintained? The *GDCS* does not respond to this, but we can say that within the *GDCS*, the emphasis is not on the basis of virtue in the heart/mind and nature, but on appropriate cultivation and mastery. To use the words of the Ming Dynasty, the stress is not on ontology, *benti* 本體, but on mastery, *gongfu* 功夫.

7. *Xing and Tian (天 Heaven) and Ming (命 Mandate; Decree)*

The *XZMC* says in the first line: "*Xing* comes out from *ming* (decree/destiny), *ming* descends from *tian* (Heaven). The *dao* begins from *qing* (emotions), and *qing* are generated from *xing* (nature)."[24] The editors and compilers of the bamboo strips have paid particular attention to this phrase, thinking that it resembles the first phrase of the *Zhong Yong*《中庸》, "the decree of heaven is called *xing* [*tianming zhi wei xing* 天命之謂性]."[25] Certainly, if we put aside the explanations of the *Zhong Yong* by later Song Confucians, then the meaning of "*xing* comes out from *ming* and *ming* descends from heaven," says that human nature comes from *ming* and *ming* comes from heaven, leading to a literal translation as "the decree of heaven is called human nature."

Really, if we set aside the explanations of the Song Confucians and only rely on "the decree of heaven is called human nature," the meaning cannot be summarized into the theory that human nature is good, but only says that human nature is given by heaven, or that that which has been born of heaven is called human nature. The *Mengzi* says:

> With a plentiful harvest, sons and younger brothers are mostly good.
> With a bad harvest, sons and younger brothers are mostly oppressive.
> It is not that the ability which heaven sends down to them is different.
> It is because they sink and drown their hearts that it is so.[26]

The "ability sent down (*jiang* 降) from heaven" is the natural/heaven born (*tiansheng* 天生) nature, which is the same as "the decree of heaven is called human nature," and is the same as "human nature comes out from *ming* and *ming* descends [*jiang*] from heaven." These statements in themselves do not entail that human nature is good.

The *XZMC* and the first line of the *Zhong Yong* are different, though, in that within the *Zhong Yong*'s phrase, "the decree of heaven is called human nature," *ming* is a decree and not an independent segment of existence. It is an activity or mode of expression of heaven, so that Zhu Xi explains *ming* here as command (*ling* 令).[27] But in the *XZMC*'s line "*ming* descends from heaven," "descend" corresponds to *ming* in the *Zhong Yong*. Hence within the *XZMC*, *ming* itself is commanded and endowed by heaven, but possesses a definite independent existence, which should be related to the ancient cultural belief in *ming*. I think that *ming* here has the meaning of life, *shengming* 生命, as *ming* is spoken of in later Daoism. The meaning of "Human nature comes out from *ming* and *ming* descends from heaven" is that human nature is rooted in the embodiment of life, and life is endowed from heaven. This aligns with the thought of the whole text in using life and *qi* to discuss human nature. Although this explanation still needs more support, it should be tenable in terms of its general line of thought.

II. MAINSTREAM THEORY OF HUMAN NATURE IN PRE-QIN CONFUCIANISM AND ITS POSITION WITHIN THE CONFUCIAN TRADITION

From the perspective of the theory of human nature, the most attractive question has been: do the *XZMC* and the other texts of the

GDCS raise the theory that human nature as good? The "likes and dislikes are human nature," and, "the *qi* of joy, anger, sadness, and sorrow are human nature," of the *XZMC* are surely not the theory that human nature is good. In other words, they do not advocate the idea that "the nature of each human is good." The last part of the *XZMC*, though, has this passage: "Without speaking, the common people have trust: this is one with fine emotions (*meiqing* 美情). Without education, the common people are constant: this is one with a good nature (*xingshan* 性善)."[28] Here the terminology of "human nature is good" appears, but it refers to certain "superiors," those who govern the common people. It says one who, without having made promises, already has the trust of the common people is a person with fine *qing* (emotions); one who, without extending education, already makes the people obtain a constant heart/mind is a person whose *xing* is good. Here *meiqing* and *xingshan* are parallel. If we connect it to the theory of "likes and dislikes are *xing*" or "the *qi* of joy anger sadness and sorrow is *xing*," this line should refer to the likes and dislikes and the joy, anger, sadness, and sorrow of the rulers beings integrated with the *dao*. This would gain the trust of and influence the common people. Here, *shan*, goodness, is similar to *mei*, fine or beautiful, which is different from the Mengzian theory that human nature is *shan*, good. This expression at most claims that only some people have a good nature, and it clearly supposes that those with a good nature are the minority. For this reason, this phrase cannot be generalized into a theory of the goodness of human nature.

According to Wang Chong 王充, "Shi Shuo of Zhou thought that human nature has good and has bad. If one raises up the goodness in our nature, nourishing and perfecting it, then goodness grows."[29] Shizi's theory says that the nature of each human being is not singular but there is a good side and there is a bad side. According to Wang Chong, the disciples of Kongzi, Mi Zi Jian, Qi Diao Kai and the second generation disciple Gongsun Nizi all advocated similar propositions to Shizi. The *Mengzi* records three types of theories on human nature.[30] One proposition is:

> Human nature can become good and can become not good.

Another proposition is:

> There are people with good nature and people with a not good nature.

Gaozi, who lived at the same time as Mengzi, clearly said:

> Human nature is not good and is not not good.

The claim that "human nature can become good and can become not good" aligns with Gaozi's claim that "human nature is not good and is not good." Gaozi also said:"Human nature is like whirling water. Give it an outlet in the east and it will flow east; give it an outlet in the west and it will flow west."[31] This is the same as can become good and can become not good. The theory that "there are people with good nature and people with not good nature," though, differs from the theory of Shizi, claiming not that the nature of everyone has good and has not good but that some people have a good nature and some people have a bad nature. That perspective could be said to be a development of Kongzi's "only the wise and the foolish do not change."[32]

While the theories of human nature of Mizi, Qi Diaozi, Gongsun Nizi, Shizi, and Gaozi are not exactly the same, they are similar, and it can be said that this general type of theory formed the mainstream Confucian theory of human nature in that era. The basic concept of human nature in the *Xunzi* was clearly influenced by this mainstream pre-Qin Confucian theory. Moreover, this early Confucian theory of human nature was not replaced by that of Mengzi but continued to spread. Thus it is not just that this type of theory of human nature can be established as the Confucian theory between Kongzi and Mengzi—it continued to spread in various forms through the Han and Tang periods, becoming the mainstream perspective of Confucian theories of human nature through the Tang Dynasty.

Nevertheless, Mengzi's theory of human nature as good became the dominant Confucian theory of human nature after the Song period. The large majority of Confucian thinkers of the Song and Ming on the theoretical level acknowledged that "human nature" is good. Therefore, if we look at the entire history of Confucian thought, we can see that theories of human nature underwent tremendous changes from the early to the later period. No doubt, the theory of the two Cheng brothers and Zhu Xi that "human nature is principle" played a decisive role in the process of this change.

It could be said that in each historical epoch, the Confucian theory of human nature presented different emphases and configurations, making it is diverse rather than singular, but during each period of history, there was usually one dominant kind of view. The whole development of the theory of human nature within Confucian thought in China can be divided into four stages. The first stage is the ancient period represented by the influence of the *Book of Odes* (*Shi Jing*《詩經》) and the *Book of History* (*Shang Shu*《尚書》); the second is the periods of the Spring and Autumn and Warring States; third is the period of the Han and Tang Dynasties; and fourth is the Song and Ming periods.

The first stage is represented by the *Book of History*, in phrases such as, "not concerned for their nature from heaven [*buyu tianxing* 不虞天性]," or what is called "restraining nature [*jiexing* 節性]," or "from practice to form a nature [*xi yu xing cheng* 習與性成]."[33] These notions of human nature, as Mou Zongsan says, "refer to what is natural [*ziran* 自然] and originary [*benran* 本然], the spontaneous or originary direction of *xing*, the ability of *xing*, the desires of *xing*, or the quality of *xing*," all referring to "the *xing* that is constructed by the natural characteristics of the original nature of life."[34] At this stage, the "good" and "bad" that evaluated the content of the original nature of life had not yet appeared.

The second stage is the Confucianism from the time of Kongzi to the end of the Warring States period. During this time the evaluation of the nature of human beings as "good" or "bad" begins, but it was highly influenced by the thought of the first stage. Taking natural likes as *xing*, this conception of human nature is a "naturalistic nature [ziran zhi xing 自然之性]" or a "descriptive nature [shiran zhi xing 實然之性]," not a "normative nature [dangran zhi xing 當然之性]." Kongzi was influenced by the ideas of the Western Zhou period in advocating the similarity of *xing*, which should refer to a naturalistic human nature.[35] The theory of human nature within the Confucian documents of *GDCS*, which use likes and dislikes or the *qi* of joy, anger, sadness, and sorrow to discuss human nature, emphasize natural feelings as the basis rather than normative principles. Therefore, it is also a way of discussing a naturalistic form of human nature. The theory represented by Gaozi that human nature is without good and without bad, or the theory that human nature can become good or bad, in taking the form of "living is what is called *xing*," also all highlight a naturalistic conception of human nature. During the period of the Kongzi's seventy disciples, they began to use the categories of good and bad to contemplate the topic of human nature. Shizi, Qi Diao Zi, Mi Zi, and Gongsun Nizi all claimed "human nature has good and has bad," which became the mainstream pre-Qin Confucian theory of human nature.

These all take natural feelings and tendencies as a basis for seeking a conception of human nature. Moreover, *GDCS* says, "in sadness and happiness, natures are similar,"[36] which clearly is a continuation of the thought of Kongzi, while its recognition that some people's *xing* is good should be similar to the concept of human nature as having good and having bad, popular in the Warring States period. Moreover, their conception of human nature clearly takes "*qi*" and "likes and dislikes" as a basis. This offers us difficult to obtain materials for understanding the conceptions of human nature from this era. Mengzi developed the concept of human nature having goodness by extending from virtuous feelings toward their common internal basis. Xunzi continued the naturalistic conception of human nature but considered it to be bad. The Confucians of the Warring States period had many different varieties of theories of human nature without any single core. It is just as indicated by Wang Chong, that "former Confucians and those of old wrote and worked on many articles and chapters, all of them with discussions and persuasions about human nature, but none had the capacity to truly decide."[37]

The third stage emphasized "a mix of good and bad." Really, this was a further development of the theory that "Human nature has good and has bad," proposed by Shizi. Dong Zhong Shu, Yang Xiong, and Xun Yue all supported this notion. What made it different from the pre-Qin period is that during this era the theory of mixed good and bad in human nature was integrated with the theory that human nature has three levels of quality. This combined the theory of mixed good and bad as the "middle quality," with the theory of human nature as good as the 'top quality' and the theory of human nature as bad as the "lowest quality." Because people of the middle rank are most numerous, the mixed theory of good and bad was applied most broadly.

The fourth stage is the Cheng-Zhu theory taking principle (*li* 理) as human nature, where human nature is the same as principle and has been endowed by the principle of heaven and earth. A normative conception of human nature became the basic concept of the "School of Principle" and the theory of human nature as good became the primary theory during the Song and Ming periods. Although the notion that human nature is good on the theoretical level was broadly affirmed, along with the dominance of a rationalistic moral nature (*yili zhi xing* 義理之性), there was also the concept of human nature as vital quality (*qizhi* 氣質), which included a naturalistic conception of human nature.

From the perspective of the history of Confucian theories of human nature from the pre-Qin to the Song and Ming periods, there is no single traditional theory. Although in general one can say that from the Southern Song on, there is an emphasis on human nature as good, looking at the entire tradition, the theory that human nature is good cannot be called a consistent position from the beginning. Because of this, the various types of Confucian doctrines of human nature, actually, are various philosophical expositions of the foundations of Confucian thought. Thus from a historical perspective, the theory that human nature is good cannot be the core that defines what counts as Confucian. Otherwise, other than Mengzi, all the Confucian thinkers from the pre-Qin to Sui-Tang periods would be considered to have deviated from the core of Confucian thought. This would equal the negation of the history of Confucianism in those periods, and would even negate many Confucians after the Song. This clearly is not the actual history.

Based on this, we should neither take the earliest form of theory on human nature as fundamental nor should we view the later mainstream theories in the development of Confucian thought as deviations from an orthodox doctrine. These views, whether intended or not, all move toward a fundamentalist style of argument. At the same time, we can understand that Confucianism is not a single philosophy but rather a system of thought encompassing different philosophical viewpoints. These different philosophical viewpoint—in different time periods, under different historical conditions, and from different angles—develop different philosophical expositions of the foundations of Confucian thought. The kind of position that condenses Confucianism down to a single philosophy usually comes from a religious perspective which is incomplete.

If the different types of Confucian theories of human nature are different expositions and justifications of the central point of Confucianism, then is there a basic and continuous standard, central point, or core structure which defines the Confucian tradition? Based on actual historical conditions, this standard is unspoken but clearly known. During each era, people have consciously recognized scholars of Confucianism and clearly distinguished those of other schools, even though these standards and distinctions are rarely expressed on the level of explicit statements. From my perspective, from the pre-Qin to the Ming and Qing periods, the standard, central point, or core of Confucianism can be said simply to be "basing in the Five Classics and Kongzi, advocating the kingly path for governing, focusing on virtue and self-cultivation, emphasizing family ethics, attending to social virtues, and respecting the transformative function of ritual (*li* 禮) and music (*yue* 樂)." From the pre-Qin to the Sui-Tang periods, Confucianism often took the form of "studying the classics" (*jingxue* 經學), and "basing on the Five Classics and Kongzi" indicates this special Confucian characteristic.

Of course, the theory that human nature is good has at least in form become the mainstream Confucian doctrine on human nature since the Song period. In this sense, we can say that as Confucianism developed, more and more Confucian thinkers had the tendency to hold that human nature is good. Thus it appears that, in contrast to other Confucian theories, the theory that human nature is good better expresses the particular characteristics of Confucianism and agrees more with Confucian thinking about education, morality, and politics. However, in researching the history of Confucianism, we should not use the ideas of orthodox–heterodox to analyze of the various theories of human nature within the system of Confucian thought.

The various Confucian theories of cosmology, metaphysics, epistemology, and human nature are all different expositions and developments of these main goals, and these theoretical demonstrations and theoretical extensions constitute the great richness of Confucianism. Moreover, the reason for the emergence of these different expositions is not only diversity of the thinkers themselves, but more so reflections of problems of different time periods, social backgrounds, and dilemmas. It is just these different, particular, and concrete expressions of Confucianism which fittingly responded to the challenges of their own times, that have contributed to the development of Confucianism. Because of this, we cannot use one kind of exposition as a gauge to abstractly weigh other kinds of expositions, because each should be applied according to the particular problems of one's own time and unique experience. Thus what we need is the most inclusive perspective on the history of Confucianism, in which every historical form of expression or style of exposition, and the whole system of thought contributed to by the developments of each historical period, all can achieve full recognition and inclusion.

TSINGHUA UNIVERSITY
Beijing, China

ENDNOTES

I would like to thank Elizabeth Li for translating this article, and to thank Franklin Perkins for his enormous editorial work on an early version, particularly his input on some of the translations of the excavated texts. I give my respectful gratitude to Professor Chung-ying Cheng for his invaluable comments, for some of which I shall discuss separately because of space reason. I also have authorized the *Journal* to work on necessary revising and condensing and proofreading of this article on my behalf, and I am thankful for their diligent work.

 1. Translated from Chinese by Elizabeth Li.
 2. This article develops and takes as its foundation from Chen Lai, "*Jingmen Chujian zhi 'Xing Zi Ming Chu' Chutan,*" *Ru Lin*《儒林》 (Studies on Confucianism) 3 (1998).
 3. *Xing Zhi Ming Chu*, Slip 4. References of the Guodian texts are from Museum of Jingmen, *Guodian Chumu Zhujian*《郭店楚墓竹簡》 (Beijing: Wenwu Press, 1998), cited by slip number.
 4. Sun Xidan 孫希旦, *Li Ji Jijie*《禮記集解》 (Beijing: Zhonghua Shuju Publisher, 1989), 984.
 5. Li Disheng 李滌生, *Xunzi Jishi*《荀子集釋》 (Taipei: Taiwan Xuesheng Publisher, 1979), 506, 460.
 6. *Xing Zi Ming Chu*〈性自命出〉(*XZMC* hereafter), 2.
 7. Wang Pinzhen 王聘珍, *Da Dai Liji Jiegu*《大戴禮記解詁》 (Beijing: Zhonghua Shuju Publisher, 1985), 191–92.
 8. Sun, *Li Ji Jijie*, 1000.
 9. Yu Cong II, 8–37.
10. *XZMC*, 9.
11. *XZMC*, 1–2.
12. *Cheng Zhi Wen Zhi*, 26–28.
13. Sun, *Li Ji Jijie*, 976.
14. Ibid., 984.

15. Ibid., 984.
16. Ibid., 998.
17. *XZMC*, 10–11; *XZMC*, 2.
18. Ibid., 9–14.
19. Wang, *Da Dai Liji Jiegu*, 51.
20. *Mengzi*, 7A1, cited from Jiao Xun 焦循. *Mengzi Zhengyi*《孟子正義》(Beijing: Zhonghua Shuju Publisher, 1987).
21. *Mengzi*, 6A7.
22. Ibid., 6A8.
23. Huang Hui 黃暉, *Lun Heng Jiaoshi*《論衡校釋》(Beijing: Zhonghua Shuju Publisher, 1996), 132–33.
24. *XZMC*, 2–3.
25. Zhu Xi, *Sishu Zhangju Jizhu*《四書章句集注》(Beijing: Zhonghua Shuju Publisher, 2003), 17.
26. *Mengzi*, 6A7.
27. Zhu Xi, *Sishu Zhangju Jizhu*, 17.
28. *XZMC*, 51–52.
29. Huang, *Lun Heng Jiaoshi*, 132–33.
30. *Mengzi*, 6A6.
31. Ibid., 6A1.
32. *Lunyu*, 17.3, cited from Liu Baonan 劉寶楠, *Lunyu Zhengyi*《論語正義》(Beijing: Zhonghua Shuju Publisher, 1990).
33. *Shisan Jing Zhushu* 十三經注疏 (Taipei: Yiwen Yinshuguan Publisher, 1955), 145, 222, 117.
34. Mou Zongsan 牟宗三, *Xinti Yu Xingti*《心體與性體》(Shanghai: Shanghai Guji Publisher, 1999), Vol. 1, 198.
35. If we follow the explanation of Ruan Yuan 阮元, who takes *xing* as *sheng* 生 (birth, living), then when Kongzi says that our natures are close to each other, this means: when people are born they are similar and it is practice or custom that pulls out the differences. With this understanding, strictly speaking, this phrase from Kongzi does not really address the topic of human nature.
36. *XZMC*, 29.
37. Huang, *Lun Heng Jiaoshi*, 132.

MICHAEL PUETT

THEODICIES OF DISCONTINUITY: DOMESTICATING ENERGIES AND DISPOSITIONS IN EARLY CHINA

The enormous number of materials being excavated from early China provides us with the opportunity to reconstruct concerns and issues that have either been excluded from or at least marginalized by the received tradition. New paleographic sources are allowing us to reconstruct legal, political, and social realms that were before almost impossible to explore, and the same is very much the case with philosophical and religious materials. The goal of this article will be to discuss one body of thought that is particularly prominent in some of the texts excavated from the Guodian 郭店, tomb—a body of thought that was to continue in works like the later *Liji*《禮記》, but that has been somewhat obscured by later intellectual developments. By taking these materials seriously, I will argue that they shed light on a number of philosophical and religious issues that deserve more attention.

For the materials that I will be discussing here, the basic vision was that, in our experience, the world we confront is one of fundamental discontinuity: the world consists of discrete things that often interact with each other poorly. This is true among humans: we have conflicting sets of dispositions that lead us to behave poorly toward each other. But it is also true among other aspects of the world as well. Accordingly, the goal of humans is to transform both ourselves and the world around us so that things come to resonate well with each other.

I am referring to these materials as "theodicies of discontinuity" to emphasize some of the larger significance that they may hold. In much of early modern Western thought, the problem of theodicy has revolved around the problem of how to account for the existence of evil and suffering in a cosmos created by a moral deity. One of the most significant and influential responses to this was to argue that

MICHAEL PUETT, Professor, Department of East Asian Languages and Civilizations, Harvard University. Specialties: Chinese philosophy, religions, and history. E-mail: puett@fas.harvard.edu

Journal of Chinese Philosophy, Supplement to Volume 37 (2010) 51–66
© 2010 Journal of Chinese Philosophy

evil and suffering were necessary in the world so that humans could exercise free will.[1] The lack of overt concern with evil in a strong sense or with free will could certainly be used to argue that theodicy as a problem had no place in early China. But another approach would be to ask what larger set of concerns underlies the issue of theodicy, and whether such larger concerns can be found elsewhere. In the case at hand, I would argue that the larger concerns—namely, the fact that humans find themselves in a world filled with suffering and injustice and that such problems require some kind of response—are certainly evident in early China. But the fact that the responses do not revolve around issues of free will is telling of a different conception of the issue. As I have argued elsewhere, a commonly perceived problem in early China was that phenomena were controlled by highly capricious ghosts and spirits.[2] The problem for humans was thus to transform themselves, the spirits, and phenomena so that a more harmonious world could be created. Instead of, for example, asserting free will, the problem was rather to connect, to transform, to domesticate.

This is why I would like to refer to the issues of concern here as theodicies of discontinuity. The equivalents of evil and suffering are seen in terms of a lack of proper interaction among discrete substances—ghosts, spirits, and humans not interacting well, humans not interacting well with each other or with the rest of the cosmos, the different energies and dispositions within humans not interacting well with each other. The solution is thus to assert more continuity—to link things, harmonize things, and transform things such that they can come to interact better.

Thus, my concern throughout this article will be to focus on problematics: what were the tensions that the authors were working through, and what were the problems that the texts in question were trying to solve? Theories aimed at asserting free will, for example, are based upon a concern with continuity: the problem is seen to be one of creating discontinuity, of breaking from an overly continuous and thus restrictive order and asserting autonomy. The texts in question here, on the contrary, were concerned that the world was overly discontinuous, and they saw the problem as one of finding ways to connect, link, transform, and domesticate the world so as to create—if only for brief periods of time—more harmonious interactions. One solution to this problem, as we will see, is to argue that there are, contrary to experience, underlying continuities that can be built upon in our projects of domesticating connecting the world.[3] But the perceived problem was not one of continuity but rather discontinuity, and the solution was one of finding ways to build a world of proper connections and proper interactions.

Before turning further to the philosophical implications of this material, perhaps a bit should be explained about the nature of these excavated texts and the reasons we possess them. The vast majority of these materials come from tombs. A brief word about these tombs may accordingly be helpful. I will then turn to a discussion of some of the relevant texts.

I. Ancestors and Tombs

Death in early China was associated strongly with concerns related to those just mentioned.[4] Humans consist of a plethora of energies, souls, and spirits. If our goal while alive is to domesticate these energies and train these dispositions, such a process of domestication—of transforming and taming these energies—would need to continue after death.

The implications of not doing so were clear. Parts of the deceased would turn into ghosts and haunt the living. The sense seemed to be that the souls—associated with the personality of the person while alive—would stay connected to the spirit, which was extraordinarily powerful. Since the process of domestication of the person while alive would be over, the ghost would be in danger of manifesting the worst energies of humanity—anger, resentment, jealousy, and so on—and these energies would often be aimed at those family members who the deceased was close to while alive and who now, precisely because they are still alive, become the objects of that anger and resentment.

To prevent this from happening, the attempt was made to separate the various parts of the deceased (particularly the souls and the spirit) and to domesticate each, albeit in different ways. To begin with, the souls would be moved into a tomb, wherein would also be kept the corpse. The concern was to keep them in the tomb and thus keep them away from the world of the living. This would be done in part through ritual requests for the deceased not to return above ground. But it would also be done by placing within the tomb things that surrounded the person when alive. This could include food and clothing, but it could also include texts. The goal was presumably twofold. Placing things that the souls enjoyed while alive would hopefully keep the souls happy in the tomb, and render them less likely to leave and haunt the living. But part of the goal probably involved an ongoing attempt to continue, or at least maintain, the process of domestication that had been occurring when the deceased was alive. Thus, those aspects of the culture that had helped to domesticate the figure while alive would be placed in the tomb such that, hopefully, the souls would remain domesticated until they either decomposed or moved into another realm of the afterlife.

Meanwhile, the spirit, which tended to float upward, was domesticated in a very different way: the spirit would be transformed into an ancestor. It would be given a ritual position based upon its lineage rank, and it would be brought down on ritual occasions to receive offerings. On such occasions, the spirit would be called upon to continue acting like an ancestor, and the living would call upon themselves to behave as proper descendants to the ancestors. In other words, ongoing rituals would continue the process of domestication, transforming the spirits and the living humans into ancestors and descendants in a proper lineage relationship.

These practices of dealing with the dead are relevant to our discussion, since the vast majority of our paleographic texts come from these rituals. To begin with the ancestors. Our first paleographic works, in fact, are Shang oracle bone inscriptions, which are divinatory records directed to the ancestors of the Shang royal family.[5] The subsequent inscribed bronze vessels of the Western Zhou were also directed to the ancestors.[6] The bronze vessels themselves were used to provide sacrifices to the ancestors: the ancestors would be called to come down to the ancestral temples to join the rituals with the living.[7]

And the rituals involving tombs are even more significant for the materials that will be of concern for this article. The aforementioned bronze vessels were buried in tombs, as were bamboo strips and silk writings during the Warring States and Han periods. In short, we possess these paleographic materials because of their involvement in the rituals concerning the entombment of the corpse and the souls.

II. Texts and Tombs

Given that we possess paleographic materials because they were utilized in rituals involving entombment, it is accordingly relevant to ask why these materials were put into tombs. This has been an object of a great deal of speculation. For example, Hiyashi Minao has speculated that the reason bronze vessels were buried in tombs was to allow the souls in the tombs to continue sacrificing to the earlier ancestors.[8] Similarly, with the later bamboo strips and silk manuscripts, there have been some attempts to argue that the contents of the texts in the tombs may be relevant to the needs of the soul of the deceased—either the ongoing cultivation of the soul in the tomb or to its later journeys to an afterlife.

Although these speculations may well be plausible in particular cases, it may rather be the case, as mentioned above, that the reason these materials—from earlier bronze vessels to the later bamboo and silk manuscripts—are in tombs is for the same reason that things like food and clothes are in the tombs: they serve the dual purpose of keeping the souls acculturated in the domesticated world created by humans, and of doing so in a way that will impel the souls to stay in the tomb rather than return to haunt the living. In other words, the texts do serve a purpose in tombs, but this is a purpose that follows directly from one of the basic purposes they serve the living—they (like food, clothing, and all other cultural artifacts) serve to domesticate human dispositions—in a living human and thereafter as well.

Thus, it is not necessarily the case that the souls would be performing sacrifices using the bronze vessels, any more than they would necessarily be reading texts. The reason these materials are placed in tombs is simply that they were associated with the personality of the person while alive. Someone involved with the law, for example, might be buried with legal materials. (Of course, this would not necessarily imply that the person had actually read the materials while alive either: the person could also be buried with significant texts because the person liked to be thought of as educated.) In other words, the concern seemed to be to place things in the tomb that represented aspects of the personality of the tomb occupant—as opposed to the spirit that would ascend to the skies and be transformed into an ancestor. As such, the souls would remain in the tomb, hopefully still domesticated and at the least not returning to attack the living.

This would imply that these materials are not being selected for any purposes related to the content of the texts (except insofar as they might be associated with some aspect of the deceased). This is fortunate for us, as it means we can expect to find a wide array of materials in tombs—legal cases, legal codes, recipes, along with philosophical texts. And such a fact is of particular interest to this article, as it means we are likely to find texts that are not being picked because they fit some larger ideological paradigm.

III. THE GUODIAN TEXTS

The Guodian tomb was sealed in roughly 300 BCE, and was discovered in 1993.[9] The texts found therein have been the object of an extraordinary outpouring of scholarship. My goal here will be to build upon this scholarship by emphasizing the theme of discontinuity as one of the central themes of a few of the texts, and then to point to some of the later instances of related types of arguments.

IV. THE TRAINING OF THE DISPOSITIONS

The *Wuxing*《五行》 discusses these issues in terms of the training of the dispositions.[10] The text opens by defining the five actions:

> As for the five actions, when humaneness is formed within, it is called
> virtuous action, when it is not formed within it is called action. When
> propriety is formed within, it is called virtuous action, when it is not
> formed within it is called action. When ritual is formed within is
> formed within, it is called virtuous action, when it is not formed
> within it is called action. When understanding is formed within, it is
> called virtuous action, when it is not formed within it is called action.
> When sagacity is formed within, it is called virtuous action, when it is
> not formed within it is called action. When the five virtuous actions
> are harmonized, it is called virtue. When the four kinds are harmo-
> nized it is called good. Goodness is the way of humans. Virtue is the
> way of Heaven.[11]

Each of these actions must be formed within, and each must also be
harmonized with the others. If humaneness, propriety, ritual, and
understanding can be formed within and harmonized, one will have
achieved goodness. If sageliness is also formed within and harmonized
with the other four, then one will achieve virtue. The former is simply
the way of humans, but the latter harmonizes with Heaven as well.

This theme of harmonizing potentially discrete things recurs
throughout the work. As the text argues at one point:

> The ears, eyes, nose, mouth, hands, and feet, these six are followers of
> the mind.[12]

The mind is thus called upon to harmonize them:

> When they harmonize, they are in accord. When they are in accord,
> there is goodness.[13]

The problem of the text is thus presented clearly. The remainder of
the text then works out how the five actions are formed within and
harmonized with the others. Intriguingly, however, the text does so not
by defining precisely what each of these values is and explaining how
to harmonize them together. On the contrary, the main method of the
text is to provide lengthy series of emotional dispositions, each of
which is to be balanced by another disposition, thus leading to a
development toward yet another disposition. Thus, for example, interaction with others is described as follows:

> If you use your outer mind to interact with others, you will be distant.
> If you are distant yet strong, you will be respectful. If you are respect-
> ful yet not lax, you will be stern. If you are stern yet reverent, you will
> be venerated. If you are venerated yet not proud, you will be defer-
> ential. If you are deferential yet extensively interact with others, you
> will have ritual.[14]

But the dispositions in each of these chains are not simply being
balanced by other dispositions in the same chain, for the chains are
constantly being folded into other chains. The result is an ever-

growing series of interlocking chains. Moreover, there is no consistent definition given to any of the terms, as each is constantly being defined in relation to other terms, all of which are constantly being defined in relation to yet other terms in other interlocking chains:

> Hearing the way of the gentleman is keenly hearing. Hearing and understanding it is sageliness. The sage understands the way of heaven.[15] To understand and put it into practice is propriety. To put it into practice at the proper time is virtue. Seeing the worthy is clearly seeing. Seeing and understanding it is understanding. Understanding and being stable, is humaneness. Being stable and being respectful is ritual. Sageliness and understanding is that from which ritual and music are generated and that from which the five actions are harmonized. When they are harmonized, there is joy. When there is joy, there is virtue. When there is virtue, the states and families are together.[16]

The text thus consists of a seemingly endless proliferation of series of interlocking chains, with each term being defined in terms of the others. The sense would appear to be that no one virtue is sufficient in itself. Thus one is constantly, in every situation, needing to develop one's dispositions by playing them off against other dispositions, and modulating each type of action by bringing it into play with the other types of actions. This is why the text does not provide stable definitions of any of its terms: each one can only be defined in terms of the others, and each is relevant only insofar as it is modulated by and harmonized with each of the others. The ultimate goal is the combining of all of the types of action, thus achieving the sagely linking of the human with Heaven.

As is clear from the argument, the achieving of continuity is at best a brief occurrence. The text instead posits a world of endless work, of constantly striving to train the dispositions, modulate them with other dispositions, and internalize and harmonize the resulting forms of action. An ethics, in short, of connecting, linking, harmonizing.

V. THE FORMATION OF A RITUAL CANON

Similar concerns underlie the *Xing Zi Ming Chu* 《性自命出》.[17] The basic view of the *Xing Zi Ming Chu* is that the world consists of discrete things that are constantly, in every situation, reacting to each other. The way things respond to each other is based upon their dispositional responsiveness. For humans, these dispositions are based on the energies of our emotions. When we encounter various things (which can include other people as well), they pull out our energies of anger, joy, and so on:

> The energies of joy, anger, sorrow, and sadness are given by nature.
> When it comes to their being manifested on the outside, it is because
> things have called them forth.[18]

Accordingly, humans tend to simply respond immediately to those
things that they encounter:

> In general, although humans possess nature, their mind is without a
> fixed purpose. They await things and only then do they become
> active; they await pleasure and only then do they move; they await
> practice and only then do they become fixed.[19]

The goal of the text, therefore is to teach us how to move from such
a state of immediate responsiveness, in which our emotions are simply
being pulled out by whatever things and situations we happen to
encounter, to one in which we have a fixed purpose. Only through the
latter, the text claims, can we achieve an ethical world.

The full argument of the text, therefore, is that the Way is simply the
endless motion in the world caused by things—with their inherent
dispositions—affecting each other. But, through training, one can
move from this immediate responsiveness to a responsiveness based
upon propriety—responding to situations properly:

> The Way begins in dispositional responsiveness and dispositional
> responsiveness is born from nature. At the beginning one is close to
> dispositions, and at the end one is close to propriety.[20]

But this ability to take an active role in shaping responsiveness is a
uniquely human capability:

> As for the Way's four techniques, only the human way can be Way-ed
> [i.e., only the human way involves a fixed will]. As for the other three
> techniques, one is moved and that is all.[21]

Everything else in the world simply consists of things reacting to other
things. Humans alone are capable of fixing a proper form of interaction. And, therefore, only humans can move from a Way of things
randomly impacting other things to one in which there is a proper
form of responsiveness.

So how do humans do this? By developing a ritual canon to train
human responsiveness. The argument is that, as humans respond to
situations, some of these responses would come to be seen later as
having been exemplary. They would thus be raised up and made into
rituals—actions that the next generations would repeat in order
to help train themselves and help refine their own dispositional
responsiveness. Out of this process eventually accumulates a repertoire of exemplary actions—poems, speeches, rituals, and musical
performances—that would become part of a canon for training the
later generations:

> As for the poems, documents, rites, and music, their first expression
> was generated among humans. With the poems, there were activities
> and they put them into practice. With the documents there were
> activities and they spoke of them. With the rites and music, there
> were activities and they raised them.[22]

The sages worked with these traditions and canonized them, creating
the rituals that would then be used to educate and train the dispositions of the latter born:

> The sages compared their categories and arranged them, analyzed
> their order and appended admonishments to them, embodied their
> propriety and put them in order, patterned their dispositions and
> both expressed and internalized them. As such, they were brought
> back for use in education. Education is the means by which one
> generates virtue within. The rites arise from the dispositions.[23]

The rituals thus come from the dispositions—they are responses that
are deemed to be exemplary and are deemed to be capable of helping
to train the next generations to pattern their dispositions as well.

The fundamental problem for the text, therefore, is again that of
discontinuity: the world consists of discrete things interacting with
each other, and usually interacting poorly. Humans, however, are
called upon to train their dispositions such that they learn to respond
well to the situations in which they find themselves. As such, humans
are capable, and uniquely capable, of moving from a world of immediate responsiveness to one of proper responsiveness—one in which
things are linked well. The key for doing this is through ritual—ritual
not in the sense of guidelines telling humans how to act but rather
rituals that train human dispositions such that one gains a fixity of
purpose and an ability to respond well to the world.

VI. A MODULATED COSMOS

Such an emphasis on training the dispositions might at first glance
seem radically at odds with other materials from the Guodian
tomb. The *Taiyi Sheng Shui*《太一生水》, for example, provides a cosmogony in part aimed at demonstrating the claim that natural processes are ultimately interlinked.[24] Such a position would at first
glance not seem to fit into the position we are describing. But here
too a general vision of discontinuity underlies the text: the thrust of
the argument is to claim that things seen as discrete are, counter-
intuitively and contrary to our experience, related. As I have argued
elsewhere,

> . . . what is going on in Chinese correlative thought is precisely
> an attempt to pull together elements that are perceived to be

distinct—an attempt to claim a form of continuity prevailing against disparate entities. Continuity is not assumed; it is created.[25]

What we thus see is the work involved in formulating cosmological arguments predicated upon the claim that, contrary to our experience of a discontinuous world, the cosmos is in fact a continuous order.

What is intriguing about the cosmogonic series provided in the *Taiyi sheng shui* is that the argument often replicates the sorts of chains we saw with the *Wuxing*, although here the series is worked out in cosmogonic terms rather than in terms of the dispositions, and the ultimate direction of the process is reversed. The text begins with *taiyi*, the Great One.[26]

> The Great One gives birth to water. Water goes back and supplements [i.e., joins with] the Great One. They thereby complete Heaven. Heaven goes back and supplements the Great One. They thereby complete Earth. Heaven and Earth [return and supplement each other].[27]

The starting point is the Great One. But note that the Great One does not generate two forces (such as Heaven and Earth or *yang* and *yin*) that then give birth to the rest of the cosmos—the type of cosmogony that would become increasingly common in third and second century BCE texts from early China. On the contrary, the Great One generates water, which then returns and supplements the Great One. The Great One and water together then complete Heaven. Heaven then supplements the Great One to complete Earth. In other words, each figure in the series needs to join with the Great One to continue the process. The Great One thus underlies the entire process, in the sense that no element can operate successfully without it.

Once Heaven and Earth are formed, they then supplement each other and start the second stage of the cosmogonic process:

> They thereby complete the spirits and the illuminated (*shen ming* 神明). The spirits and the illuminated return and supplement each other. They thereby complete the yin and yang. *Yin* and *yang* return and supplement each other. They thereby complete the four seasons. The four seasons return and supplement each other. They thereby complete the cold and hot. Cold and hot return and supplement each other. They thereby complete the wet and dry. The wet and dry return and supplement each other. They thereby complete the year and then stop.[28]

In this second stage, the cosmos is already formed. The spirits and illuminated supplement each other to complete the yin and yang, which in turn supplement each other to complete the four seasons. These in turn supplement each other to complete hot and cold, and the same process leads to wet and dry. The entire cosmos is

accordingly created through each element returning and supplementing that which came before or that with which it is paired:

> Therefore, the year was generated by wet and dry. Wet and dry were
> generated by cold and hot. Cold and hot were generated by the four
> seasons. The four seasons were generated by yin and yang. *Yin* and
> *yang* were generated by the spirits and numinous. The spirits and the
> illuminated were generated by Heaven and Earth. Heaven and Earth
> were generated by the Great One.[29]

The Great One accordingly underlies everything—not in the sense
of actually guiding the cosmos but rather in the sense of being that
which began the process and that with which everything is ultimately
(even if indirectly) supplemented:

> Therefore the Great One is stored in water and moved in the seasons.
> Circulating and again [four graphs missing, probably: starting, it takes
> itself as] the mother of the myriad things. At times diminishing, at
> times flourishing, it takes itself as the alignment of the myriad
> things.[30]

As such, the Great One is not something that any one element of the
cosmos can control or regulate:

> This is what Heaven is unable to kill, what Earth is unable to regu-
> late, and what yin and yang are unable to complete. The gentleman
> who understands this is called . . . [characters missing][31]

Although we are missing a key set of graphs here, the point is clear:
the gentleman is being called upon to recognize the workings of the
cosmic processes:

> Heaven and Earth, the style-name and name, were established
> together. Therefore, if one transgresses the other's boundaries, each
> fits[32] with each other without thinking. [When Heaven was insuffi-
> cient in][33] the northwest, that which was below raised itself through
> strength. When the Earth was insufficient in the southeast, that which
> was above [seven graphs missing; the last four are probably: If there
> is insufficiency above], there is excess below; if there is insufficiency
> below, there is excess above.[34]

Given the way the cosmos operates, any insufficiency in one area of
the cosmos inherently brings about the play of its pair to compensate.

There is, therefore, no one element that runs the cosmos. The align-
ment is provided by the Great One, meaning that each element must
supplement prior and/or partnered elements in order to be generative. The resulting argument is a series very much along the lines of
that seen in the *Wuxing*, only here the argument is worked out in
reverse. Instead of beginning with humans and calling on them to
train their dispositions to respond effectively to situations to build a
more harmonized world, the concern is rather to argue that, counter-

intuitively, the cosmos itself operates by processes of modulation and interaction, and humans should accordingly do the same. But note that the text is not claiming that the cosmos provides guidelines to follow. It rather shows the means by which proper action should occur. Like the *Xing zi ming chu*, it is calling on humans to constantly interact with other things properly. And like the *Wuxing*, it builds its arguments through chains of elements that are to be endlessly modulated against other elements. Here again, the attempt is to assert continuity, rather than assert discontinuity, to try to link things, rather than to assert automony.

VII. CONCLUSION

In all three of these texts, the problematic is one of discontinuity. Our goal as humans is therefore seen to be one of creating continuity—of transforming ourselves and operating with the world such that, ideally, everything can be made to interact well and resonate well with everything else. And, as this is a human project of domestication and transformation, it is also a never-ending one: most humans will never be fully transformed, and, of course, the next generation of humans will then have to go through the same process of transformation and domestication anyway.

Such a problematic results in a number of significant consequences.

To begin with, there is relatively little concern in this body of materials with issues like the assertion of free will and autonomy. Such concerns arise when the fundamental problem is seen to be one of continuity, and the fundamental goal is seen to be the assertion of discontinuity—the assertion of free will and autonomy as against a world seen to be too continuous and thus too limited.

But there is, on the contrary, a tremendous concern with issues like ritual, education, and cultivation. The first of these requires further clarification. From the perspective of a tradition (as is certainly the case for a great deal of nineteenth, twentieth, and twenty-first century Western thought) that emphasizes assertions of discontinuity, ritual is often seen as one of the things from which we need to break. Following ritual, from such a perspective, means following a heteronomous set of guidelines, when one should on the contrary be asserting one's autonomy and free will. But, from the concerns of the traditions under consideration here, ritual is often seen as crucial, and not because it provides guidelines for our behavior. Because it is rarely the case that a given ritual will flawlessly fit every situation, ritual rarely provides a perfect guide to us. Ritual is crucial instead because it helps us train our dispositions such that we become better and better able to live in a discontinuous world where things often interact poorly and more capable of playing a role in creating better forms of interaction.

Such a position of cultivation as a means of working within and transforming a discontinuous world—articulated in powerful terms in three texts that were not handed down in the received tradition—allows us to see the philosophical significance of works that have tended to be dismissed in the history of philosophical reflection in early Chinese texts. Several chapters of the *Liji*, for example, build upon these ideas.[35] One of the chapters—the "*Li Yun* 〈禮運〉"—discusses the ritual domestication of humanity as being comparable to the domestication of the natural world through agriculture. In both cases, one is taking a world in which things interact poorly—humans often dying from inadequate amounts of food, wild animals eating humans, humans being horrible to each other, and so on. Humans then transform the world—domesticating crops and animals as well as domesticating themselves through ritual. The result is a world in which everything is transformed such that it at least potentially works as a perfect unity, with the seasonal shifts of Heaven and the produce of the earth being connected through the domesticating acts of humanity. Humans thus form a triad with Heaven and Earth.[36] Arguments such as these that begin with a fundamental premise of discontinuity as being the problem that needs to be solved should be treated with the philosophical significance they deserve.

But the problematic outlined here not only helps us to refocus our attention on works that have perhaps not received the full attention they deserve. It may also help us to rethink some of these texts that have become more strongly associated with early Chinese thought in general. For example, all too frequently the texts of correlative cosmology that became increasingly significant over the course of the late Warring States and Han periods are read as representing an assumption that the world is inherently connected and harmonious. But, as we have seen from the *Taiyi sheng shui*, it may be more accurate to see these materials as working out of a problematic of discontinuity, arguing a position that would have been seen as clearly counterintuitive at the time, in order to make an argument for how humans must organize the world through constantly modulating, supplementing, and connecting elements. In short, by having materials like this, we may be in a position to rethink some of our standard ways of reading the early tradition.

And, finally, as alluded to above, these materials may help us to rethink early Chinese notions of death as well. If here too the problem was one of discontinuity, with the deceased falling back into being undomesticated and thus highly capricious and dangerous ghosts, then much of early Chinese tomb construction and ancestral sacrifice makes a great deal more sense—both were ongoing efforts to domesticate the ghosts, just as efforts were being equally made to domesticate the living.

In short, modern scholars may have themselves unintentionally domesticated much of early Chinese thought by reading it according to later paradigms. The excavated materials can help us to see some of the philosophical strength and terrifying power of some of these early traditions.

HARVARD UNIVERSITY
Cambridge, Massachusetts

Endnotes

I would like to thank Chung-ying Cheng and Franklin Perkins for their invaluable comments on this article.

1. For an outstanding discussion of theodicy in both European and Chinese thought, see Franklin Perkins, "Reproaching Heaven: The Problem of Evil in Mengzi," *Dao: A Journal of Comparative Philosophy* 5, no. 2 (2006): 293–312.
2. Michael Puett, *To Become a God: Cosmology, Sacrifice, and Self-Divinization in Early China* (Cambridge: Harvard University Asia Center, 2002).
3. For an excellent study of how this solution develops, see Chung-ying Cheng, "On Harmony as Transformation: Paradigms from the *Yijing*," in *Philosophy of the Yi: Unity and Dialectics (Book Supplement Series to the Journal of Chinese Philosophy)*, ed. Chung-ying Cheng and On-cho Ng (Malden: Wiley-Blackwell, 2010), 11–36.
4. On notions of death in early China, see Poo Mu-chou, *In Search of Personal Welfare. A View of Ancient Chinese Religion* (Albany: State University of New York Press, 1998); Constance A. Cook, *Death in Ancient China: The Tale of One Man's Journey* (Leiden: Brill, 2006); Cook, "Ancestor Worship during the Eastern Zhou," in *Early Chinese Religion: Shang through Han (1250 BC–220 AD)*, ed. John Lagerwey and Marc Kalinowski (Leiden: Brill, 2009), 237–79; Anna Seidel, "Traces of Han Religion in Funeral Texts Found in Tombs," in *Dôkyô to shûkyô bunka*, ed. Akitsuki Kan'ei (Tokyo: Heibonsha, 1987), 21–57; Kenneth E. Brashier, "Han Thanatology and the Division of 'Souls,'" *Early China* 21 (1996): 125–58; Yu Ying-Shih, "'O Soul, Come Back!' A Study in the Changing Conceptions of the Soul and Afterlife in Pre-Buddhist China," *Harvard Journal of Asiatic Studies* 47, no. 2 (1987): 363–95; Puett, "The Offering of Food and the Creation of Order: The Practice of Sacrifice in Early China," in *Of Tripod and Palate: Food, Politics, and Religion in Traditional China*, ed. Roel Sterckx (New York: Palgrave Macmillan, 2005), 75–95; Puett, "Combining the Ghosts and Spirits, Centering the Realm: Mortuary Ritual and Political Organization in the Ritual Compendia of Early China," in *Early Chinese Religion: Shang Through Han (1250 BC–220 AD)*, ed. John Lagerwey and Marc Kalinowski (Leiden: Brill, 2009), 695–720.
5. The best introduction to the Shang oracle bone inscriptions in English are David N. Keightley, *Sources of Shang History: The Oracle-Bone Inscriptions of Bronze Age China* (Berkeley: University of California Press, 1978), and Keightley, *The Ancestral Landscape: Time, Space, and Community in Late Shang China (ca. 1200–1045 B.C.)* (Berkeley: Institute of East Asian Studies, 2000).
6. The best introduction to Western Zhou bronze inscriptions is Edward L. Shaughnessy, *Sources of Western Zhou History: Inscribed Bronze Vessels* (Berkeley: University of California Press, 1991).

7. Lothar von Falkenhausen, *Chinese Society in the Age of Confucius (1000–250 BC): The Archaeological Evidence* (Los Angeles: Cotsen Institute of Archaeology, 2006).
8. Hayashi Minao, "Concerning the Inscription 'May Sons and Grandsons Eternally Use this [Vessel],'" *Artibus Asiae* 53, no. 1/2 (1993): 51–58.
9. For fuller discussions of the Guodian materials, see Sarah Allan and Crispin Williams, ed., *The Guodian Laozi: Proceedings of the International Conference, Dartmouth College, May 1998* (Berkeley: The Society for the Study of Early China and Institute of East Asian Studies, University of California, 2000); Ding Sixin, *Guodian Chumu Zhujian Sixiang Yanjiu* (Beijing: Dongfang Publisher, 2000); Guo Yi, *Guodian zhujian yu xian Qin xueshu sixiang* (Shanghai: Shanghai Jiaoyu Publisher, 2001); Kenneth W. Holloway, *Guodian: The Newly Discovered Seeds of Chinese Religious and Political Philosophy* (Oxford: Oxford University Press, 2009); Dirk Meyer, "Texts, Textual Communities, and Meaning: The Genius Loci of the Warring States Chu Tomb Guodian One," *Asiatische Studien/Études asiatiques* 63, no. 4 (2009): 827–56; Edward Slingerland, "The Problem of Moral Spontaneity in the Guodian Corpus," *Dao: A Journal of Comparative Philosophy* 7, no. 3 (2008): 237–56; Paul Goldin, "Xunzi in the Light of the Guodian Manuscripts," *Early China* 25 (2000): 113–46; Scott Cook, "The Debate over Coercive Rulership and the 'Human Way' in Light of Recently Excavated Warring States Texts," *Harvard Journal of Asiatic Studies* 64 (2004): 399–440; Attilio Andreini, "The Meaning of *Qing* in Texts from Guodian Tomb No. 1," in *Love, Hatred, and Other Passions: Questions and Themes on Emotions in Chinese Civilization*, ed. Paolo Santangelo and Donatella Guida (Leiden: Brill, 2006), 149–65.
10. My understanding of the *Wuxing* has been helped dramatically and deeply influenced by the excellent discussions by Mark Csikszentmihalyi, *Material Virtue: Ethics and the Body in Early China* (Leiden: Brill, 2004); Holloway, *Guodian*; Scott Cook, "Consummate Artistry and Moral Virtuosity: the 'Wu Xing 五行 Essay and Its Aesthetic Implications," *Chinese Literature: Essays, Articles, and Reviews* 22 (2000): 113–46; Pang Pu, *Zhu Bo "Wu Xing" Pian Jiao Zhu Ji Yan Jiu* 竹帛五行遍校注及研究 (Taipei: Wanjuanlou Publisher, 2000); Ikeda Tomohisa, *Baôtai Kanbo Hakusho Gogyôhen Kenkyû*「馬王堆漢墓帛書五行遍研究」(Tokyo: Kuko Shoin Publisher, 1993); Pang Pu, *Boshu Wuxingpian Yanjiu*《帛書五行遍研究》(Shandong: Qilu Publisher, 1980).
11. *Wuxing*, strips 1–4, *Guodian Chumu Zhujian*《郭店楚墓竹簡》(Beijing: Wenwu Publisher, 1998), 149. My translations from the *Wuxing* here and throughout have been helped greatly by those given by Csikszentmihalyi, *Material Virtue*, 277–310; Holloway, *Guodian*, 131–39.
12. *Wuxing*, strip 45, *Guodian Chumu Zhujian*, 150.
13. *Wuxing*, strip 46; *Guodian Chumu Zhujian*, 150.
14. *Wuxing*, strips 36–37; *Guodian Chumu Zhujian*, 150.
15. Following Ikeda in reading *er* 而 as *tian* 天. See his *Baôtai Kanbo Hakusho Gogyôhen Kenkyû*, 364.
16. "*Wuxing*," strips 26–29, *Guodian Chumu Zhujian*, 150.
17. For excellent studies of the *Xing zi ming chu*, see Holloway, *Guodian*; Andreini, "Meaning of *Qing*," 149–65; Erica Brindley, "Music and 'Seeking One's Heart-Mind' in the '*Xing Zi Ming Chu*,'" *Dao: A Journal of Comparative Philosophy* 5, no. 2 (2006): 247–55. I have also discussed the text in Puett, "The Ethics of Responding Properly: The Notion of *Qing* in Early Chinese Thought," in *Love and Emotions in Traditional Chinese Literature*, ed. Halvor Eifring (Leiden: Brill, 2004), 37–68; Puett, "Innovation as Ritualization: The Fractured Cosmology of Early China," *Cardozo Law Review* 28, no. 1 (2006): 28–30; Puett, "The Haunted World of Humanity: Ritual Theory from Early China," in *Rethinking the Human*, ed. J. Michelle Molina and Donald K. Swearer, with Susan Lloyd McGarry (Cambridge: Center for the Study of World Religions, 2010), 95–111.
18. *Xing Zi Ming Chu*, strips 2–3, *Guodian Chumu Zhujian*, 179.
19. *Xing Zi Ming Chu*, strip 1; *Guodian Chumu Zhujian*, 179.
20. *Xing Zi Ming Chu*, strip 3; *Guodian Chumu Zhujian*, 179.
21. *Xing Zi Ming Chu*, strips 14–15; *Guodian Chumu Zhujian*, 179.

22. *Xing Zi Ming Chu*, strips 15–16; *Guodian Chumu Zhujian*, 179.

23. *Xing Zi Ming Chu*, strips 16–18; *Guodian Chumu Zhujian*, 179.

24. For an excellent discussion of the *Taiyi sheng shui*, see Allan, "The Great One, Water, and the Laozi: New Light from Guodian," *T'oung Pao* 89, no. 4–5 (2003): 237–85. I have also discussed the text in Puett, *To Become a God*, 160–64.

25. Puett, *To Become a God*, 164.

26. Taiyi appears as a god in the Baoshan divination texts from the state of Chu in the fourth century BCE, and was thereafter elevated into a high god or high cosmic power more powerful or more primordial than Heaven. For an excellent study of the paleographic materials related to Taiyi, see Li Ling, "An Archaeological Study of *Taiyi* (Grand One) Worship," *Early Medieval China*, 2 (1995–1996): 1–39.

27. *Taiyi Sheng Shui*, strip 1; *Guodian Chumu Zhujian*, 125.

28. *Taiyi Sheng Shui*, strips 2–4; *Guodian Chumu Zhujian*, 125.

29. *Taiyi Sheng Shui*, strips 4–6; *Guodian Chumu Zhujian*, 125.

30. *Taiyi Sheng Shui*, strips 6–7; *Guodian Chumu Zhujian*, 125.

31. *Taiyi Sheng Shui*, strips 7–8; *Guodian Chumu Zhujian*, 125.

32. Following Qiu Xigui, *Guodian chumu zhujian*, 126 n. 17.

33. Ibid.

34. *Taiyi Sheng Shui Sheng Shui*, strips 12–14, *Guodian Chumu Zhujian*, 125.

35. Puett, "Human and Divine Kingship in Early China: Comparative Reflections," in *Religion and Power: Divine Kingship in the Ancient World and Beyond*, ed. Nicole Brisch (Chicago: The Oriental Institute of the University of Chicago, 2008), 199–212.

36. Puett, "Ritualization as Domestication: Ritual Theory from Classical China," in *Ritual Dynamics and the Science of Ritual, Volume I: Grammars and Morphologies of Ritual Practices in Asia*, ed. Axel Michaels, Anand Mishra, Lucia Dolce, Gil Raz, and Katja Triplett (Wiesbaden: Harrassowitz, 2010), 365–76.

SARAH ALLAN

ABDICATION AND UTOPIAN VISION IN THE BAMBOO SLIP MANUSCRIPT, *RONGCHENGSHI*

History in received literature from the Warring States period conventionally begins with the time of Yao 堯, who transmitted the rule to the virtuous Shun 舜 rather than to one of his sons. A few texts from the end of this period refer to rulers from an earlier age, but the manner in which they transmitted rule to their successors is never articulated. *Rongchengshi*《容成氏》, a bamboo slip manuscript in the Shanghai collection, is the only known example in which the practice of abdication to the most worthy, rather than to a son, is attributed to rulers in an era of high antiquity before Yao.[1] It does so in the context of a narrative history, which is unique in form, as well as in content.

This history begins with a utopian vision in which, under the first rulers, everyone in the world served according to their ability, from the sage, who became ruler, to those suffering from anxiety disorders, who fished in the marshes. It is followed by the time of Yao and Shun and ends with the establishment of the Zhōu 周 Dynasty. As history progresses, political institutions, especially taxation, criminal punishments, and warfare, increase; and personal morality declines. However, rule by men of worth (*xian* 賢), who institute good government throughout the world, periodically establishes stability. These men of worth achieve their position either by abdication of the previous ruler or by attracting the allegiance of all of the people.

In the following, I will first summarize the content of the manuscript and discuss its form. I will then give a detailed explication of the first part. Finally, I will place the manuscript in its philosophical context. I will argue, (i) that, although the manuscript takes the form of a narrative history, it should be understood as a philosophical statement, not as history; (ii) that the effect of placing a period of perfection at the beginning of history is to produce an evolutionary (or devolutionary) paradigm of historical change as opposed to the

SARAH ALLAN, Professor, Department of Asian and Middle Eastern Languages and Literatures, Dartmouth College; Chair, Society for the Study of Early China. Specialties: early Chinese thought, paleography, archaeology. E-mail: sarah.allan@dartmouth.edu

Journal of Chinese Philosophy, Supplement to Volume 37 (2010) 67–84
© 2010 Journal of Chinese Philosophy

dynastic cycle; this view of history is associated with the late Warring
States period; (iii) and that the manuscript argues for rule by the most
worthy, to be achieved by abdication in ideal conditions, but when
abdication is not possible, by attracting the loyalty of the people
through lenient and frugal government. In the author's own age,
attracting the loyalty of the people through good government would
have been the most appropriate and possible way.[2] While it relates to
a range of received and unearthed manuscripts, the historical scheme
and the philosophy contained therein are significantly different from
those of other known texts.

I. The Manuscript

The source of *Rongchengshi* and the other Chu script bamboo slip
manuscripts now held by the Shanghai Museum is unknown.
However, most scholars take the manuscripts to be of similar date
and provenance to the manuscripts found in Tomb No. 1 at
Guodian, Jingzhou, Hubei Province; that is, to have been composed
before *ca.* 300 BCE, or, at the latest, 278 BCE, when the state of Qin
overran the nearby Chu capital. *Rongchengshi* is often grouped with
two other manuscripts that discuss abdication, *Tang Yu Zhi Dao*
《唐虞之道》, from Guodian Tomb No. 1, and *Zigao* 《子羔》, also in
the Shanghai Museum collection.[3] I shall argue below that the historical scheme found in the *Rongchengshi* is related to that found in
texts of the third century BCE and so it was probably composed
shortly before burial; that is at the end of the fourth century or
beginning of the third.

   With fifty-three bamboo slips, *Rongchengshi* is one of the longest
of the Chu script bamboo slip manuscripts yet discovered. The
title, *Rongchengshi*, is taken from three characters written on the
back of slip 53.[4] Some of the slips are damaged and one or more
slips are missing at the beginning and the end. Most scholars have
rejected the initial bamboo slip sequence proposed by Li Ling 李零
in *Shanghai Bowuguan Cang Zhanguo Chu Zhushu* in favor of an
alternative sequence offered by Chen Jian 陳劍, with or without
minor modifications. Herein, I follow Chen Jian's revised sequence,
as modified by Guo Yongbing 郭永秉.[5] Although this sequence of
bamboo slips is different from that published in *Shanghai Bowuguan Cang Zhanguo Chu Zhushu*, I retain the original slips numbers
herein for ease of cross reference. These numbers are marked in
subscript in my translation and in the Chinese edition appended to
this article.

II. Summary of the Narrative

In this article, I will only discuss the first three sections of the manuscript in detail. Thus, before turning to my discussion of the narrative form of the manuscript, I will first summarize the content of the manuscript as a whole:

1. A period of perfect harmony beginning with Rongchengshi. Rule was not passed down hereditarily, but bestowed by a worthy upon another worthy, and all people, even the disabled, had work suitable to their abilities (slips 1–3).

2. The name of the first ruler is missing because a slip is damaged. Taxes are sparse and there is no criminal punishment. Everyone is able to live the full span of their years. The ruler cedes the rule to Youyu Tong 有虞通 (slips 35B, 4–6).

3. The rule of Yao. Yao gained rule by attracting the allegiance of the people with lenient government. Before accepting, he searched for a worthy to whom he could cede the rule, setting a model for the whole world. He then met Shun and appointed him, finally ceding the rule to him, rather than to one of his seven sons, when his physical powers had diminished (slips 6–7, 43, 9–11, 13).

4. The rule of Shun. The formation of the civilized world, including the taming of the waters and dredging of the rivers by Yu 禹, the creation of crop rotation by Hou Ji 后稷, the hearing of legal plaints by Gao Yao 皐陶, and the creation of the musical scale by Kui 夔. Shun ceded the rule to Yu, rather than to one of his five sons, when his physical powers had diminished (slips 13–14, 8, 12, 23, 15, 24–30, 16–18).

5. The rule of the lineage of Yu. A time of frugal government, simplicity, and peace under Yu, who organized the people into five regions, with emblems for each. Yu ceded the rule to Gao Yao, rather than to one of his five sons, but Gao Yao refused and then died. Yu then ceded the rule to Yi 益, but his son, Qi 啓, attacked Yi and took the rule from him. Yu's lineage continued to rule until Jie 桀 appeared. (This is the Xia Dynasty, but the dynastic name is not given.) (slips 18–22, 31, 33–34, 32, 35A).

6. The rule of the lineage of Tang 湯. Tang first assisted Jie in collecting taxes and levies, but the afflicted rose up. Finding that he could not change Jie, Tang began secretly appointing worthies and plotted with Yi Yin 伊尹, who gained the support of the people by getting rid of arms and taxation. Jie was extravagant, licentious, and foolhardy militarily. Tang attacked him, was given the backing of the armies throughout the world, and decimated

Jie and his lineage. Tang's lineage continued to rule until Zhòu 紂 appeared (the Shang Dynasty, but not named as such) (slips 35A, 38–41, 36–37, 42).

7. Zhòu and King Wen 文. Zhòu did not pass on the way of the former kings. He made a tower with coals at the bottom, and forced people to walk on a pole over them. He made a lake of wine and was dissolute. The nine lands rebelled. King Wen heard of this, but did not consider it correct to rebel. Wen subdued the nine lands on behalf of Zhòu and all but Feng 峰 and Hao 豪 submitted. Responding to moral suasion by King Wen, Feng, and Hao also submitted (slips 42, 44–49).

8. The rule of the lineage of King Wen. When King Wen died, King Wu 武 wished to replace Zhòu, who did not follow the Way. Declaring that sky/heaven was about to replace Zhòu and he wished to assist it, he marshaled his forces against Zhòu (and overthrew him—the end of the manuscript is missing. This is the Zhōu Dynasty, but, again, the dynastic name is not used) (slips 49–53).

III. The Narrative Form

In an earlier study, *The Heir and the Sage: Dynastic Legend in Early China*, I analyzed the manner in which historical legend in texts composed from the fifth to first centuries BCE was used to express political philosophy.[6] Although philosophical texts sometimes include short narratives about ancient history, they usually cite historical examples in highly abbreviated forms. In these citations, the stress is commonly placed on a value-laden verb, describing the relationship between two ancient figures or a deed of significance. By listing figures and actions from different periods in parallel form, the philosopher suggests a pattern of history from which he can then draw a conclusion for his own time. While certain basic facts must remain the same, each philosopher is free to transform aspects of the legends. By this means, he expresses his own understanding of the patterns of historical change and their implications for his own time. For example, Yao passed the rule to Shun, who is never described as his son. But, the manner in which he passed the rule may be described as an abdication (personal bestowal), a recommendation to heaven, or as a usurpation.

In the received texts, the same motifs recur in the legends of abdication by Yao and Shun and the formation of the Shang and Zhōu Dynasties. Thus, for example, Yao's raising up of Shun from the fields to become his minister in the predynastic period might parallel Tang's raising up of Yi Yin from the kitchen at the beginning of the Shang, and Wen Wang's raising up of Taigong Wang 太公望 from the river-bank at the beginning of the Zhōu. The predynastic rulers raised up their successors, whereas the dynastic founders raised up the future ministers who assisted them in founding a new dynasty. Similarly, Shun acted as a regent for Yao in his old age, just as Yi Yin and Zhōu Gong 周公 served as regents for Tai Jia 太甲 and the young King Cheng 成 after the Shang and Zhōu were established. In this manner, the breach of heredity implicit in the abdications of the predynastic period serves to support the idea of a changing mandate of heaven in the dynastic period.

The dynastic cycle embodies a paradox of conflicting values of rule by virtue and rule by hereditary right, and this inherent conflict is played out again and again in the legends of change of rule of both the predynastic and dynastic periods. Different philosophers expressed their social and political positions by transforming the legends in a coherent manner. The philosophical text that most consistently favors merit over hereditary right is the *Mozi*《墨子》and, in that text, the future rulers and their founding ministers were described as having very low social status before they were raised up. The *Mozi* also described the transfers of rule in the predynastic eras straightfor-wardly as abdications and those of the dynastic era as the result of military action. The *Mencius*, on the other hand, described the found-ing ministers as retired gentlemen, rather than as truly poor, and argued that neither abdication nor overthrow was possible, because only heaven could change its mandate. This was manifested in the allegiance of the people in both the predynastic and dynastic eras. In the *Hanfeizi*《韓非子》, on the other hand, Shun forced the rule from Yao and King Wu committed regicide.

The transformations of historical legend found in each of the major philosophical works of the Warring States period are generally coher-ent; that is, each philosophical text includes systematic manipulations of the legends about the ancient past and the manner in which legends of one period are related coheres philosophically with the manner in which the legends of other periods are expressed.[7] However, the received tradition does not include historical narratives that might have served as sources for the particular forms of the legends associ-ated with particular philosophers and their followers. They may have been lost to history or passed down orally as part of a master's teaching, in which case they would not necessarily have taken a nar-rative form. In any case, *Rongchengshi* is the only such narrative known—a history from the most primitive times to the beginning of the Zhōu, which is clearly informed by a political philosophy. Taken as history, it would be the earliest history in the Chinese tradition that bridges historical periods.[8] However, the manner in which the historical legends are transformed for polemical purpose suggests that it is a philosophical work, rather than an historical one; that is, in traditional Chinese terminology, it is the work of a master (*zi* 子) rather than a historian/scribe (*shi* 史). As we shall see below, that philosophy is different in significant ways from known philosophical schools and some of the transformations of historical legend are unique. Nevertheless, the pattern of transformations presents a coherent political philosophy, which stresses rule by a worthy, who practices lenient and frugal government, as the key to a harmonious society.

IV. THE PERIOD OF PERFECT VIRTUE

Now let us look at the first three sections of the manuscript as outlined above. The manuscript begins with a list of names. Although a slip is missing at the beginning, as its title is *Rongchengshi*, we may assume that it began with Rongchengshi, as does a similar list of names in the "*Qu Qie*〈胠篋〉(Rifling Trunks)" chapter of the *Zhuangzi*《莊子》, which I will discuss below. The slip numbers are given in subscript and correspond to those given in the edition at the end of this article:

> [When Rongchengshi, . . . ₁ Zun]lushi 尊盧氏, Hexushi 赫胥氏, Qiaojieshi 喬結氏, Cangjieshi 倉頡氏, Xianyuanshi 軒轅氏, Shennongshi 神農氏, Weiyishi 樺乙氏, and Lubishi 壚畢氏 had [rule over] all-under-sky/heaven, they all did not give it to their sons, but gave it to a man of worth. Their virtue (*de* 德) being still clear, those above loved those ₂ below, people's intentions were as one, arms were laid down, and offices awarded according to ability. Hence, the deaf and mute carried the candles; the blind played the drums and stringed instruments; the lame guarded the gates; the dwarfed made arrows; the gigantic thatched the houses; those who were stooped, leveled mounds; those with goiters ₃boiled salt, the anxious fished in the marshes. The hurt and rejected were not discarded. Whoever was humble and worn out, the (rulers) taught and instructed. They gave them drink and food. They controlled the multitudinous officials and gave them monthly receptions. Thus, at that time there were no. . . .

In received texts, personal names are notoriously variable, often written with different graphs in different texts. Chu script manuscripts, in which many words are written with graphs that are different from those found in the modern scripts, present even more complex problems in identifying personal names, and the identity of most of the figures on this list is open to question. Some of the names can be reasonably identified as variants of the names of well-known figures, including Rongchengshi, Xianyuanshi, and Shennongshi; others are identified with probability, such as Zunlushi and Hexushi; still others can only be identified by a determined assumption that the names in the manuscript will correspond to known figures. With this strong assumption, my list above of (Zun)lushi, Hexushi, Qiaojieshi, Cangjieshi, Xianyuanshi, Shennongshi, Weiyishi, and Lubishi, might be further refined to read as: Zunlushi, Hexushi, Gaoxinshi 高辛氏 (or Gao Ku 高嚳), Cangjieshi, Xianyuanshi, Shennongshi, Hundunshi 混沌氏, and Fuxishi 伏羲氏.[9] However, many of the phonological arguments for the phonetic loans used as evidence for the proposed identifications are difficult to follow.

The use of the title *shi* for figures placed before Yao in late Warring States and Han texts suggests that they may have originated as the mythical ancestors of different lineages, who have been joined onto an existing historical scheme by placing them at the beginning. However, we know very little about the origin and implications of the list found here. For example, Rongchengshi appears in association with Laozi 老子 and Huang Di 黃帝 in the *Liezi*《列子》 and *Huainanzi*《淮南子》 and is a well-known figure in medieval Daoist religion. He is also closely associated with sexual cultivation techniques. But, these roles have no obvious relationship to this manuscript.[10]

After listing the names, the passage goes on to state that all these figures abdicated to men of worth rather than to their sons. This is the only example in the extant literature that states that rulers before the time of Yao abdicated to their successors. Indeed, to my knowledge, it is the only statement from the Warring States period in which there is any mention at all of how rulers before Yao succeeded to the throne. Hereditary right plays no role in this utopian vision. These rulers of high antiquity appoint men of worth to succeed them even though they have sons, as do Yao, Shun, and Yu, who had nine, seven, and five sons, respectively. There is no suggestion that the sons of those who abdicated were evil, or even inept. Because none of the sons who were passed over in favor of a man of worth are described in negative terms, the abdications were clearly matters of preference for merit over heredity.

The passage continues with a description of utopian harmony. This includes the employment of people with various afflictions in positions consistent with their abilities (i.e., disabilities). A related discussion of the employment of people with "eight afflictions" (*ba ji* 八疾) when King Wen of Zhōu reigned is found in the *Guo Yu*《國語》.[11] The effect of attributing this motif to the rulers in the era of high antiquity in the *Rongchengshi* is to frame the abdication of the rulers of high antiquity within a context in which all people were selected and employed appropriately, whether they were a sage ruler or a deaf torch-carrier. The justification for choosing the most meritorious was thus that, in an ideal society, everyone would be employed in the manner in which they would be most useful, considering both their abilities and disabilities.

V. The Development of the Historical Scheme

In the *Gushibian*《古史辨》, Gu Jiegang 顧頡剛 and his colleagues argued that the earlier the figures in the historical scheme, the later the text.[12] The scheme found in early Zhōu texts is that of the three dynasties: Xia, Shang, and Zhōu. Warring States texts begin history with Yao, as does the *Shang Shu*《尚書》. Then, under the influence of five-phase theory, there are five emperors, beginning with Huang Di 黃帝, as found in the *Shi Ji*《史記》. This hypothesis is founded on a textual history which has many problems in light of recent evidence. Nevertheless, there is still no evidence to contradict the general hypothesis concerning the development of historical thinking. More-over, whereas there were undoubtedly numerous mythical heroes and lineage ancestors in the Zhōu period, it is only at the end of the Warring States period that these begin to appear at the beginning of king lists, in what Bernhard Karlgren in another seminal study called "free" as opposed to "systematized" texts.[13]

The period of perfect peace found in *Rongchengshi* is related to passages found in the "*Qu Qie*" chapter of the *Zhuangzi* and the "*Wu Du*〈五蠹〉(Five Vermin)" chapter of the *Hanfeizi*, although both the philosophies expressed in these passages are quite different from that in the manuscript. The "*Qu Qie*" chapter of the *Zhuangzi* begins with a condemnation of Tian Cheng, who is equated with the Robber Zhi for having usurped the rule of Qi from its hereditary lord, and a declaration that only when the sages die will the great robbers cease. Then, it states:

> Do you alone not know of the era when virtue was at its fullest? Formerly, in the time of Rongchengshi, Datingshi 大庭氏, Bohuang-shi 伯皇氏, Zhongyangshi 中央氏, Lilushi 栗陸氏, Lixushi 驪畜氏, Xianyuanshi, Hexushi, Zunlushi, Zhurongshi 祝融氏, Fuxishi, and Shennongshi, people made use of tied knots (for writing), found their food sweet and their clothes beautiful, were happy with their customs and content in their dwellings. The people of neighboring lands might glimpse one another and hear one another's roosters and dogs, but they grew old and died without visiting one another. As for that era, it was one of utmost order.[14]

Although the beginning of the list of names found in *Rongchengshi* is missing and there are some differences, there is clearly some relation-ship between the two lists. The description of utopian bliss in the

Zhuangzi passage is also different from that found in *Rongchengshi*, but it similarly presents an era in antiquity in which people lived in harmonious simplicity.

The *Zhuangzi* passage goes on to contrast this utopian era of high antiquity with its own period. Now, people look for men of worth to whom they may give their allegiance and states are stolen from the rightful, hereditary rulers:

> Today, [virtue] has declined to the point that people crane their necks and stand on tiptoe, saying, "In such a place there is a man of worth," pack their grain and hasten to him. Within their family, they desert their parents; outside, they abandon the service of their lord, . . . [15]

Philosophically, this is in stark contrast to the *Rongchengshi*, which advocates rule by men of worth. Indeed, this situation that *Zhuangzi* warns against is precisely the one that led to the establishment of rule by Yao, as well as the founding of the Shang and Zhōu dynasties in the *Rongchengshi*. Thus, although both texts refer to a list of rulers before Yao beginning with Rongchengshi, their messages could not be more different.

The "*Wu Du*" chapter of the *Hanfeizi* also includes a period of primitive simplicity before the time of Yao but, like Thomas Hobbes, who famously declared that life in primitive times was "nasty, brutish, and short," Hanfeizi takes primeval life as dangerous and uncomfortable until the inventions of the sage kings of antiquity improved human living conditions:

> In high antiquity, there were few people and many birds and beasts. The people could not overcome the birds, beasts, insects, and snakes. When a sage arose and crossed branches to make nests so that they could avoid the various [sources of] harm, the people were pleased with him and made him king over all under sky/heaven. They called him "Youchaoshi 有巢氏 (Of the Nest-clan)." The people ate fruit and berries and shellfish. Because [their food] putrified and stank, it injured their stomachs and people were often ill. When a sage arose, he struck flint to make fire with which he transformed its rotting, and the people were pleased with him, and made him ruler over all under sky/heaven, and called him "Suirenshi 燧人氏 (Of the Fire-making-clan)." In middle antiquity, there was a great flood in the world and Gun 鯀 and Yu made irrigation ditches. In recent antiquity, Jie and Zhòu were violent and disorderly and Tang and Wu smote them. [16]

As in the *Rongchengshi* and the "*Qu Qie*" chapter of the *Zhuangzi*, the pattern of historical time in this passage is one of cultural and material change over the ages.

As noted above, in received Warring States texts, the legends of Yao and Shun are linked by repeating motifs to those of dynastic formation. Thus, they serve to reenforce rather than challenge the idea of a changing mandate of heaven manifested in the dynastic cycle. The effect of placing a time of perfect peace and harmony—or primeval danger—before the time of Yao is to change the paradigm from a correlative one in which the same archetypal motifs, representing the competing demands of heredity and merit, appeared at critical intervals, into one in which the sense of historical change predominates. This paradigm of historical change, beginning with a time of perfect simplicity, does not appear until the late Warring States period. Moreover, it never gained much force in the orthodox historiography of later periods, as the of use the five-phase correlative system revived and recast the cyclical pattern; with the newly orthodox scheme of "five emperors" (Huangdi, Zhuan Xu 顓頊, Yao, Shun, and Yu), found in the *Shi Ji*《史記》serving to reenforce the idea of correlative change embodied in the idea of three dynasties preceded by Yao and Shun, rather than replacing it.[17]

The use of the paradigm of devolutionary change thus reflects conditions in which the idea of dynastic cycle determined by a moral spiritual force (sky/heaven) had become increasingly difficult to defend. The rejection of the paradigm of correlative patterns is most notable in the *Hanfeizi*, which uses the idea of material change to argue against followers of Confucius. Indeed, its ultimate manifestation may be the declaration by the king of Qin that he was the "first emperor," of a lineage would last ten thousand years. Although both the *Hanfeizi* and *Zhuangzi* passages refer to a period before the time of Yao in which life was simple, they are conceptually, rather than textually, related to one another. The names of the rulers in *Rongchengshi*, on the other hand, are related to those in the "*Qu Qie*" chapter of the *Zhuangzi*. Hanfeizi's dates are 280–233 BCE and the bulk of the text that bears his name, including the "*Wu Du*" chapter, is generally attributed to Hanfeizi himself. The "*Qu Qie*" chapter of the *Zhuangzi* refers to "twelve generations" of rule by the Tian 田 clan, who usurped the rule of the state of Qi 齊 in 481 BCE, so it could not have been written before the middle of the third century BCE.[18] Because the Shanghai manuscripts were probably written before 278 BCE, *Rongchengshi* should predate the *Zhuangzi* passage. However, as this paradigm does not appear earlier in the received tradition, *Rongchengshi* was probably composed close to the time of its burial.

VI. YOUYU TONG

There is serious damage to the manuscript in the next section. Because the top of the slip is damaged, the name with which this part begins is missing except for the suffix "shi," indicating a clan name. This ruler, or a subsequent one, cedes the rule to Youyu Tong 有虞通. This name is not found in any extant text.[19] The prefix "you" often precedes clan names (as in Hanfeizi's "Youchaoshi" above) and Shun's clan name was Yu 虞 Thus, this passage could be interpreted to mean that the clan of Shun ruled before that of Yao, but as there is nothing in the extant literature to support this, we cannot be certain. Youyu Tong did not reward or punish; there were no starving people on the roads; and everyone, noble or humble, achieved their full span of years. When Youyu Tong had held sway over the world for nineteen years and ruled as king over the world for thirty-seven years, he died. "*Kuang* 匡," which I have translated here as "held sway," is used in many Warring States texts to describe the rule of the hegemons, especially Duke Huan of Qi. Here, it probably means that he acted as regent for the ruler before he became king, but the circumstances are unclear.

VII. The Time of Yao

Youyu Tong appears to have died without abdicating or appointing a successor. We do not know if he and Yao had any relationship with each other or what role Yao played in Youyu Tong's time. Indeed, the story of Yao starts anew in a manner that suggests two narratives may have been pieced together:

> Formerly, Yao lived between Dan Fu 丹府 and Huan Ling 蘹陵. Yao followed [the precedents] in what he bestowed and offered tribute according to the season. He did not exhort the people, and yet they were hard-working. He did not mutilate or kill, and yet there were no robbers or thieves. He was lenient and yet the people were submissive. Thereupon, from within [a territory with] the range of one hundred *li*, he led all the people in the world. They came to make obeisance and set him [on the throne], regarding him as the son of sky/heaven. Within a range of one thousand *li*, [officials] holding tablets took their proper position.[20] The [people in the] four directions became harmonious and, by cherishing them, he caused all the people under the sky/heaven come [to him].

References to the first rulers of the Shang and Zhōu Dynasties, beginning with one hundred *li* (sometimes seventy for Tang) and achieving rule over the entire world, are very common in Warring States period texts (found in the *Mozi*, *Mencius*, *Xunzi*, and *Hanfeizi*), but to my knowledge, there are no such references to Yao as having begun with a small territory.

In received Warring States texts, the trope of movement of the people from a ruler belonging to one lineage to someone of another lineage functions to establish the legitimacy of the dynasties founded after the overthrow of the heirs of the previous dynasty. It is particularly important in the *Mencius*, which denies the possibility both of abdication, as only sky/heaven can appoint the ruler, and of dynastic overthrow, as rule can only be changed by a celestial mandate.[21] The movement of the people is the sign of the change of mandate and the *Mencius* extends this concept back to the predynastic era: the people go from Yao to Shun and Shun to Yu, just as they did from Jie to Tang and Zhòu to Wen and Wu (but did not go to Yi after Yu's death). With this trope, the predynastic breaches of heredity and those of the dynastic founders are equated. This serves to reenforce the legitimacy of dynastic change, albeit limiting its potential circumstances to those in which the nonhereditary ruler was meritorious enough to gain the loyalty of the people while the hereditary ruler oppressed his people. To my knowledge, however, no received text states that Yao became king by attracting the allegiance of the people.

In contrast to the *Mencius*, *Rongchengshi* does not take the movement of the people as a unifying theme for change of rule throughout history. There is no mention of movement of the people in the era of high antiquity, when all the rulers abdicated, or when Yao abdicated to Shun and Shun to Yu. Those were simply cases of abdication, in which the ruler clearly had the power to give the rule to his successor. In this, the manuscript resembles the *Mozi*. *Rongchengshi* also tells us that Qi forcibly took the rule from Yu's minister Yi, to whom Yu had abdicated, whereas, in the *Mencius*, the establishment of the hereditary dynasty was explained in terms of Yi's inability to attract the loyalty of the people.[22]

Concomitantly, *Rongchengshi* is not interested in the mandate of heaven. The only reference to heaven (*tian* 天) as a power in the entire narrative is when King Wu finally moves to attack Zhòu, whose tortures are described with details not found in other texts. There, we are told that Wu knew that heaven was about to punish Zhòu—presumably to explain why it was that, although Wen served Zhòu loyally but attracted the allegiance of the people, Wu used military force. Moreover, the names of the three dynasties are never used in the manuscript, only those of their first and last rulers. This lack of interest in the role of heaven is further evidence of the development of a historical paradigm which recognized material progression, be it good or bad, and loss of faith in the idea of a spiritually transferred mandate. When history begins with Yao's rule, the question of how Yao became ruler does not arise. Presumably, the placement of an era before Yao in a continuous narrative required the author to explain how Yao became king. However, by describing Yao's accession as one of attracting the allegiance of the people and applying this trope again to the era of Tang and King Wen, the manuscript makes attracting the allegiance of the people the appropriate alternative to abdication, applicable to the author's own era.

Yao did not immediately assume the throne. He first searched for another man of worth to whom he might cede. By this search, he established a model of letting the most meritorious rule that was emulated by everyone beneath him:

> ₉Thus, [Yao] examined the men of worth, with his feet on the ground and the sky on his head, he looked for the principled (*yi* 義) and trustworthy (*xin* 信). His kindness filled the space between the sky and earth and his embrace, all within the four seas. If he succeeded in accomplishing his task, he would establish (the worthy) as the son-of-sky/heaven. Yao then gave instructions for this purpose, saying, "After I have gone inside, I will₁₀ secretly look out in order to find one who is a man of worth to whom I will cede [the rule]." Yao wished to cede [the rule over] all-under-sky/heaven to a man of worth, but of the men of worth in the world, none were adequate to receive it. The rulers of the myriad lands, all wished to cede their lands to a man of worth, ₁₁ [but of the men of worth in their lands, not one was fit to receive it. The heads of the noble estates all wished to cede their estates] to a man of worth, but of the men of worth [on their estates], not one was fit to receive them. Thereupon, everyone under sky/heaven ₁₃saw Yao as being good and promoting men of worth, and, in the end, they set him [on the throne].

Thus, only when Yao did not succeed in finding a man of worth capable of ruling the empire, did he finally accept the rule himself.

The motif of attempting to cede the rule to another man of worth before accepting succession to the throne is, once again, common in Warring States period texts, but not in association with Yao.[23] It is Shun and Yu who are usually said to have attempted to yield the throne to other men of worth before accepting it—and they do so later in this manuscript. The function of the motif in which a future ruler yields to someone else before he accepts the throne in these legends is to allow the nonhereditary successor to remove the stigma of greed and usurpation by demonstrating that he is not interested in power, only the good of the world. On the other hand, especially in the *Zhuangzi*, the implied comparison of the purity of those who refuse to be tainted by rule to which they have no right with the nonhereditary successors serves to highlight the compromised position of those who accept the rule. Here, Yao did not receive the rule by abdication, but by attracting the allegiance of the people. Thus, the appearance of this motif at this point in the narrative implicitly equates his mode of succession—attracting the loyalty of the people—with abdication. In light of Yao's prestige as the commonly accepted first ruler in most Warring States periods texts, this description of his rise by attracting the allegiance of the people is significant for our understanding of the message of the manuscript as a whole.

VIII. Philosophical Implications

This manuscript argues, by means of its historical narrative, that in order to have a harmonious society, all people must be employed appropriately, according to their abilities. Thus, the ruler must be a man of worth—and his officials, the most meritorious in their domains. The ideal means of political succession was for a good ruler to appoint a man of worth as his successor—this was the means by which the rulers of the utopian era before Yao achieved position, as did Shun and Yu—but, in the absence of a meritorious ruler who might abdicate, a man of worth from a different lineage than the reigning monarch could legitimately establish himself as king by good administration of a small area, thus attracting the allegiance of people from the entire world. By placing this alternative means of achieving a harmonious society ruled by a man of worth in the time of Yao, the manuscript puts attracting the loyalty of the population on a par with receiving an abdication.

Structurally, the placement of a period of high antiquity, in which life was simple and government undeveloped, before the time of Yao results in a paradigm of historical change. Here, that change is devolutionary in the sense that human society became progressively more depraved. Thus, according to the latter part of the manuscript, Tang and Wen, under the evil Jie and Zhòu, had to secretly enact governmental measures which would attract the loyalty of the people. They did not at first challenge the right of the hereditary rulers and even served them, but eventually they, too, became rulers over the whole world. In light of the devolutionary scheme of the manuscript—and the historical circumstances which led to the final collapse of the Zhōu Dynasty—attracting the loyalty of the people was not only equally legitimate, but much more appropriate to the times.

Tang Yu Zhi Dao from Guodian Tomb Number One explicitly advocates the "Way of Tang Yao and Yu Shun," that is, abdication, as the ideal form of government. In contrast, *Rongchengshi* simply argues for rule by the most worthy, which it takes as the key to establishing a harmonious society in which all people were cared for and played an appropriate role according to their ability. This might be established by abdication of a man of worth to another man of worth, as in the time of high antiquity and the predynastic era. Alternatively, it might be established by a man of worth, who, by ruling a small area well, attracted the allegiance of people throughout the world, as did Yao, Tang, and Kings Wen and Wu. In the devolutionary scheme of the manuscript and the conditions of the late Warring States period, this would have been the only possible model.

IX. CHINESE TEXT OF *RONGCHENGSHI*

The following Chinese text is the basis of my translation above. The slip numbers given in subscript are those given in *Shanghai Bowuguan Cang Zhanguo Chu Zhushu*. The readings of individual characters are those given in that publication, except where indicated by a subscript slip number followed by a comma and the number of the character on the slip, such as "$_{1,16}$" (i.e., slip 1, sixteenth character). Notes keyed to these numbers follow the text and provide the sources for the alternative readings that I have chosen. Where my readings are different from a direct transcription of the Chu graph, the original graph is supplied in parentheses. However, I have omitted direct transcriptions of those Chu graphs that do not correspond to a modern character. The phonetic reconstructions are those of Bernhard Karlgren, *Grammata Serica Recensa, Bulletin of the Museum of Far Eastern Antiquities*, no. 29 (1957).

Section I

[容成氏、.... 、尊] $_1$盧氏（是）、赫（蒼）胥（疋）氏（是）、喬結氏（是）、倉頡氏（是）、軒轅（緩）氏（是）、$_{1,16}$神（慎）農（戎）氏（是）、$_{1,19}$樟乙氏（是）、壚畢氏（是）之有（又）天下也，皆不$_{1,31}$授（受）其子而授（受）賢。其德$_{1,39}$猶（酉）清，而上愛$_2$下，而一其志，而寢其兵，而官其材(才)。 於是乎喑聾執燭，瞽瞽鼓瑟，跛躄守（獸）門，侏儒（需）爲矢，長者$_{2,35}$秀宅，傻（婁）者$_{2,39}$劇（坆）壞，癭$_3$者煮鹽，$_{3,4}$宅（厇）憂者漁$_{3,9}$澤，害棄不廢。凡民$_{3,15}$蔽（俾）$_{3,16}$芾者，教而誨之，飲而食之，$_{3,26}$使(思)役百官而月請（青）之。故(古)當是時也，無（亡）并......

Section III

　　昔堯處於丹府與藋陵之閒，堯$_{6,17}$踐（戔）施而{時時}$_{6,22}$賓，不勸而民力，不刑（型）殺而無盜賊（側），甚緩而民服(備)。於是乎方$_7$百里之中，率天下之人就，$_7$奉而立之，以爲天子。 於是$_7$乎方圓千里（之中），〈於是乎〉（於）持板正位(立)，四向$_{7,35}$委和（禾），懷以徠天下之民。$_9$是以視賢，履地戴天，$_{9,9}$督（篤）義與信。$_{9,14}$惠（會）在(才)天地之間，而保（包）$_{9,21}$在四海之內，畢能其事，而$_{9,31}$立爲天子。堯$_{9,36}$乃爲之教曰："自$_{10}$入（內）焉，余穴窺焉，以求賢者而讓（壤）焉。"堯以天下讓於賢者，天下之賢者莫之能受也。君皆以其邦讓於賢$_{11}$[者]............[讓於]賢者，而賢者莫之能受也。於是乎天下之人，以$_{13}$堯爲善興賢，而卒立之。

1,16 神. Following Su Jianzhou 蘇建洲, "*Rongchengshi Yishi* 〈容成氏〉譯釋." In Ji Xusheng 季旭昇 et al. *Shanghai Bowuguan Cang Zhanguo Chu Zhushu (Er) Duben*《上海博物館藏戰國楚竹書(二)》讀本》(Taipei: Wanquanlou, 2003), 107. **1,19** 乙, **1,39** 猶. Following Qiu Dexiu 邱德修, *Shangbo Chu Jian Rongchengshi Zhuyi Kaozheng*《上博楚簡〈容成氏〉注譯考證》(Taipei: Taiwan Guji Publisher, 2003), 147, 154.

2,35 秀. Following Huang Dekuan 黃德寬, *Xinchu Chu Jian Wenzi Kao*《新出楚簡文字考》, (Hefei: Anhui Daxue Press, 2007), 170–71. **2,39–40** 劇壞. Following Li Ruohui 李若暉. "*Shi Rongchengshi 'Louzhe* XX' 釋《容成氏》 '婁者XX'." In *Shangboguan Cang Zhanguo Chu Zhushu Yanjiu Xubian* 上博館藏戰國楚竹書研究續編, ed. Zhu Yuanqing 朱淵清 and Liao Mingchun 廖名春 (Shanghai: Shanghai Shudian Publisher, 2004), 391–96.

3,4 宅; **3,9** 澤 **3,26** 使; Following He Linyi 何琳儀. "*Di Er Pi Hu Jian Xuanshi* 第二批滬簡選釋." In *Shangboguan Cang Zhanguo Chu Zhushu Yanjiu Xubian*, 444–55. **3,15–16** 蔽芾. Following Qiu Xigui 裘錫圭. "*Du Shangbo Chu Zhujian Rongchengshi Zhaji Er Ze* 讀上博楚竹簡《容成氏》札記二則," *Guwenzi Yanjiu* 25 (2004): 314–16.

6,17 踐. Following Qiu Dexiu, *Shangbo Chu Jian Rongchengshi Zhuyi Kaozheng*, 2,11. **6,22** 賓. Suggested by Chen Jian 陳劍, "*Shangbo Jian Rongchengshi de Chu Jian Pinhe Yü Bianlian Xiaoyi* 上博簡《容成氏》的竹簡拼合與編連問題小議." In *Shangboguan Cang Zhanguo Chu Zhushu Yanjiu Xubian*, 328.

7,35 委. Following He Linyi. "*Di Er Pi Hu Jian Xuanshi*."

9,9 The Chu graph, 竺 (*tôk), is a variant of 篤 (*tôk), which I read as the homophone 督 (*tôk). For examples of these interchanges in received and unearthed texts, see Gao Heng 高亨, *Gu Zi Tongjia Hui Dian*《古字通假會典》(Beijing: Qi Lu Shushe Publisher, 1989), 744; Wang, Hui 王輝, *Guwenzi Tongjia Zidian*《古文字通叚字典》(Beijing: Zhonghua Shuju Publisher, 2008), 330 (2352). **9,14** 惠 (*g'iwəd) is homophonous with 會 (*g'iwəd) and **9,20** 包 (*pôg) with 保 (*pôg). I suggest these readings for their semantic and grammatical values. **9,36** 乃 is missing in the original transcription.

DARTMOUTH COLLEGE
Hanover, New Hampshire

Endnotes

I would like to thank Yuri Pines for allowing me to read an early draft of his manuscript, "Political Mythology and Dynastic Legitimacy in the *Rong Cheng shi* manuscript," which will appear in *Bulletin of the School of Oriental and Asian Studies* 73, no. 3 (2010): 1–27.

A version of this article was presented at the Association for Asian Studies Annual Meeting, March 28, 2010, in Philadelphia, and I am also grateful for comments received at that time.

1. *Shanghai Bowuguan Cang Zhanguo Chu Zhushu*《上海博物館藏戰國楚竹書》, ed. Ma Chengyuan 馬承源 (Shanghai: Shanghai Guji Publisher, 2001), vol. 2, 91–146 and 247–93.

2. In Sarah Allan, "The Way of Tang Yao and Yu Shun: Appointment by Merit as a Theory of succession in a Warring States Bamboo Slip Text," in *Rethinking Confucianism: Selected Papers from the Third International Conference on Excavated Chinese Manuscripts, Mount Holyoke College, April 2004*, ed. Wen Xing *International Research on Bamboo and Silk Documents: Newsletter*, 5, no. 2 (Special Issue, 2006): 22–46; Ai Lan 艾蘭, "*Tang Yu zhi Dao: Zhanguo Zhujian zhong Renming yi De de Jiwei Xueshuo*《唐虞之道》: 戰國竹簡中任命以德的繼位學說," *Ruxue Wenhua Yanjiu* 1 (2007): 118–54; and Allan, "Not the *Lun Yu*: The Chu Script Bamboo Slip Manuscript, *Zi Gao*, and the Nature of Early Confucianism," *Bulletin of the School of Oriental and African Studies* 51, no. 2 (2009): 115–51, I referred to *Rongchengshi* as a manuscript that advocates abdication, but I have revised this position and argue against it below. For a reading of *Rongchengshi* as advocating abdication, see Pines, "Disputers of Abdication: Zhanguo Egalitarianism and the Sovereign's Power," *T'oung Pao* 91, no. 4–5 (2005): 263–68; see also, Pines, "Subversion Unearthed: Criticism of Hereditary Succession in the Newly Discovered Manuscripts," *Oriens Extremus* 45 (2005–2006): 169–75; Pines, *Envisioning Eternal Empire: Chinese Political Thought of the Warring States Period* (Honolulu: University of Hawaii Press, 2009), 65–71.

3. The text of *Tang Yu Zhi Dao* is published in *Guodian Chu Mu Zhujian* 《郭店楚墓竹簡》, ed. Jingmenshi Bowuguan 荊門市博物館 (Beijing: Wenwu Publisher, 1998), 39–41 and 157–59; that of *Zi Gao*, in *Shanghai Bowuguan Cang Zhanguo Chu Zhushu*, vol. 2, 31–47 and 183–89. My own editions, with full translations and analysis of these texts, as well as of the *Rongchengshi* and *Baoxun* 保訓, from the Tsinghua University collection, will be included in my forthcoming book, *Written on Bamboo: Political Theory and Pre-Dynastic Legend in Early Chinese Manuscripts*. This book will also review what little is known about the source of the Shanghai Museum collection.

4. The first character is actually written as *song* 頌, but this graph is commonly read as *rong* 榮 in bamboo slip manuscripts. See Wang Hui 王輝, *Guwenzi Tongjia Zidian*《古文字通叚字典》(Beijing: Zhonghua Shuju Publisher, 2008), 475 (no. 3260). *Shi* 氏 in the title is also written with the graphic variant, 氐. On the face of the slips, it is written with the homophone *shi* 是, a substitution that is also common in these manuscripts. This suggests that the title was added to the manuscript by another hand.

5. Chen Jian 陳劍, "*Shangbo Jian Rongchengshi de Chu Jian Pinhe yu Bianlian Xiaoyi*" 上博簡《容成氏》的竹簡拼合與編連問題小議, in *Shangboguan Cang Zhanguo Chu Zhushu Yanjiu Xubian*《上博館藏戰國楚竹書研究續編》, ed. Zhu Yuanqing 朱淵清 and Liao Mingchun 廖名春 (Shanghai: Shanghai Shudian Publisher, 2002), 327–34; Guo Yongbing 郭永秉, "*Cong Shangbo Chu Jian Rongchengshi de 'You Yu Tong' Shuo Dao Tang Yu Chuanshuo de Yiwen*" 從上博楚簡《容成氏》的 "有虞迵" 說到唐虞傳說的疑問, *Chutu Wenxian yu Guwenzi Yanjiu*《出土文獻與古文字研究》1 (2006): 295–312; Guo Yongbing 郭永秉, *Di Xi Xin Yan*《帝系新研》(Beijing: Peking University Press, 2008), 43–56. Guo Yongbing's sequence is based upon his identification of the name in slip 32 as the same as those in slip 5, but with duplication marks after each of the three graphs. If this is accepted, then these slips should be part of a single section, which could only be before the time of Yao and after the list of rulers in highest antiquity. See also note 19 below.

6. Allan, *The Heir and the Sage: Dynastic Legend in Early China* (San Francisco: Chinese Materials Center, 1981) provides a detailed analysis of the manner in which historical legend was used in texts from the fifth to first centuries BCE.

7. See Allan, *Heir and the Sage*, 123–40. Considering the composite nature of most of the texts, this is somewhat surprising and it may reflect Han editing, but the exceptions are rare.

8. Cf. Pines, *Envisioning Eternal Empire*, 65ff. Pines recognizes the polemical purpose of the manuscript, but still seems to regard it as an historical work.

9. For Gao Xin and Fuxishi, see Liao Mingchun 廖明春, "*Du Shangbojian Rong-chengshi Zhaji* 读上博简《容成氏》札记 (一)," http://www.jianbo.org/Wssf/2002/liaominchun03.htm; for Gao Ku see Qiu Dexiu 邱德修, *Shangbo Chu Jian Rongcheng-shi Zhuyi Kaozheng* 《上博楚簡《容成氏》注譯考證》, *Chutu Sixiang Wenwu yu Wenxian Yanjiu Congshu* 《出土思想文物與文獻研究叢書》, 15 (Taipei: Taiwan Guji Publisher, 2003), 139; for Hundunshi, see He Linyi 何琳儀, "*Di Er Pi Hu Jian Xuanshi*" 第二批滬簡選釋, in Zhu Yuanqing and Liao Mingchun, *Shangboguan Cang Zhanguo Chu Zhushu Yanjiu Xubian*, 450.

10. For discussion of the identity of Rongchengshi, see Bing Shangbai 邴尚白, "*Rongchengshi de Pianti ji Xiangguan Wenti*" 《容成氏》的篇題及相關問題, in Zhu Yuanqing and Liao Mingchun, *Shangboguan Cang Zhanguo Chu Zhushu Yanjiu Xubian*, 367–71. His role in medieval Daoism is discussed in Gil Raz, *Creation of Tradition: the Emergence of Daoism* (London: Routledge, 2011). I would also like to thank him for bringing this to my attention.

11. *Guo Yu* 《國語》 (Shanghai: Shanghai Guji Publisher, 1978), *Juan* 10, 387.

12. Gu Jiegang 顧頡剛, ed., *Gu Shi Bian* 《古史辯》 (Beijing and Shanghai: 1926–41 [rpt.: Shanghai: Shanghai Guji Publisher,1982]).

13. See Bernhard Karlgren's seminal study, "Legends and Cults in Ancient China," *Bulletin of the Museum of Far Eastern Antiquities* 18 (1946): 199–365.

14. *Zhuangzi Jishi* 《莊子集釋》 (Taipei: Heluo Tushu Publisher, 1974), *Juan* 4 (*Zhong*), 357.

15. Ibid.

16. *Hanfeizi Jishi* 《韓非子集釋》 (Taipei: Heluo Tushu Publisher), *Juan* 19, 1040.

17. See Gophal Sukhu, "Yao, Shun, and Prefiguration: The Origins and Ideology of the Han Imperial Genealogy," *Early China* 30 (2006): 91–154, for the use of the legend of Yao and Shun in Han ideology.

18. Qian Mu 錢穆, *Xian Qin Zhuzi Xinian* 《先秦諸子繫年》 (Taipei: Dongda Tushu Publisher, 1990), 163.

19. The graph that I transcribe as *yu* 虞, following Guo Yongbing (see n. 5 above), is written as *wu* 吳. This accords with *Tang Yu Zhi Dao*, where Yu 虞, is written as 吳; see *Guodian Chu Mu Zhujian*, 39–41 and 157–59. Li Ling, *Shanghai Bowuguan Cang Zhanguo Chu Zhushu*, vol. 2, 254, reads 吳 (*ŋo)as *wu* 無 (*mi̯wo), but this borrowing is not attested in received or unearthed texts and is phonologically problematic. The inability to explain these three graphs adequately except as a name provides support for Guo's argument. 迵 clearly functions as a loan graph for 通 on slips 24–27 of *Rongchengshi*, so the name here should probably be read in the same way.

20. There is a second "thereupon" (*yushi hu* 於是乎) here, which I have omitted in translation.

21. See Allan, *Heir and the Sage*, 31, 134. *Mengzi Yizhu* 《孟子譯註》, ed. Yang Bojun 楊伯峻 (Beijing: Zhonghua Shuju Publisher, 1984), 171 (4A.9), 219 (5A.5), 221–22 (5A.6); 4A.9; see also *Xunzi Jijie* 荀子集解 (Beijing: Zhonghua Shuju Publisher, 1988) *Juan* 12, 321–40. which places less stress on the movement of the people and more on the definition of kingship.

22. *Mengzi Yizhu*, 221–22 (5A.6).

23. See Allan, *Heir and the Sage*, 39–43, 59–61.

LIANG TAO

RETURNING TO "ZISI": THE CONFUCIAN THEORY OF THE LINEAGE OF THE WAY[1]

I. The Lineage of the Way: Premises and Theories

Confucianism has roots that stretch back into the distant past and it holds a deep and rich content of its own, within which there are not only distinctions, such as that between "the learning of the masters" (*zixue* 子學) and "classical learning" (*jingxue* 經學), but also oppositions, as between "Han learning" (*hanxue* 漢學) and "Song learning" (*songxue* 宋學). Each of these schools of learning can further be divided into various branches. Thus when later generations talk about a theory of the "Lineage of the Way," *daotong* 道統, they necessarily make particular discriminations, decisions, or evaluations regarding this content. While every school of thought is complex, each must still have a center. The notion of a Lineage of the Way is a way of expressing what lies at the center of a tradition of thinking.

While the concept of a Lineage of the Way of Confucianism is extremely old, it was Han Yu 韓愈 from the mid-Tang Dynasty who systematically expressed it. Han Yu believed that a Confucian Lineage of the Way started not with Confucius, but with the ancient sages Yao, Shun, Yu, and Tang. This shows that Confucianism as he understood it entirely inherited and continued the culture of the Pre-Axial Age, rather than starting with Confucius in the Axial Age, which certainly has some historical basis. Even so, he excluded Xunzi from the Lineage of the Way, claiming "that after the death of Mencius, no one received the transmission." Han Yu explained his view as follows:

> Benevolence and rightness are fixed terms [*dingming* 定名], while the Way and virtuous power [*de* 德] are empty positions [*xuwei* 虛位].... Thus, when I mention the Way and virtuous power, I speak of them in terms of benevolence and rightness. This is the shared vocabulary of the world.[2]

LIANG TAO, Professor, School of Chinese Classics, Renmin University. Specialties: Chinese intellectual history, excavated texts, Confucian thought. E-mail: liangtao1965@ 163.com

Journal of Chinese Philosophy, Supplement to Volume 37 (2010) 85–100
© *2010 Journal of Chinese Philosophy*

Han Yu saw benevolence and rightness as the essence of the Way, and the continuous lineage of Yao, Shun, Yu, Tang, Wen, Wu, the Duke of Zhou, and Confucius was this Way of benevolence and rightness. After Confucius, the one who truly and correctly proclaimed this Way was Mencius. After the death of Mencius, Xunzi was like Mencius in that "the words he uttered became classic," "he was deeply concerned with becoming a sage," and "he rarely deviated from the thought of Confucius."[3] However, in terms of benevolence and rightness "he grasped them, but did not refine them; he spoke of them, but not in much detail," and, "[Xunzi] was by and large exemplary, but not without defects." As such, Xunzi could not but be excluded from the Lineage of the Way. Han Yu's theory of the Lineage of the Way existed under conditions of decline known as "the waning of Confucianism" (*rumendanbo* 儒們淡薄), attempting to fend off Buddhism and Daoism, illuminate benevolence and rightness, and to newly reestablish a position of orthodoxy for Confucianism. As such, his influence on later generations was tremendous, and his point of view was accepted by later Neo-Confucians who were similarly concerned with fortifying the Way.

Han Yu's theory of a Lineage of the Way was not only accepted by many of the Song and Ming Neo-Confucians, but has also been echoed by Contemporary New Confucians. Mou Zongsan 牟宗三 (1909–1995), a representative of Contemporary New Confucianism, believed that Han Yu's theory of the Lineage of the Way was accepted because it corresponded to objective facts, not just because it was Han Yu's personal opinion. However, even though Mou Zongsan believed that the source of the Lineage of the Way was in the Pre-Axial Age age of Yao and Shun, he more emphasized the positive significance of Confucius establishing the teaching of benevolence for the "original Lineage of the Way" (*daozhibentong* 道之本统). He also emphasized the uniqueness of the form and orientation of Confucius's way of life.

In Mou Zongsan's view, the Way passed on from Yao, Shun, Yu, and the Three Dynasties was the Way of "government rules and accomplishments" (*zhenggui yexu* 政規業續), which was a way of culture and institutions (*wenzhizhidao* 文制之道). In short, this was the Way of the "outer king" (*waiwang* 外王) and not the Way of the "inner sage" (*neisheng* 內聖). The Way of the inner sage started with Confucius and his teachings of benevolence. Integrating Confucius' teaching of benevolence with the teachings of Yao, Shun, Yu, and the Three Dynasties provides the holistic meaning of "the Way of inner sageliness and outer kingliness." As such, Confucius's role in the original Lineage of the Way initiated a new breakthrough and another founding of the Way.[4]

Viewing things from this angle, the Lineage of the Way comes from Confucius and not from Yao, Shun, Yu, Tang, Wen, Wu, or the Duke of Zhou. We can clearly see that Mou Zongsan emphasized Confucius's breakthrough and transcendence of Pre-Axial Age culture rather than his inheritance from it or his connections to it. In this sense, in the eyes of Mou Zongsan, Confucius was one who "broke from the flow of the masses" (*jieduanzhongliu* 截斷眾流). Therefore, Mou opposed Han and Tang Confucians who saw Confucius as the transmitter of the Classics. This was because, according to Mou,

> Transmitting the Classics by means of teaching is one thing; the unique life of Confucius is another thing. Simply practicing the Six Arts does not necessarily enable one to truly understand the unique life of Confucius. Believing that practicing the Six Arts and transmitting the Classics are what constitutes a Confucian bypasses Confucius, taking the ancient Classics as a standard rather than the basic orientation of Confucius's life wisdom. They believed that Confucius was no more than a mediator.[5]

On the basis of this understanding, Mou excluded Han and Tang Confucians from the Lineage of the Way, and affirmed the contributions of Song and Ming Confucians in continuing the Lineage of the Way.

The account of the Lineage of the Way that began with Han Yu, was accepted by the majority of Song and Ming Neo-Confucians, and was further developed by Contemporary New Confucians is the standard view within Confucian history, with the greatest and most profound influence. However, we should also take note of another theory of the Lineage of the Way that developed in opposition to this. The Tang Dynasty scholar Yang Liang 楊倞 (sixth century CE) believed that the *dao* which the Duke of Zhou inherited from the Three Sovereigns and Five Emperors included things such as ritual, musical performances, benevolence, rightness, transforming through virtue (*dehua* 德化), and governing through law (*xingzheng* 刑政). It also included the *Book of Poetry*, the *Book of History*, and other texts that recorded the virtuous acts and punishments carried out by the early kings. This "way" obviously has a broad meaning, as the way is not only a conceptual view but also embodies transforming through virtue and governing through law. Thus he called it "the Way of the true king" (*wangdao* 王道), and claimed that it was transmitted through the lineage of the Duke of Zhou, Confucius, Mencius, and Xunzi. Even through the Spring and Autumn and Warring States periods where "the four barbarian groups attacked each other" (*siyijiaoqin* 四夷交侵) and the constant human relations fell into disuse, the line was not broken.

We can now see the distinctive points of this theory of the Lineage of the Way. For one, it expands the contents of the Way—the Way is not limited to benevolence and rightness, but also contains rituals, musical performances, and so on. Two—and this relates to the previous point—it does not exclude Xunzi from the Lineage of the Way, but rather sees him as an important link in propagating the Lineage of the Way.

The modern historian Qian Mu 錢穆 (1895–1990) opposed the theory of the "heart/mind and human nature" (*xinxing* 心性) put forth by Mou Zongsan and others, who considered it the main criteria by which they were able to pick and choose what they considered the Confucian tradition. Qian Mu thus criticized the theory of the Lineage of the Way of Han Yu and the Song and Ming Neo-Confucians and suggested taking the Chinese cultural tradition in its entirety as the real Lineage of the Way. What Qian Mu discussed was not restricted to Confucianism but an even more general theory of the Lineage of the Way.[6] The contemporary scholar, Li Zehou 李澤厚, in direct opposition to Mou Zongsan's theory of "three periods" (*sanqishuo* 三期説) of Confucianism, put forth a theory of "four periods" (*siqishuo* 四期説) with "Confucius, Mencius, and Xunzi as the first period; Confucians of the Han Dynasty as the second period; Song and Ming Neo-Confucians as the third period; and current and future developments—even if inheriting the previous three time periods, but possessing considerably different characteristics—as the fourth period."[7] Although Li Zehou does not explicitly mention the Lineage of the Way, he believes that the distinction between three and four periods relates to how Chinese culture, and in particular how the Confucian tradition is understood. He thereby concerns himself with the fundamental question of how to develop this tradition. On some level this most certainly reflects his understanding and comprehension of the Confucian Lineage of the Way.

II. AN ANALYSIS OF THE CONFUCIAN THEORY OF THE LINEAGE OF THE WAY

While the above survey of the two theories of the Lineage of the Way reveals several disparities and even some large differences within each, generally speaking, we can understand the first as speaking of "Lineage" from the perspective of the "Way," and the latter as speaking of the "Way" from the perspective of "Lineage." In speaking of Lineage from the perspective of the Way one first establishes what the Confucian Way is, and then takes this Way as a standard to distinguish and establish a Confucian genealogy. Whoever accords with this Way is placed in the Lineage. Whoever does not accord with this Way is excluded. As such, this view is first of all a philosophical or transcendental conception of the Lineage of the Way and not a historical or cultural conception. It does not pay attention to the history of Confucianism or the evolution and development of certain aspects of society; rather it focuses on a transcendental spirit, set of values, or ideology beyond history and society.

Second, and corresponding to the first point, it has the characteristics of a "classification of teachings" (*panjiao* 判教)—in an effort to separate the orthodox Confucians from the unorthodox. Because Han Yu, Zhu Xi, Mou Zongsan, and others believed benevolence and rightness to be the main essentials of the Way—and that benevolence and rightness manifest themselves in the principles of the heart/mind and human nature—they therefore believed that after Confucius, Mencius and the Song and Ming Dynasty Neo-Confucians inherited the Lineage of the Way. They therefore excluded Xunzi and the Han and Tang Dynasty Confucians from the Lineage of the Way.

We should also note that the "transmission" (*chuan* 傳) of the Lineage of the Way that these figures have in mind does not entail the usual meaning of the term, where a teacher passes it on to a student. Instead it is a "deep creation obtained from the self" (*shenzaozide* 深造自得) or a spiritual enlightenment. As such they can claim that the Lineage of the Way sometimes breaks—that there are periods of darkness where heaven and earth lack their brilliance—but then believe that after a time of interruption the Lineage of the Way can be rediscovered and continued. In short, their view is that regarding the early sages and the later sages, their heart/minds fit together perfectly.

In contrast, speaking of the "Way" from the perspective of "Lineage" concentrates on the entirety of the Confucian tradition, so that everything within the successive tradition of Confucianism can be seen as constituting the Way. For example, Yang Liang believed that benevolence, rightness, ritual, musical performances, transforming through virtue and governing through law, the *Book of Poetry*, the *Book of History*, and the Six Arts were all the fundamentals of the Way, the dao which Shi Jie 石介 (1005–1045) put forward as the "three powers" (*sancai* 三才) (heaven, earth, and human beings), "nine parcels of land" (*jiuchou* 九疇) discussed in the *Book of History*, and the "five enduring virtues" (*wuchang* 五常) (benevolence, rightness, ritual, wisdom, and trust).[8] Although Qian Mu's theory of the Lineage of the Way was not limited to Confucianism, practically speaking we can say that it contains the entirety of the Confucian tradition. This adequately illustrates the notion of speaking of the Way from the perspective of Lineage. Li Zehou affirmed Xunzi and the Han and Tang Confucians, the latter because they exerted a great influence in establishing institutions and shaping the psychology of the people.

While taking a different approach, Li's results amount to speaking of the Way from the perspective of Lineage. Speaking of the Way from the perspective of Lineage is a historical and cultural view of the Lineage of the Way. It pays more attention to the actual development and evolution of Confucianism, rather than some transcendent value or ideal. Furthermore, it does not require distinctions between orthodoxy and unorthodoxy within Confucianism, or it at least does not make this a focal point. Instead it completely envelops the systematic thought, internal structure, and social function of Confucianism. At the same time it does not emphasize breaks in the Lineage of the Way or the loss of ideal values, but rather views the Confucian tradition as one of "ceaseless generation" (*shengshengbuxi* 生生不息), with the earlier and later in continuous connection.

Now that we have compared two theories of the Lineage of the Way, how should they be regarded? How should one engage in an analysis, examination, and judgment of a reconstruction of a Confucian theory of the Lineage of the Way? This undoubtedly is a major theoretical question for the future development of Confucianism. In answering this question, the following points must be examined and pondered.

First of all, we must reflect on the difference between the Lineage of the Way, and "lineages of learning" (*xuetong* 學統) or "lineages of government" (*zhengtong* 政統). Confucianism is a bountiful tradition with a deep source and long history. The *Book of Poetry*, *Book of History*, *Book of Ritual*, *Book of Music*, and the Six Arts constitute its "learning." Its transmission through history can be called a "lineage of learning," but it is not the Lineage of the Way, because while the Six Arts reside in and include the Way, they are not themselves the Way. Rituals, musical performances, punishments, and the institutions used to govern can be regarded as government. This government, through the transition of successive dynasties, can be called a "lineage of government" or a "lineage of order" (*zhitong* 治統), but this also is not the Lineage of the Way, because while ritual, musical performances, punishments, and the institutions used to govern, originate in the Way and apply the Way in practical governing, they are not themselves the Way.

The Confucian Lineage of the Way can only be its core value ideals and its systematic thought. This ideal and system, when implemented in historically situated cultural traditions, follows the development and progression of a historical culture and manifests itself as a certain transcendent, long-lasting but ever renewing, continually transmitted, cultural spirit (*wenhua jingshen* 文化精神) and cultural life (*wenhua shengming* 文化生命). The existence of this cultural spirit and cultural life is certainly the most essential element of a Confucian Lineage of the Way.

The notion of speaking of the Way from the perspective of Lineage gives prominence to the holistic and continuous nature of Confucianism. It ties together the Lineage of the Way and concrete historical processes, which is its most reasonable point. However, it is inadequate in lacking a clear awareness of the difference between the Lineage of the Way and concrete historical processes. In comparison, speaking of Lineage from the perspective of the Way gives prominence to the core value ideals of Confucianism, and in using the transmission of these ideals to understand the Confucian Lineage of the Way, it is no doubt more reasonable. It is insufficient, though, in that it understands the contents of the Way as nothing more than benevolence and rightness, thereby neglecting other dimensions.

Next, one must address the difference between the cultures of the Pre-Axial Age and Axial Age. Put concretely, should the Confucian Lineage of the Way begin with Yao, Shun, Yu, and Tang, or should it begin with Confucius? Historically, Han Yu, Yang Liang, Sun Fu (992–1057), Shi Jie, Zhu Xi, and others believed that the Confucian Lineage of the Way began with Yao, Shun, Yu, Tang, Wen, and Wu, and not with Confucius. They believed that from the Pre-Axial Age times of Yao, Shun, Yu, and Tang down to the Axial Age of Confucius and Mencius there was a common thread that tied the Way together and was continually transmitted. This view, however, while giving prominence to the origins of the Lineage of the Way also neglects the differences between the Pre-Axial Age and the Axial Age.

In contrast to this, Mou Zongsan put forth the notion that Confucius established the teaching of benevolence, making a creative breakthrough regarding the "original Lineage of the Way" and establishing it anew. On this view, the Confucian Lineage of the Way begins with Confucius and not with Yao, Shun, Yu, Tang, Wen, Wu, and the Duke of Zhou. This position pays attention to the differences in the culture of the Pre-Axial Age and the Axial Age and certainly is one step more profound. Mou Zongsan believed that the Confucian Lineage of the Way was the learning of the inner sage and the heart/mind and nature (*neisheng xinxing* 內聖心性). This learning of the inner sage and the heart/mind and nature is none other than Confucius's notion of benevolence, but this obviously is not sufficiently comprehensive. Confucius's reestablishing the original Lineage of the Way was not only in the new invention of benevolence but also in advocating ritual, which has a much more complex connection with Pre-Axial Age culture. On the one hand, Confucius explained ritual in terms of benevolence.

On the other hand, he implemented benevolence by means of ritual. Benevolence and ritual are exactly the core contents of Confucius' reconstruction of the original Lineage of the Way, and the relationship between benevolence and ritual is the core question for the Lineage of the Way. Although when discussing ritual, Confucius integrated the rites and ceremonies of his times, the difference between Confucius and those who came after him was that Confucius emphasized the spirit, value, and significance of ritual. The specific practices of rites and ceremonies can be relegated to the realm of history—becoming simply footprints of the past. But the spirit, value, and significance of rituals are most definitely transcendent, following through the developments and evolution of each era.

The place of Mencius and Xunzi in the Lineage of the Way remains an issue worthy of investigation. Ever since Mencius and Xunzi diverged and became opposed, the issue of who was more representative of the Confucian Lineage of the Way has been a greatly contested question. Historically speaking, the shift from Confucius to Mencius and Xunzi was really a process of internal diversification. This diversification had an indirect influence on later schools of thought such as Han and Tang Classical Studies and the Song and Ming Neo-Confucianism. Thus if we do not want to hold a view of the Lineage of the Way that is subjective, singularly transmitted, or easily broken, then we should not view the Lineage of the Way from the division and opposition between Mencius and Xunzi or by following the divisions of later Confucianism. Rather, we should see the Lineage of the Way in terms of the abundant fruitfulness of its source. Thus we should acknowledge that the original cultural life of the source is ceaselessly generating and that the early and later forms are mutually continuous. This is indeed where to find the Lineage of the Way.

However, the Lineage of the Way is not one singularly transmitted line, taking form once and never changing. Rather it has twists and turns as well as innovations and breakthroughs. Certain aspects of the Way can be hidden and concealed, becoming hidden and opaque in certain periods of time, making the form of the way incomplete. At the same time, if other aspects of the Way linger—continuing and even gaining in abundance and development—then the Lineage of the Way has not been truly cut off. Furthermore, in the continuation of the Lineage of the Way, one should not lament when the form of the Way is incomplete, taking those covered up aspects of the Way as orthodox. Rather, through a process of "removing the blinders" (*qubi* 去蔽) one should illuminate the lost aspects of the Way, causing the diverse aspects of the Way to reconverge and be rewelded together. As such, the precise process of differentiation from Confucius to Mencius and

Xunzi deserves further investigation. The transitional figure of Zisi—
his thought and position in the tradition—therefore, comes into
prominence.

III. RETURNING TO "ZISI"—RECONSTRUCTING A CONFUCIAN THEORY OF THE *DAOTONG*

In 1993 a cache of bamboo strips was unearthed in the village of
Guodian (in the province of Hubei) from a tomb dating back to the
ancient state of Chu. The tomb was sealed sometime between the
middle of the fourth century and the late third century BCE—thereby
coming from the middle to late Warring States period. The texts
recorded on the bamboo strips, however, are most likely from an
earlier period—probably coming after Confucius, but before Mencius.
These bamboo strips provide us with important documents and materials to understand a history that had been under a cloud of obscurity
for those researching the ancient past. Especially valuable was the fact
that these bamboo strips touched on the writings of Zisi, and provided
for us the rare opportunity to understand the thought of Zisi as well
as the Confucianism of Zisi's time.

These bamboo texts change some of our long-held views, giving us
a new understanding and comprehension of Confucianism during this
time period. For instance, the scholarly world traditionally believed
that the theory that "benevolence is internal and rightness is external"
(*rennei yiwai* 仁內義外) was the view of Gaozi, and was criticized and
opposed by Confucians. However, the bamboo texts from Guodian
have many discussions relating to the theory of "benevolence as internal and rightness as external." They demonstrate that this theory was
commonly accepted by earlier Confucians.

In the Guodian manuscripts, although the concept of "benevolence
as internal and rightness as external" is complex and holds various
meanings. One meaning is directed toward internal and external stat-
utes of morality, implying that some moral principles are "born from
the inside" (*shengyunei* 生於內) and others are "obtained from the
outside" (*shengyuwai* 生於外). Benevolence is born from the internal,
and rightness is obtained from the external; the practice of morality
begins with both aspects of "benevolence as internal" and "rightness
as external"—in essence integrating the two. This notion of "benevolence as internal and rightness as external," however, has obvious
differences from Gaozi's emphasis on the opposition between
benevolence as internal and rightness as external.

The progression from the Guodian manuscript's theory of
"benevolence as internal and rightness as external" to Gaozi's theory

and then to Mencius' theory of "benevolence and rightness as internal" (*renyi neizai* 仁義內在) passed through a complex and winding process of conceptual development. This was also an exploratory process for Confucian theorization. More importantly, the theory of "benevolence as internal and rightness as external" in the Guodian manuscripts is one that Zisi probably accepted; in other words, Zisi must have taken a similar position. As such, although Mencius and Xunzi seem in opposition, they both have direct and indirect connections with Zisi's ideas. The development of Confucianism after Zisi was not monolithic, but rather multidimensional. Mencius and Xunzi simply represent different dimensions of this process of differentiation.

In addition, much of the Guodian texts, particularly the "*Xingzimingchu*《性自命出》*,*" discuss the notion of "sentiment" (*qing* 情) in a way that challenges many of our long held assumptions. Traditionally, scholars believed that notions of a transcendent dimension of human nature—where human nature came down from the mandate of heaven (*tianming* 天命) and was necessarily good (*shan* 善), were a recent development in the tradition, different from an earlier tradition of taking human nature as rooted in physiology and natural desire—the idea that "the processes of life are human nature" (*sheng zhiwei xing* 生之謂性). However, the "*Xingzimingchu*" states, "Human nature comes forth from the mandate. The mandate comes down from Heaven." It then goes on to say that "the *qi* of joy, anger, sorrow, and grief is human nature," and "likes and dislikes are human nature." So, while it speaks of human nature as coming from the mandate of Heaven, or from a transcendent dimension, the human nature it discusses is most certainly a "naturalistic human nature" (*ziran renxing* 自然人性) and not a "moral human nature" (*daode renxing* 道德人性).

Traditionally, scholars also believed that human sentiment does not contain morality and is opposed to ethical principles; they therefore interpret human sentiment from a negative angle. However, the "*Xingzimingchu*" differs from this. It praises and affirms human sentiment, saying, "Any genuine human sentiment can be pleasing," and "if done with genuine sentiment, even if erring it is not hated."[9] It thereby interprets human sentiment from a positive angle.

This reveals that our previous framework of explanation may not be entirely plausible, unable to explain the actual conditions of ancient theories of human nature. In this ancient time, China already held a tradition of interpreting human sentiment from a transcendent perspective. The early Chinese did not simply discuss sentiment from the perspective of human experience, but rather discussed it in connection with Heaven and Earth. They understood human sentiment in terms of the six *qi* of Heaven and Earth, and claimed that the six *qi* are bestowed upon the bodies of the people and generate the sentiments of pleasure, anger, sorrow, and joy.[10] This tradition does not primarily concern itself with the issue of human nature being good or bad, but with the issue of human nature being harmonious. It believes that Heaven and Earth have a harmonious and organic existence. Heaven and Earth bestowed our nature, which generates our sentiments. The nature we obtain from the very beginning is necessarily in a condition of primordial harmony.

In the past, scholars liked to discuss a "metaphysics of morals" (*daode xingshangxue* 道德形上學), desiring to find a metaphysical foundation for goodness. However, according to the "*Xingzimingchu*" and other ancient texts, it seems we should also discuss a "metaphysics of sentiment" (*qinggan xingshangxue* 情感形上學), seeking a metaphysical foundation for human sentiment. We should discuss human sentiment not only from the dimension of experience, but we should also connect it with a dimension of transcendence, discussing human sentiment in connection with its roots in Heaven and Earth. It is precisely on this point that the way the ancients, including the "*Xingzimingchu*," understood human nature and sentiment, particularly natural sentiments, is not the same as that of later generations.

The material above demonstrates that Zisi is not simply a key figure in early Confucianism, but also that the period that he represents in the development of early Confucianism is a pivotal point. Before Zisi, Confucius absorbed and synthesized the culture of ritual and musical performances created by Yao, Shun, Yu, and the Three Dynasties. He furthermore fashioned, developed, and gave form to the Confucian thought that took the notions of benevolence and ritual as its core. This coalesced in Zisi, who inherited and continued it almost completely. After Zisi, this rich Confucian tradition began to diversify, developing in different directions. From Zisi to Mencius and Xunzi, the Confucian tradition underwent a process of internal deepening but at the same time of narrowing. The division between Mencius and Xunzi developed different sides of the Confucian tradition that came from Confucius. This caused certain aspects of Confucianism to be fully developed such that they became more nuanced and profound. However, other aspects of Confucianism were neglected or went astray. Thus they did not truly inherit and continue the whole of the Confucian tradition passed down from Confucius.

In terms of standing in the Lineage of the Way, if we take benevolence and ritual as its core content, then we must affirm that in its transmission, there is that which Mencius lost. By primarily emphasizing the internal aspect of the tradition (the heart/mind and human nature), he developed the study of benevolence, but neglected the external dimensions of practice and training, insufficiently transmitting the Confucian study of ritual and thus leaving gaps.

On the other hand, Xunzi also had his biases. He primarily developed the side of external institutions and ritual practices, also integrating law into ritual, giving rise to the tendency to mix Legalism with Confucianism. However, he did not sufficiently emphasize the Confucian study of benevolence, and did not truly grasp the spirit of benevolence, thereby causing benevolence to become shallow and narrow. These are the deviations that developed in his thought.

Therefore, in confronting the divide between Mencius and Xunzi we should not simply value one position and repress the other. In the ceaseless debate about who is more representative of the Confucian Lineage of the Way, we should return to "Zisi." But this return is not a return in a historical or genetic sense but rather a return in a hermeneutic sense—namely a restoration of the rich cultural life of the source. It is on this foundation of plentitude that the Confucian Lineage of the Way should be reestablished. "Zisi" does not simply stand for Zisi himself or his thought, but stands for a rich era of thought in Confucianism, as well as a rational conceptual framework. If we say that the transition from Zisi to Mencius and Xunzi was the beginning of the differentiation, but also the deepening of various strains of Confucian thought, then returning to "Zisi" means enacting a unification to create and reestablish the Confucian Lineage of the Way on the foundation of these deepened strains.

So, returning to "Zisi" is first of all engaging in a renewed understanding and elucidation of the relationship between benevolence and ritual—enabling the Confucian study of benevolence and study of ritual to organically unite together. This would entail inheriting the positive results of Mencius' thought, borrowing the reasonable core of Xunzi's thought, giving prominence to the subjectivity and internality of benevolence, and discarding certain aspects of the content of rituals, such as the ranking of "superior and inferior" (*zunbei* 尊卑), but preserving the positive forms of ritual to differentiate, order, and harmonize things. In short it means developing the study of benevolence, transforming the study of ritual, and establishing a school of thought based on the unity of benevolence and ritual. Returning to "Zisi" in terms of a theory of human nature means unifying conceptions of our nature as "benevolent (*renxing* 仁性)," "knowing (*zhixing* 知性)," and "sentimental (*qingxing* 情性)" (as in, "The likes, dislikes, pleasure, anger, sorrow, and joy of human nature is what we call sentiment," or, "What is human sentiment? It is pleasure, anger, sorrow, fear, like, dislike, and desire").[11] In other words this is a process of constructing a rich and comprehensive framework for a theory of human nature.

Returning to "Zisi" in terms of political thought means unifying the Confucian notions of "choosing the worthy and able" (*xuanxian yuneng* 選賢於能) and "power being publicly held" (*quanli gongyou* 權力公有), with notions of benevolent governing and taking "the people as the root (*minben* 民本)." At the same time it also means absorbing the ideals of Western democracy—removing what is coarse and preserving what is refined—and developing a new model of Confucian democratic thought. Returning to "Zisi" from the point of view of the received culture means managing the relationship between the cultures of the Pre-Axial Age and the Axial Age. More concretely, this is the relationship between the "Five Classics" and the "Four Books."

In terms of the evolution and development of Confucianism, Song and Ming Neo-Confucianism may be closer to the form of early Confucianism. The Confucians of these periods absorbed and borrowed the theoretical perspectives of Buddhism and Daoism thereby creating a new interpretation of Confucianism. They also made the Confucian doctrines of the "heart/mind and nature" and "rightness and principle (*yili* 義理)" progress another step. At the same time, while the Four Books esteemed by Song and Ming Confucians have a positive meaning, they were not necessarily able to encompass or reflect the spirit of early Confucianism; and while this was done in the service of their theory of the Lineage of the Way, it had the effect of simplistically "adding to and subtracting from" (*sunyi* 損益) early Confucianism.

In my view, if we do not stand on a narrow view of the Lineage of the Way as "one thread with a single transmission," but rather see the Lineage of the Way as that original cultural life of the source—as the process of ceaseless generation or an unfading cultural spirit—then what can truly represent and reflect the cultural spirit and life of early Confucianism should be the four books of the *Analects*, the *Book of Ritual* (*Li Ji* 《禮記》), the *Mencius*, and the *Xunzi*. Of these, the *Analects*, the *Mencius*, and the *Xunzi* can be classified as the records and reflections of the spirit and cultural life of Confucius, Mencius, and Xunzi, respectively, while the *Book of Ritual* can be classified as the works of Confucius' seventy-two disciples and their followers (including Zengzi, Ziyou, Zisi, and others), collected and discovered by Han scholars. The *Book of Ritual* also sorts and arranges their discussions of rituals, ceremonies, and writings. Thus the relevant content of the bamboo texts from Guodian and the Shanghai Museum should be included among these. As such the *Analects*, the *Book of Ritual*, the *Mencius*, and the *Xunzi* truly cover the content of the cultural life and spirit of early Confucianism, and can be called "the New Four Books" (*Xinsishu*《新四書》). We should, however, not view the *Analects*, the *Book of Ritual*, the *Mencius*, and the *Xunzi* as transmitting an identical Way "united by one thread" (*yiyiguanzhi* 一以貫之); rather we should view these texts as part of the ceaseless regeneration of Confucian cultural life, a process of growth and development but also with twists and turns.

So neither Mencius nor Xunzi are capable of taking up the Confucian Lineage of the Way alone. Regarding the Confucian Lineage of the Way as a ceaselessly generating cultural life, they both have that which they "lost" and that which they are "biased toward." Only through unifying Mencius and Xunzi—allowing them to supplement each other—can the Lineage of the Way be reestablished, and the life spirit and vital force of Confucianism be recovered. The oppositions and divergences in the thought of Mencius and Xunzi are just what render it necessary to mix them to supplement each other. As such, in studying the *Mencius* one must append the *Xunzi*, and in studying the *Xunzi* one must return to the *Mencius*—especially in regards to the topic of human nature. As stated in the *Zhongyong*, "The myriad things are enriched together and do not harm each other. [The various] Ways move together and do not pervert [each other]."[12]

The Song and Ming Confucians were able to take returning to early Confucianism (and to Confucius and Mencius in particular) as their goal, and take the theory and metaphysics of Buddhism and Daoism as their points of reference, in their words, "Going in and out of the realm of Daoism and Buddhism to garner their ideas, and then returning with these ideas to the Six Classics."[13] They thus were able to complete a great restoration of Confucianism through a creative interpretation of the Four Books. In the same way, then the discovery of the Guodian and the Shanghai Museum materials may enable us to have an even more vivid understanding of the development of Confucian thought from Confucius to Mencius and Xunzi, to feel the pulse of the cultural life of early Confucianism, and to unearth and rediscover the sources of early Confucian thought.

Therefore, we can learn from the practices of Song Confucians by going in and out of Western learning (Kant, Hegel, Heidegger, Rawls, and others) to gather ideas, and then return to the "Six Classics." We would take a new theory of the Lineage of the Way as our lead and take a new Four Books as our fundamental classics, using the notions of "The Six Classics comment on me" (*liujing zhuwo* 六經注我) and "I comment on the Six Classics" (*wozhu liujing* 我注六經) to accomplish a new beginning and reestablishment of contemporary Confucianism, which would become one of the great responsibilities and missions that we face. On one side, the value and significance of the "Six Classics" flows into "my" life, enriching "me" and nourishing "me"—this is called "the Six Classics comment on me." On the other side, the sentiments of "my" time, the concerns of "my" life, and "my" critical consciousness are taken and read into the "Six Classics"—this is called "I comment on the Six Classics." It is on just this level of meaning that we can say "the Six Classics are histories" (*liujing jieshi* 六經皆史)—the "Six Classics" are histories of the development and growth of a people, histories of the spirit of a culture, and histories of freedom. These histories of spirit and freedom are the places where the Confucian Lineage of the Way and the spirit of Confucius, Zengzi, Youzi, Zisi, Mencius, and Xunzi are found. They are also the greatest revelation given to us in light of our study of the Guodian manuscripts and the Zisi-Mencius school of thought.

RENMIN UNIVERSITY
Beijing, China

ENDNOTES

I am deeply grateful to Dr. Michael Ing's translation of my article from Chinese. My writing was based on a presentation delivered at the International Conference on "*Ruxue yu Rensheng Xinyang* 儒学与人生信仰" (Confucianism and Human Faith), Renmin University, Beijing, China, December 12, 2009. Meanwhile I am indebted to the support of Renmin University's Project for Academic Publications in English Periodicals. Moreover, I thank the *Journal of Chinese Philosophy* for inviting me to join this special issue, and I am respectfully grateful to Professor Chung-ying Cheng's important comments and suggestions. I have authorized the editors of this journal to proofread and edit both the manuscript and page-proofs, and my much thanks go to them particularly to Professor Franklin Perkins for their time and labor.

1. Translated from Chinese by Michael Ing.
2. Han Yu 韩愈, *Han Yu Quanji*《韩愈全集》(Shanghai: Shanghai Guji Publisher, 1997), 120.
3. Ibid., 131, 128.
4. Mou Zongsan 牟宗三, *Xinti yu Xingti I*《心體與性體》(一) (Taipei: Zhongzheng Shuju Publisher, 1968), 13–14.
5. Ibid., 12.
6. Qian Mu 錢穆, *Zhongguo Xueshu Tongyi*《中國學術通義》(Taipei: Taiwan Xuesheng Shuju Publisher, 1993), 94.
7. Li Zehou 李澤厚, "*Shuo Ruxue Siqi* 説儒學四期," in *Yuandao*《原道》(Guizhou: Guizhou Renmin Publisher, 1999). Regarding the latest viewpoint on theories for the division of the Ruxue 儒學 into time periods, see Chung-ying Cheng, "The Development of Confucianism in Its Fifth Stage and the Positioning of Neo-Neo-Confucianism," 〈第五阶段儒学的发展与新新儒学的定位〉, *Wen Shi Zhe*《文史哲》5 (2002).
8. Shi Jie 石介, "*Guai Shuo Zhong* 〈怪説中〉," in *Culai Shi Xiansheng Wenji*《徂徠石先生文集》, vol. 5, *Siku Wenyuan Geben*《四庫文淵閣本》.
9. "*Xingzimingchu* 〈性自命出〉," strips 50–51, in *Guodian Chumu Zhujian*《郭店楚墓竹简》, ed. Jingmen City Museum 荊門市博物館 (Beijing: Wenwu Publisher, 1998).

10. *'Zuo Zhuan "Zhao Gong Ershiwu Nian"*《左傳・昭公二十五年》, where Zidashu
子大叔 quotes the words of Zichan 子產 (Yang Bojun, *Chunqiu Zuozhuan Zhu*
《春秋左傳注》[Beijing: Zhonghua Shuju Publisher, 1981], vol. 4, 1357–58).

11. *"Li Yun"*〈禮運〉, in *Li Ji*《禮記》(Shanghai: Shanghai Guji Publisher, 1997), 376.

12. *"Zhong Yong"*〈中庸〉, *Li Ji*, 922.

13. Cheng Yi 程颢 and Cheng Hao 程颐, *Er Cheng Ji*《二程集》(Beijing: Zhonghua Shuju
Publisher, 1981), 489.

SCOTT COOK

"*SAN DE*" AND WARRING STATES VIEWS ON HEAVENLY RETRIBUTION

The question of divine retribution has long been a central one in Chinese religious, philosophical, and political thought. The term "Heaven's Mandate" (*tianming* 天命) became synonymous with morally justified political overthrow from the Zhou Dynasty onward, and the notion that Heaven served as the supreme arbiter of justice in the world was never seriously challenged until the Warring States period. Even then, the concept of Heavenly reward and retribution remained a mainstream one, the Moists going so far as to advocate a philosophical program centered on "Heaven's will," the notion that a propriety-loving Heaven consciously ensured social order by rewarding the good and punishing the depraved. This traditional belief would continue to underlie the basic tenets of the religious sects that would gain widespread followings in the imperial era, finding a direct descendent in the calculations of merit and demerit in religious Daoism, and to some extent paving the way for acceptance of the notion of karmic retribution that would come to China as part of the Buddhist worldview.

The recently unearthed text "*San De* 《三德》," or "The Three Virtues," gives us a new understanding of the nature of such beliefs during the Warring States period, revealing a certain strand of thought in which Heavenly reward and retribution underlay an intricate program of ethical directives and prohibitions. The present article will offer an overview of this newly unearthed text by first examining it in conjunction with the criticisms of Xun Zi's 荀子 (*ca.* 315–240 BC) "*Tian Lun* 〈天論〉," with which it shows a number of intriguing parallels and oppositions, and then briefly exploring its program of proscriptions in the context of early instances of "seasonal ordinance" (*shiling* 時令) literature, with which the text appears to be most closely affiliated.

SCOTT COOK, Professor, Department of Chinese and Japanese, Grinnell College. Specialties: early Chinese intellectual history, Pre-Qin textual studies. E-mail: cook@grinnell.edu

Journal of Chinese Philosophy, Supplement to Volume 37 (2010) 101–123
© 2010 Journal of Chinese Philosophy

I. *"San De"* and *"Tian Lun"*

The manuscript of *"San De"* consists of twenty-two strips or strip fragments—of which fifteen are complete—plus one strip fragment from the Chinese University of Hong Kong collection that would also appear to belong to this manuscript. The contents of the manuscript were published in December 2005 as part of volume 5 of the *Shanghai Bowuguan Cang Zhanguo Chu Zhushu* 《上海博物館藏戰國楚竹書》, a collection of Warring States bamboo manuscripts housed in the Shanghai Museum that were unearthed in the early-to-mid-1990s and can confidently be identified as having come from a Chu-state tomb located somewhere in modern-day Hubei Province and most likely datable to roughly 300 BC. Full-scale photographs of the strips of *"San De"* were published along with the arrangement and transcription of Li Ling 李零, which also included his brief annotations to the text. The manuscript is not self-titled; Li chose the title on the basis of the content of what would appear to be its first strip.[1]

"San De" is at once both a philosophically rich and philologically difficult text. Much of the difficulty lies in the nature of its literary form, as it consists of a series of individual stanzas in which rhyme predominates. The penchant to rhyme obscures the meaning as much as the presence of the rhyme itself may help us to determine the reading of certain graphs, and even in this latter regard its use is somewhat limited given that the rhyme often tends to be irregular or inexact.[2] Couple this with the fact that a number of the strips are either incomplete or missing altogether, and we thus have a text for which any sort of full restoration or precise determination of strip-order remains frustratingly hopeless. Nonetheless, many of the strips may still be confidently strung together and read contiguously, and even with all the gaps and uncertainties that are left, enough of this fascinating text remains to give us a sense of its philosophical import and intellectual-historical significance. Space here will not permit anything approaching a close examination of all the interpretive particulars or any complete exploration of this manuscript's contents—a prerequisite, if largely impracticable, task that I have already attempted elsewhere.[3] Instead, we shall focus on identifying some of its salient features, and investigating ways in which it might help us fill out the intellectual-historical picture of the mid-to-late Warring States.

If Li Ling is correct in his identification of the manuscript's initial strip, the text of *"San De"* opens with a most interesting tripartite division:

天供時 ■ ［之部］ Heaven supplies the seasons,
地供材 ■ ［之部］ Earth the resources,
人供力 ■ ［職部］ Humans the labor.

明王無思 ■ ［之部］ The enlightened king forgoes contemplation:
是謂參德 ［職部］ this is what we call a "triumvirate of virtues."[4]
(strip 1)

Such a symbiotic relationship between Heaven, Earth, and man-kind is by no means unheard of in pre-Qin literature, but the ways in which this relationship is conceived and the precise nature of each member's contribution is subject to variation. Of all currently extant texts, those that bear the greatest overall similarity to "*San De*"—in terms not only of ideological content, but, as we shall see, of termi-nology and literary form as well—may be the so-called *Huangdi Sijing* 《黃帝四經》texts of Mawangdui 馬王堆, found at the head of the same silk scroll that contains the *Laozi B*《老子乙本》text (hereafter "Four Lost Texts [of Mawangdui]").[5] Regarding these opening lines in par-ticular, there are at least two instances in which the "Four Lost Texts" speak of a "triumvirate participation" (*can* 參) of Heaven, Earth, and mankind: "In the way of he who rules as king over the world, Heaven, Earth, and man are all involved. By utilizing these three in tandem (*sanzhe can yong zhi* 參［三］者參用之), one may . . . (lacuna) . . . and possess the world" ("*Jing Fa* 經法," "*Liu Fen* 六分"); and again: "Thus kings do not rule their states through serendipity, but inherently possess a pre-established way: above, they understand the timing of Heaven, below, the benefits (*li* 利) of the Earth, and in between, the affairs (*shi* 事) of mankind" ("*Shi Da Jing*〈十大經〉," "*Qian Dao*〈前道〉").[6]

As Cao Feng has rightly pointed out, the notions of "Heaven" or "Heaven and Earth" in both "*San De*" and the "Four Lost Texts" represent an eternal, unchanging standard "demanding that mankind take the operational system of Heaven and Earth as its model and standard, before it may receive 'Heaven's' protection and not be subject to its punishments," and thus both works concern themselves in no small measure with the respective prohibitions of Heaven, Earth, and mankind.[7] We shall examine such prohibitions in greater detail below. The Mawangdui texts are far from the only ones that share this basic ideological framework of triadic cooperation, and others bear even closer similarities to the "*San De*" opening in terms of shared terminology. In particular, we may cite the opening passage from the "*Shanquan Shu*〈山權數〉" chapter of the *Guanzi*《管子》—a chapter that largely deals with the principles of natural resource management and sound economic policies—in which the respective attributes of Heaven, Earth, and mankind are precisely equivalent to those of our text: "Guanzi replied, 'Heaven has the seasons as its balance (*quan* 權), Earth has its resources as its balance, mankind has its labors as its balance, and the ruler has his commands (*ling* 令) as his balances. If the balance of Heaven is lost, then the balance of mankind and Earth will be lost as well.' "[8] The consistent idea in all of these texts is that successful rulership of the realm is dependent upon achieving the harmonious operation and appropriate utilization of the seasonal, environmental, and labor resources of Heaven, Earth, and mankind.

At issue, however, is just how that triadic harmony is to be achieved. In this regard, by far the most interesting parallel to the "*San De*" opening is to be found in a text that in terms of overall philosophy is in many ways its diametric opposite: the "*Tian Lun* 〈天論〉" chapter of the *Xunzi*, which begins as follows:

> There is constancy in Heaven's movement (*tian xing* 天行): it neither persists for the sake of [a sage like] Yao or perishes for the sake of [a tyrant like] Jie. If you respond to it with order, there will be good fortune, but if you respond to it with disorder, there will be ill fortune. If you strengthen resources and moderate consumption, Heaven cannot make you destitute ... [whereas] if your resources are neglected and your consumption extravagant, Heaven cannot make you wealthy. . . . You will starve even before floods or droughts arrive, get sick even before frigid or scorching weather presses in, and find ill fortune without the arrival of any anomalous portents. Though you receive the same timing of the seasons (*shi* 時) as an orderly age, your [having of] disasters will differ from it; for this you cannot blame Heaven—that is just the way things work. Thus [only] when you comprehend the division (/separate lots) between Heaven and mankind (*tian ren zhi fen* 天人之分) can you be called a "man of attainment."[9]

Heaven thus operates in accordance with its own principles, in a course that is constant unto itself just as it may be unpredictable in its manifestations. It is most certainly not a sentient operator that responds *directly* to the ethics of human conduct, but rather a natural order whose bounty we may work to harvest for our own benefit, or whose threats of disaster we may neglect to prepare against at our own peril. It is in this sense, then, that Xun Zi wishes to draw a clear division between "Heaven" and "mankind."[10]

Xun Zi's discourse here, as always, is largely directed against prior or contemporary doctrines, not the least of which is certainly that of the Moists, who advocated the more traditional view of a willful Heaven who ensures the common good by rewarding the righteous and inflicting punishments upon the wicked. But the Moists were far from the only ones to adopt such a belief, which was, after all, an ancient one, and which still found many advocates in Xun Zi's time. In order to strengthen his own position and effectively counter those of his opponents, Xun Zi's favorite tactic was always to adopt and assimilate the more acceptable portions of his rivals' doctrines while simultaneously attacking their more pernicious elements. In this case, let us note that the "constancy" of Heaven's ways here is in fact a *premise* that Xun Zi has accepted; what he wants to discuss, though, is what, exactly, constitutes that constant way, and what implications that may have for human society. Xun Zi, again, denies to Heaven any direct role as *arbiter* in the process of moral retribution. But Heaven still *does* have a relationship with mankind, in the sense that Heaven and Earth are the ones that provide us with the means for our sustenance, and thus our task is to make use of those means wisely, with timeliness, preparation, and moderation. Thus we still need to "respond to" (*ying* 應) Heaven's constancy and follow in accordance with its seasons before we may begin to speak of putting ourselves in order.

"*Tian Lun*" goes on to define Heaven's duties (*tian zhi* 天職) in terms of those for which it acts or strives to no purpose:

> Accomplishing without acting for a purpose (*wei* 為),
> attaining without striving (*qiu* 求)
> —this is what is meant by "Heaven's duties."
>   Upon such things as this,
> to not apply deliberation (*lü* 慮), however profound;
> to not apply one's capabilities, however great;
> to not to apply investigation, however refined
> —this is what is meant by "not competing for duties with Heaven."

At which point come the lines of resonance with our text:

天有其時，	Heaven has its seasons,
地有其財，	earth its resources,
人有其治，	and humans their order
夫是之謂能參。	—this is what is meant by "able to form a triad."
舍其所以參，	To forsake the means by which to form the triad
而願其所參，	and yet wish to form it nonetheless
則惑矣。	—this is delusion.[11]

Mankind, most emphatically, should "not try to compete with Heaven for its duties," should not attempt to fill the role of "acting to no purpose." We must, however, form a triad with Heaven and Earth, so as to accord with their natural patterns and bring their works to ultimate fruition in the human sphere. In having this common goal of triadic co-participation, Xun Zi differs little from the philosophies of many of his rivals and predecessors. The key, however, is to know the proper means by which one is to form this triad, and this lies in the mutual coordination of their very separate duties: Heaven has its seasons, the earth has its resources, and mankind has its *order*. That Xun Zi, in his own reformulation of the triumvirate, has a definite object of criticism in mind here could not be clearer: it is those who "wish to form the triad" but "forsake the means by which to do so." Just whose philosophy is he criticizing while, simultaneously, adopting its premises and adapting them to his own purposes?

The discovery of "*San De*" would appear to give us a much clearer answer to that question than previously ascertainable.[12] Aside from the highly significant "substitution" of *zhi* 治, "order," for *li* 力, "labor," "muscle," Xun Zi's formulation of the Heaven-Earth-Man triumvirate is otherwise precisely the same as that found at the head of "*San De*." The context, however, is entirely different, beginning with the one line from the "*San De*" opening that is not virtually replicated here: "The enlightened king forgoes contemplation" (*mingwang wu si* 明王無思). The "enlightened king" itself is a term that does appear in the *Xunzi*, as in the "*Wang Zhi*〈王制〉" chapter, where he is one who models his ritual system after the natural hierarchies of Heaven and Earth: "There is Heaven and there is Earth, and disparities between high and low; when the enlightened king first takes his position, the state is made to have regulations." The "enlightened king" of "*San De*," however, is much different, as he is by definition one who pursues a path of "non-contemplation" (*wu si* 無思), a term which in the *Zhuangzi* is synonymous with a lack of all evaluating deliberation, of accomplishing the Way without acting to any definite purpose whatsoever, as in "*Zhi Beiyou*〈知北遊〉:"

> The Yellow Emperor said: "Only without contemplation or deliberation (*wu si wu lü* 無思無慮) will you comprehend the Way; only without habitat or compliance will you be secure in the Way; only without following or guidance will you attain to the Way."

Or again in "*Tian Di*〈天地〉": "The man of virtue is one who in repose lacks contemplation (*wu si*), and in action lacks deliberation (*wu lü*), harboring no [evaluations of] right or wrong, beauty or ugliness."[13]

For Xun Zi, on the other hand, such thoughtless accomplishment, such acting to no purpose, is the role of Heaven, not of mankind. Although one is thus not to "apply deliberation" to the duties of Heaven, the enlightened king most certainly must apply conscious thought and action to the ways of man, who decidedly does not "accomplish without acting to a purpose" or "attain without seeking."[14] It is presumably for this reason that in lieu of the *li* ("muscle," "strength," "labor") for the "virtue" of mankind that we find in "*San De*," "*Tian Lun*" instead gives *zhi* ("order"): rather than reiterating an emphasis on human agricultural labor, Xun Zi makes the point of establishing "order" as the quintessential human characteristic, the mark of a humanity driven by conscious action and deliberation, clearly distinguished from the "acting to no purpose" of Heaven and Earth. Whereas "everyone knows how" Heaven's works "are brought to completion," but "no one knows their formless" (*wu xing* 無形) origins, the achievements of man are invariably structured by the manifest and self-conscious structure of ritual order.

To be sure, humanity is itself the offspring of Heaven, so that we are inherently endowed with our "heavenly affections" (*tianqing* 天情), our "heavenly officers" (*tianguan* 天官) (sense organs), and our "heavenly ruler" (*tianjun* 天君) (the mind)—the terms themselves ironically suggesting that Heaven might indeed have a conscious design in our creation after all—and our efficient use of the resources of Heaven and Earth provide us with "heavenly nourishment" (*tianyang* 天養)," to be taken in accordance with the dictates of "heavenly governance" (*tianzheng* 天政).[15] So long as we use well what Heaven has given us, our order is secure, but only disaster awaits lest we fail to do so. In a sense, a stanza from strips 3–4 of "*San De*" could still be used to sum up this particular aspect of "*Tian Lun*"'s philosophy: "Revere it, revere it! Heaven's mandate is truly enlightened. Should you turn against it, you are bound to meet with disastrous misfortune." "*Tian Lun*" in fact describes such misfortune wrought by violations against the heavenly in its own series of rhymed lines:

> To benight one's heavenly ruler,
> wreak havoc upon one's heavenly officers,
> forsake one's heavenly nourishment,
> turn against one's heavenly governance,
> and disregard one's heavenly affections,
> so as to suffer the loss of Heaven's achievements
> —this is what we call "great misfortune."[16]

Xun Zi's borrowing here of both form and vocabulary from the quasi-mantic literature of Heavenly ordinances and prohibitions is, however, deeply ironic, and his appending of the adjective "great" to the key term "misfortune" clearly signals his radical reinterpretation of the term against its common meaning.[17] On the one hand, "*Tian Lun*" does show conceptual similarity with certain aspects of the thought of "*San De*": the former's notion that "placing people in offices to maintain the heavenly (*guan ren shou tian* 官人守天), one maintains the way for himself,"[18] for instance, may well closely resonate to the latter's notions of "entrusting offices to people" (*tuo guan yu ren* 托官於人) (strip 7) and "complying with Heaven's seasons" (*shun tian zhi shi* 順天之時) (strip 18). Yet Xun Zi is fundamentally opposed to the central thought of a text like "*San De*" insofar as he denies all possibility of *direct* retribution and vehemently asserts the separation of Heaven and mankind: "Heaven has its constant course (*dao* 道), Earth has its constant configuration (*shu* 數), and the noble man has his constant structure (*ti* 體)," thus "the noble man is reverent toward what lies within his self and does not aspire to what lies in

Heaven."[19] What "lies in the self" is naturally itself Heavenly endowed, and it is this aspect of Heaven that mankind must revere, not those aspects of its mysterious workings that inherently lie beyond our comprehension. Mankind must therefore stick to its own sphere in order to uphold Heaven's way, not emulate that way directly. In other words, mankind must find Heaven in his *own* conscious activity, and it is only by abandoning that and trying to emulate the natural nonpurposiveness of Heaven that we bring forth negative "retribution," so to speak—truly "great misfortune" as opposed to the direct vengeance of an angered Heaven.

Let us now turn back to "*San De*" to better examine the pervasiveness of the latter conception. The second half of strip 1 reads as follows:

卉（草）木須昔(時）而句（後)畚(奮）■ [文部]   Vegetation must await its season before it bursts forth;

天亞（惡）女（如）忻（欣）■ [文部]   Loathing Heaven is just like delighting in it:

榑（平）旦毋哭 ■[屋部]   Do not cry at the crack of dawn;

🍃（暝）毋訶（歌）■ [歌部]   do not sing at dusk

弦望齊佰(宿）[覺部]， At the time of half- and full moons, fast overnight.

是胃（謂）川（順）天之棠(常）■ (1) [陽部]

　　　　　　—this is called "according with Heaven's constancy"[20]

This passage is a particularly difficult one to interpret, but on the whole we might understand it in the sense that we should accept Heaven's way with equanimity and forgo any emotional attachment to outcomes that would have us futilely attempt to forcibly anticipate its seasonal course. Worth noting is Yan Changgui's observation that such proscriptions as to "not cry at the crack of dawn" or "not sing at dusk" would appear to derive from numerological prohibitions seen in other (albeit later) works, wherein the violation of such ordinances leads to a shortening of one's life-span.[21] The "*Feng Cao* 〈風操〉" chapter of the *Yanshi Jiaxun*《顏氏家訓》(sixth century AD), for instance, quotes a certain "Book of the Way" (*dao shu* 道書) as stating: "Both singing at dusk (*hui* 晦) and crying at dawn (*shuo* 朔) (or perhaps: last and first days of a lunar month) merit punishment, and Heaven will deduct one's [life span] counters (*suan* 算)."[22] Given that similar temporal prohibitions against crying and singing are found in earlier excavated calendrical works as well (although still somewhat later than our manuscript), they would appear to have derived from deeply rooted origins.[23] Yan Zhitui 顏之推 (531–591) cites this in his "Feng Cao" chapter as an example of a kind of superstitious folklore to which the uneducated cling, even to the point of precluding their proper observance of mourning for their departed. But whereas Xun Zi would no doubt approve of Yan Zhitui's later reproach to such beliefs as they persisted in his day, the authors of "*San De*" freely incorporate the language of such tenets into their own philosophy, merely citing the phrase in question as an example of "according with Heaven's constancy."

For "*San De*," it is not just what may seem to us as arbitrary calendrical taboos, but decidedly more "rational" or at least common-sense ethical proscriptions also that are couched in terms of violations against the will of "August Heaven" or the "Lord-on-high," and the negative consequences of their violation are not simply a result of "the way things work," but rather take the form of direct retribution from an angry supreme deity. Strip 7, for instance, states:

喜樂無堇（期）乇（度）[鐸部]		If you indulge in limitless pleasures,
是謂大巟（荒）■	[陽部]	this is known as "great dissipation."
皇天弗京（諒）	[陽部]	August Heaven will not abide by it,
必復（報）之以憂喪。■[陽部]		and invariably requite you with worry and loss.
凡食飲無量諂（計）■[質部]		If you take no measure in food and drink,
是謂滔皇	[陽部]	this is known as "ravenous indulgence."
上帝弗京（諒）■	[陽部]	The Lord-on-high will not abide by it,
必|逡（報）之以康（荒）。■[陽部]		and will invariably requite you with famine;
上帝弗京（諒）■	[陽部]	The Lord-on-high will not abide by it,
以祀不享。■（7）	[陽部]	and thus decline to receive your sacrifices.[24]

It is of course always possible that this personified "August Heaven" or "Lord-on-high"—which would seem to be two different names for essentially the same supreme being—might simply be a rhetorical device here, much in the way that Heaven-as-arbiter is occasionally invoked in some of the more exclamatory passages of the *Lunyu* 《論語》. But the insistence with which this language of divine retribution is repeated throughout the text suggests otherwise: that moral reckoning is not merely an inevitable consequence of the inherent order of things, but that our deeds directly beckon the conscious intervention of Heaven above. This is even clearer in the passage of strips 2–3:

訊(忌) 而不訊(忌)	[之部]	If you do not avoid what you [should] avoid,
天乃隆(降)材(災)▬[之部]		Heaven will send down disasters;
已而不已 (2)	[之部]	If you do not stop what you should stop,
天乃隆(降)㲋(異)▬[之部]		Heaven will send down anomalies;
其身不昊(没)	[物部]	They will not come to an end with your own self,
至於孫＝（孫子）	[之部]	but will reach to your descendants.[25]

This, to be sure, is an undeniably direct and grim set of consequences. The contrast with "*Tian Lun*," which expressly warns us against confusing natural occurrences with divine retribution, could not be any starker. For Xun Zi, such agricultural disasters as "unseasonal wind and rain" are nothing more than "the changes of Heaven and Earth, the transformations of *yin* and *yang*, those things that occur but infrequently," and when we partake in rituals to seek divine assistance for disaster relief, "the noble man treats it as cultural, whereas the common man treats it as divine; to treat it as cultural is auspicious, but to treat it as divine is inauspicious."[26] To the extent that it, too, emphasizes the role of proper human action in the avoidance of disaster, "*San De*" differs little from "*Tian Lun*." For the former, however, Heaven remains the direct mechanism for moral retribution, and disasters are as much Heaven-sent as they are the immediate result of human negligence and disorder—the authors of "*San De*" cannot escape Xun Zi's accusation of "treating it as divine," and "true auspiciousness" remains very much beyond their reach.

For Xun Zi, what may truly be feared are "human anomalies" (*ren yao* 人祅): that "governmental commands are not clear, implementations are not timely, agricultural tasks are not managed, and human labor is used out of season"; that "rituals and propriety are not cultivated, there is no distinction between internal and external, and male and female engage in chaotic transgressions;" that "invaders and turmoil arrive all at once," and so on.[27] In point of fact, there is not a single one of these "human anomalies" that "San de" does not also strenuously urge us to avoid, no less insisting that we "accord with Heaven's seasons," and, most emphatically, that if we "frequently rob the people of their seasons, Heaven-sent famine will certainly arrive" (strips 15–16). Not only does this text treat violation of the agricultural calendar as a crucial issue, it also does not remain silent on the issue of ritual prohibitions for male and female, as in this passage from strips 3–4:

齊＝（齊齊）節＝（節節）	[質部]	Orderly and regular,
外內又（有）訤(辨)	[元部]	with inner and outer distinguished,

男女又（有）節	［質部］	and male and female regulated,
是胃（謂）天豊（禮）■	［脂部］	this is called "Heaven's ritual."
敬＝之＝（敬之敬之）	［耕部、之部］	Revere it, revere it!
天命孔明■（3）	［東部、陽部］	Heaven's mandate is truly enlightened;
女（如）反之	［元部、之部］	Should you turn against it,
必禺（遇）凶央（殃）■	［東部、陽部］	You will invariably meet with disastrous misfortune.[28]

The notion here of "Heavenly ritual" (*tian li* 天禮) would certainly appeal to any Confucian thinker, and it is not, after all, far off from what "*Tian Lun*" would refer to as "Heavenly governance" (*tian zheng* 天政).[29] The mechanism of retribution for its violation, however, remains fundamentally different. For Xun Zi, ritual order is the distinguishing characteristic of conscious human action in its fulfillment of the possibilities given to it by Heaven. By the phrase "humans have their order," Xun Zi means specifically that they "daily cultivate the proprieties of ruler and minister, the affections of father and son, and the distinctions of husband and wife, without cease"—for among what "lies with mankind," "nothing is greater than ritual propriety" (*li yi* 禮義), and thus while "the fate of mankind lies in Heaven, the fate of the state lies in ritual."[30] For Xun Zi, these are not simply natural distinctions that can be adhered to without reflection, through the "non-contemplation" of "acting to no purpose," but rather ones which may be upheld only through a gradual process of *conscious* cultivation. This fundamental point of departure from the thought characterized by "*San De*" is most succinctly encapsulated in the final lines of the main section of "*Tian Lun*":

> Rather than marvel at Heaven and ponder it,
> 　better to domesticate its creations and regulate it!
> Rather than follow along with Heaven and extol it,
> 　better to tailor Heaven's mandate and utilize it!
> Rather than look forward to the seasons and await (*dai* 待) them,
> 　better to respond to the seasons and direct them!
> Rather than rely upon things and yield to their multiplicity,
> 　better to exert our capabilities and transform them!
> Rather than ponder things and consider them as things,
> 　better to put things in order and not lose them!
> Rather than aspire to that by which things come into being,
> 　better to possess that by which they achieve completion!
> Thus when we set mankind aside and ponder Heaven,
> 　we lose the true nature (*qing* 情) of the myriad things.[31]

While the term translated "ponder" here (*si* 思) is in fact the same as that "contemplation" that the enlightened king of "*San De*" must be without, "*Tian Lun*," in disparaging it, is in fact stressing the opposite approach: for to "contemplate Heaven" entails, for Xun Zi, precisely the failure to contemplate the ways of mankind. Whereas "*San De*" speaks of "according with the seasons" (*shun shi* 順時) and "awaiting" them (*xu shi* 須時), "*Tian Lun*" talks of "responding" (*ying* 應) to them and "directing" (*shi* 使) them; better than to simply "ponder things" (*si wu* 思物), one must consider the human capability to actively "order" them (*li wu* 理物)—it is only in this way that humankind can effectively form a triumvirate with Heaven and Earth and bring their works to ultimate fulfillment. Once Heaven and Earth have "given birth to" things (*sheng zhi* 生之), mankind must follow by "bringing them to completion" (*cheng zhi* 成之)—such is the point of emphasis by which "*Tian Lun*" differs itself from our excavated text.[32]

None of this is to say that "*Tian Lun*" was formulated in direct response to "*San De*" or even some text that closely resembled it, as it clearly had other rival philosophies in mind as well, not the least of which being the Moists' doctrine of "Heaven's will." What is certain is that the mode of thought exemplified in "*San De*" was of some prevalence by the time Xun Zi came on the scene, as "*Tian Lun*" shows much evidence of both accepting many of its core tenets at the same time that it radically opposes its central take on them. That we must not disrupt the agricultural seasons, that there must be distinction between internal and external relations and divisions between male and female, that governmental posts are to be entrusted to those capable of handling the tasks—all of these are clearly emphasized in "*San De*," and being long-standing Confucian positions as well, Xun Zi would by no means oppose them. Yet insofar as it emphasizes that when humanity reaps what it sows, this has nothing to do with Heavenly retribution, and that the human way is marked not by "non-contemplation" or "acting to no purpose," but rather depends upon conscious cultivation and active management in order to achieve orderly control over society and the economic resources of the natural word—in these aspects "*Tian Lun*" proffers a fundamentally different philosophy indeed. The "triumvirate of virtues" remains the goal, but mankind's role in it cannot be one of merely passive accordance—for man is precisely the one that brings this trinity to fulfillment.

II. "*SAN DE*" AND SEASONAL PROHIBITIONS

If we examine further into "*San De*," we find that the emphasis on the "timeliness" of the agricultural seasons and the need to not deprive the people of their ability to tend to their fields at the appropriate times is indeed the most central focus of the text. This is perhaps most clearly expressed in a passage (strips 15–16) that would later be incorporated wholesale into the *Lüshi Chunqiu*《呂氏春秋》:

聚（驟）攴（奪）民峕（時）■[之部]	When the people are frequently robbed of their seasons,
天餂（飢）必夌（來）。■(15) [之部]	Heavenly famine will certainly arrive.[33]
攴（奪）民峕（時）以土攻（功）:	When the people are robbed of their seasons by construction works,
是胃（謂）頡（稽）■[脂部]	this is known as "stagnation."
不絀（絕）悬（憂）卹（恤）■[質部]	Incessant will be the worry and anxiety,
必龚（喪）其㳄（粃）■[質部]	and invariably lost will be the harvest.[34]

The text goes on to give two further parallel stanzas on the results of robbing the people of their seasons by "water works" (*shui shi* 水事) and "military affairs" (*bing shi* 兵事), with similarly disastrous results.[35] That the *Lüshi chunqiu*, with its seasonal emphasis, would adopt this passage wholesale should not be surprising, particularly since the central message of the passage was one that had long since cut across any doctrinal boundaries. We already alluded above to the early Confucian absorption of this message, and the major Warring States works of that tradition are rife with similar lines, as in the *Mengzi*: "If you do not violate (*wei* 違) the agricultural seasons (*nongshi* 農時), there will be even more grain than can be eaten"; or again in the *Xunzi*: "If you seldom undertake corvée projects and do not rob from the agricultural seasons (*duo nongshi*), then no farmer will fail to exert simple labor and keep [his pursuit of extraneous] talents to a minimum."[36]

The *Mengzi* passage adds two further parallel, conservation-minded admonitions not to fish excessively or cut down trees out of season, admonitions that are also closely reminiscent of lines from "*San De*." There, however—given the text's more thoroughgoing emphasis on acting to no purpose—the advice takes the much stronger form of a series of prohibitions, much like those to be seen in calendrical texts, but minus the specifics of being tied to any particular days. Strip 10, for example, states:

毋雝（壅）川 ■	[文部]	Do not damn up rivers.
毋剅（斷）陸（洿）■	[魚部]	Do not cut off pools of water.
毋威（滅）宗（崇）■	[冬部]	Do not level lofty hills.
毋虛牀 ■	[陽部]	Do not excavate [land-]beds.[37]

Here the call appears to be to not interfere with the natural balance
of the land and waterways by way of excessive construction works or
mining projects. Elsewhere we see appeals to not hinder the natural
growth cycles of living things, as in strip 14:

方縈（櫻）勿伐 ▬	〔月部〕	Do not ax down what is still in flux.
牲（將）壆（興）勿殺 ▬	〔月部〕	Do not kill what has yet to prosper.
牲（將）齊勿桍（刳）▬	〔魚部〕	Do not cut open what is not yet complete.
是奉（逢）凶朷（孽）▬	〔月部〕	—for to do so will incur grave misfortune.[38]

Similar sets of prohibitions are seen throughout a number of chapters
of the *Guanzi*《管子》, where they take the form of seasonal ordinances. These include, among others, "*Jin Cang*〈禁藏〉" and, most
elaborately, "*Qingzhong Ji*〈輕重己〉," where the prohibitions are proclaimed as commands from the Son of Heaven, and incorporate such
seasonal proscriptions as "do not decapitate large hills" (*wu zhan
da shan* 毋斬大山), "do not despoil large marshes" (*wu lu da yan*
毋戮大衍), and "do not obstruct large rivers" (*yu sai da shui*
毋塞大水).[39] The "*Jin Cang*" chapter even concludes its prohibitions
with lines somewhat reminiscent of the "*San De*" opening:

> "If the affairs of the four seasons are in good order, the works of the
> people will be a hundred-fold. Thus humane in the spring, faithful in
> the summer, urgent in the autumn, and stored-up in the winter, we
> accord with the seasons of Heaven (*shun tian zhi shi*), are in agree-
> ment with the proprieties of Earth (*yi* 宜), and are faithful to the
> harmonies (*he* 和) of mankind."[40]

Such texts can all be seen as more or less direct expansions of the line
of thought exemplified in "*San De*," although with their much more
elaborate forms of seasonal and five-phase correspondence theories,
they would appear to exemplify a much more developed stage of that
tradition. The culmination of this tradition can be seen in such works as
the "Twelve Almanacs" ("*Shi'er Ji*〈十二紀〉) of the *Lüshi chunqiu* (or
"Monthly Ordinances" ["*Yue Ling*"〈月令〉] of the *Li Ji*《禮記》), where
the correspondences and prohibitions are laid out in fully systematic
fashion. Even here, though, the central concerns remain the same, as a
summarizing statement from the "Annals of the First Month of Spring"
("*Mengchun Ji*"〈孟春紀〉) reveals: "Do not change the ways (*dao*) of
Heaven; do not reject the patterns (*li* 理) of Earth; do not wreak havoc
upon the order (*ji* 紀) of mankind."[41] The proscriptions in these annals
reveal numerous parallels with those of "*San De*," with much emphasis
again on not disrupting the timing of agricultural labor, and also

show close affinity with them in terms of their use of rhyme and even specific idiosyncratic terminology.[42]

Such texts derive unmistakably from the intellectual tradition of which "*San De*" is a product, but they are also manifestly more systematic in their proscriptions and reveal detailed schemes of correspondences and calendrical specifics that are lacking in this earlier work. In terms of both general philosophy and formal features, the text that bears perhaps the greatest similarities to "*San De*" is the stylistically more archaic "*Xing Shi*〈形勢〉," a relatively early chapter of the *Guanzi* that repeatedly extols the virtues of "complying with the way of Heaven" (*shun tian zhi dao* 順天之道). Compare, for example, its lines:

失天之度，	[鐸部]	Lose the standards of Heaven,
雖滿必涸。	[鐸部]	and even that which is full must run dry.
上下不和，	[歌部]	When those above and below lack harmony,
雖安必危。	[微（或歌）部]	even the most secure must come to peril.[43]

with those of "San De," strip 8:

邦四益	[錫部]	When the state expands in all directions,
是胃（謂）「方芋（華）」	[魚部]	this is called "momentary flowering,"
唯（雖）盈（盈）必虛 ▬	[魚部]	—even once full, it must turn empty.
宮室迱（過）尼（度）▬	[鐸部]	When residences and rooms exceed standards,
皇天之所亞（惡）▬	[鐸部]	this is what August Heaven abhors.
唯（雖）成弗居。▬■	[魚部]	—even when finished, they may not be occupied.[44]

The parallels in form and wording are difficult to miss. And "Xing shi," like "San De," speaks of Heaven in very much the personified terms of direct retribution:

其功順天者天助之，	Those whose achievements accord with Heaven, Heaven assists.
其功逆天者天違之：	Those whose achievements contravene Heaven, Heaven turns against.
天之所助，[魚部]	What Heaven assists,
雖小必大；[月部]	though small, must turn great;
天之所違，[微部]	What heaven turns against,
雖成必敗；[月部]	though established, must break down.

順天者有其功，[東部]   Those who accord with Heaven retain
                            their achievements.
逆天者懷其凶，[東部]   Those who contravene Heaven
                            embrace ill-fortune,
不可復振也。   never to rise up again.[45]

As the commentarial ("*Jie* 解") chapter to "*Xing Shi*" puts it: "The enlightened ruler neither goes against Heaven above nor abandons Earth below, thus Heaven gives him its seasons (*shi*), and Earth produces for him its resources (*cai*)."[46] Here, too, mankind achieves its triumvirate with Heaven and Earth only by following Heaven's will and receiving its bounty in the form of divine assistance.

In summary, "*San De*" is representative of an important early body of philosophical literature in which the language of divine retribution remains very much at the forefront, offering a detailed series of warnings and prohibitions against everything from ethical misdeeds to environmental malfeasance, all couched in terms of an affront against a supreme arbiter on high. Echoes in the received literature suggest that it may well have been a seminal text in this early tradition, precursor to both major intellectual responses and later philosophical developments, ranging from Xun Zi's redefinition of triadic participation with an emphasis on absolute human responsibility devoid of any notion of divine retribution, to the more regularized literature of seasonal ordinances and taboos entailing a much more elaborate system of cosmic correlations. In both these responses and developments, the philosophical tendency was to move away from the conception of a supreme deity as moral arbiter to a more impersonal or mechanistic view of the natural world. The religious character of this tradition, however, would certainly not die out, and centuries later such thought would still find reflection in the detailed ethical precepts and temporal taboos of the early Daoist religious canon, wherein the role of divine judgment and the laws of karmic retribution are still very much at the forefront.[47]

Although "*San De*" is found written on a manuscript that was likely produced near the very end of the fourth century BC, the text itself may date from much earlier, or at least be closely reflective of a style of philosophical literature of more ancient origins than its actual date of composition. In the "*Fei Yue, Shang*〈非樂上〉" chapter of the *Mozi*, Master Mo is given to demonstrate the authority of the practice of denouncing music by recourse to a couple of "writings of the former kings" (*xianwang zhi shu* 先王之書), including the following lines there attributed to the "Officials' Punishments" ("*Guan Xing* 〈官刑〉") of Shang founder King Tang 湯, but which evidence suggests may instead come from the early Zhou document "Great Declaration" (*Tai Shi* 太誓), attributed to its dynastic founder King Wu 武王, who would thus be drawing lessons from the downfall of his Shang predecessors:[48]

嗚乎！		Alas!
舞佯佯，	［陽部］	Dancing in vast multitudes,
黃言孔章，	［陽部］	with reeds and flutes in great display;
上帝弗常，	［陽部］	the Lord-on-high did not sanction this,
九有以亡；	［陽部］	and the nine regions were lost thereby.
上帝不順，		The Lord-on-high was not favorable,
降之百殃，	［陽部］	and rained upon them a hundred misfortunes,
其家必懷喪	［陽部］	so that their household was invariably brought to ruin.[49]

Were it not for their being applied to a specific historical context, the lines of this ancient text could just as well have come straight out of "*San De*," with its manifest parallels in wording, rhyme, and doctrinal inclination (compare again the passage from strip 7 above). Regardless of whether or not the quoted text is an authentic work of the early Zhou, the fact that it is cited in one of the earlier core chapters of the *Mozi* as a "writing of the former kings" is already sufficient to demonstrate that it derives from a relatively early point in time, and thus that "*San De*" is part of a literary and philosophical tradition with long-standing origins indeed. It is one in which Heaven and Earth not only provide the model and the resources for human achievement, but maintain a direct interest in seeing that their design be steadfastly adhered to as well. Or, as "*San De*" itself sums it up:

敬天之攷（戒）	［魚部］	Respect the prohibitions of Heaven,
壆（興）地之歫（矩）■■［魚部］		foster the regularities of Earth,
亙（恆）道必基（著）	［魚部］	and the constant Way is bound to manifest.[50]

GRINNELL COLLEGE
Grinnell, Iowa

ENDNOTES

I first explore some of the philosophical themes that begin to emerge from "San De" in my (Gu Shikao 顧史考), "*Shangbo Wu 'San De' Pian yu Zhuzi Duidu*" 〈上博五〈三德〉篇與諸子對讀〉, *Jianbo*《簡帛》2 (2007): 307–32; that article is in some ways a precursor to the present article. I am grateful for the assistance of the editors of both that journal and the *Journal of Chinese Philosophy* for helping me to improve the quality of these articles.

1. The Shanghai-Museum manuscripts were looted from their tomb and eventually purchased by the Shanghai Museum after their strips began appearing in the Hong

Kong antiquities market in spring 1994. The strips numbered over 1,200 in all, and were sold in two separate batches; additionally, as many as ten individual strips missing from texts in the corpus could be identified with those that had found their way into the collection of the Chinese University of Hong Kong; the additional "*San De*" strip is one such case. It is probable that many strips in the corpus were lost or irretrievably damaged during the process of looting and illicit exchange, and thus most of the Shanghai Museum texts come to us in a state of incompleteness, with few that can be read coherently from beginning to end. Inscriptional evidence links these strips closely with those of the Chu-tomb Manuscripts of Guodian (*Guodian Chumu Zhujian* 《郭店楚墓竹簡》), and scholars speculate that they had been looted from roughly the same area and date from a comparable time. For details on all this, see Ma Chengyuan, ed., *Shanghai Bowuguan Cang Zhanguo Chu Zhushu, Vol. 1* (Shanghai: Shanghai Guji Publisher, 2001), Ma's "Introduction," 1–4, and Chen Xiejun's "Preface," 1–4. For the "San De" manuscript text and Li Ling's transcription, see volume 5 of that publication (2005), 125–48 and 285–303. Note that a number of the strips referred to here as "complete" were actually pieced back together from broken segments.

2. Four-character lines predominate, but there are also stanzas of three-character lines, as well as those with lines of uneven length—not to mention stanzas with different numbers of lines and of a number of varying rhyme schemes. The rhyming itself is often less than exact—the rhymes frequently occurring between different, proximally close rhyme groups—but it is nonetheless unmistakable. I indicate the rhyme groups of the rhyming characters by their customary Chinese nomenclature in brackets at the ends of lines within the transcription itself; in the interest of space, I do not discuss the rhyme schemes any further in this article. Note that most of the rhymed phrases in the "San De" manuscript are identified or punctuated by horizontal markers placed underneath the final graph of each phrase; these are identified in my transcription by the symbol "▬."

3. See my (Gu Shikao) "*Shangbo Zhushu 'San De' Pian Zhuzhang Qianshi*" 〈上博竹書〈三德〉篇逐章淺釋〉, in *Qu Wanli Xiansheng Baisui Danchen Guoji Xueshu Yantaohui Lunwenji* 《屈萬里先生百歲誕辰國際學術研討會論文集》, ed. Guojia Tushuguan et al. (Taipei: Guojia Tushuguan et al., 2006), 269–309. This article also contains the full, running text of my version of the transcription, in which I adopt the following tentative ordering of strips (contiguous blocks separated by semicolons): 1; 2–5; 22, 6, 17, 15–16; 7; 8; 9; 10–12a; the Chinese University of Hong Kong strip fragment; 12b, 20; 13–14, 19; 21, 18. This strip reordering largely follows the suggestions of Chen Jian, taking into account also proposals by Li Rui and Cao Feng. For full references to "San De" scholarship invoked throughout these endnotes—mostly internet contributions—please refer to the articles cited in the aforementioned article.

4. As a translation of *de* 德, "virtue" is not to be understood as an exact equivalent to what that term has come to mean in the Western cultural tradition, but, in referring to a notion that involves at once the senses of charismatic power, good will, and accumulated merit, it remains preferable to the much more limiting rendering of "power."

5. Guojia Wenwuju Guwenxian Yanjiushi, ed., *Mawangdui Hanmu Boshu* (*Yi*) 《馬王堆漢墓帛書（壹）》 (Beijing: Wenwu Publisher, 1980), 43–88. The four texts, the first two of which are further broken down into titled sections, are respectively entitled "*Jing Fa* 〈經法〉," "*Shi Da Jing* 〈十大經〉" (alternatively read "*Shiliu Jing* 〈十六經〉"), "*Cheng* 〈稱〉," and "*Dao Yuan* 〈道原〉." The idea that these texts are indeed a version of the *Huangdi Sijing* texts preserved in early bibliographic records was first offered by Tang Lan, but as Qiu Xigui has pointed out, there are many doubtful aspects to this identification. See Qiu Xigui, "*Mawangdui Boshu Laozi Yiben Juanqian Guyishu Bing Fei Huangdi Sijing* 馬王堆帛書《老子》乙本卷前古佚書並非《黃帝四經》," in *Daojia Wenhua Yanjiu* 《道家文化研究》, v. 3: *Mawangdui Boshu Zhuanhao* 《馬王堆帛書專號》 ed. Chen Guying (Shanghai: Shanghai Guji Publisher, 1993), 249–55. The "Four Lost Texts of Mawangdui" follows from the title adopted by Qiu for these texts. Robin D. S. Yates has translated these four along with a fifth text, "*Jiu Zhu* 九主," from among the texts appended to the *Laozi A* 《老子甲本》 scroll, and refers to them collectively as the "Five Lost Classics" of Mawangdui; see his *Five Lost Classics:*

Tao, Huang-Lao, and Yin-Yang in Han China (New York: Ballantine Books, 1997). The close relationship between "*San De*" and the "Four Lost Texts" has already been explored in detail by Cao Feng, "'*San De*' yu *Huangdi Sijing Duibi Yanjiu*《三德》與《黃帝四經》對比研究," in his *Shangbo Chujian Sixiang Yanjiu*《上博楚簡思想研究》(Taipei: Wanjuanlou Publisher, 2006), 241–66.

6. Guojia Wenwuju Guwenxian Yanjiushi, *Mawangdui Hanmu Boshu* (*Yi*), 49 & 76. Cf. Yates, *Five Lost Classics*, 69 & 143.

7. Cao Feng, "'*San De*' yu *Huangdi Sijing Duibi Yanjiu*," 245–46.

8. Li Xiangfeng 黎翔鳳, *Guanzi Jiaozhu*《管子校注》(1964), ed. Liang Yunhua (Beijing: Zhonghua Shuju Publisher, 2004), 1300. Cf. W. Allyn Rickett, *Guanzi: Political, Economic, and Philosophical Essays from Early China, v. II* (Princeton: Princeton University Press, 1998), 396. Rickett translates "*yi* 以 ... *wei quan* 為權" as "displays its changes ... in terms of"; I opt here for a more literal rendering of *quan* as "balance," that is, the "weighing-scale" upon which the relative merits of different choices are assessed.

9. Wang Xianqian 王先謙, *Xunzi Jijie*《荀子集解》, ed. Shen Xiaohuan and Wang Xingxian (Beijing: Zhonghua Shuju Publisher, 1988), 306–8. Cf. John Knoblock, *Xunzi: A Translation and Study of the Complete Works, Volume III (Books 17–32)* (Stanford: Stanford University Press, 1994), 14–15; Robert Eno, *The Confucian Creation of Heaven: Philosophy and the Defense of Ritual Mastery* (Albany: State University of New York Press, 1990), 198; and Edward J. Machle, *Nature and Heaven in the Xunzi: A Study of the* Tian Lun (Albany: State University of New York Press, 1993), 77–78, 86. Note that the phrase "*qi dao ran* 其道然" ("that is just the way things work") could also be understood—as it is more commonly interpreted here—in the sense of "this is a result of the way one [chooses to] follow."

10. In this we should note that "*Tian Lun*" shares language with the almost certainly earlier "*Qiongda Yi Shi*〈窮達以時〉" manuscript of Guodian, which opens with the words: "There is [that which is controlled by] Heaven, and there is [that which is within the power of] mankind, and each has its separate lot. Once one has examined the division between Heaven and mankind (*cha tian ren zhi fen* 察天人之分), one will know how to act." "*Tian Lun*" undoubtedly owes something to the ideas represented in this manuscript, but it is much more complex than the latter, which is more exclusively concerned with the matter of individual moral constancy in the face of all that is fated or beyond our control. Insofar, however, as they both express the idea that Heaven's course is unpredictable, but how we prepare for this unpredictability is entirely within our power, the two texts share a core idea in common. For the text of "*Qiongda Yi Shi*," see Jingmen Shi Bowuguan, ed., *Guodian Chumu Zhujian*《郭店楚墓竹簡》(Beijing: Wenwu Publisher, 1998), 25–28 & 143–46.

11. Wang Xianqian, *Xunzi Jijie*, 308. Cf. Knoblock, *Xunzi, v. III*, 15; Eno, *Confucian Creation*, 198; Machle, *Nature and Heaven*, 86. There is some ambiguity as to whether the attributes of *shen* 深 ("profound"), *da* 大 ("great"), and *jing* 精 ("refined") refer to the objects to which one might apply *lü* 慮 ("deliberation"), *neng* 能 ("capabilities"), and *cha* 察 ("investigation"), or to these acts of "deliberation," and so on themselves; given that *shen*, at least, is a fairly common attribute of *lü* in Warring States texts, I tentatively understand it in the latter sense.

12. Note that throughout the remainder of this article I will be assuming that the composition of "*San De*" indeed preceded that of "*Tian Lun*." If the Shanghai-Museum manuscripts, like those of the closely related Guodian manuscripts, were interred by around 300 BC, or by the sacking of Chu's capital in 278 BC at the latest, then it is difficult to imagine that the composition of "*San De*" could have been much later than 300 BC. While Xun Zi's precise dates are uncertain, his more commonly accepted birth year of roughly 315 BC entails that Xun Zi would at best have been a young man when "*San De*" was written, if he was even alive by then.

13. Guo Qingfan 郭慶藩, *Zhuangzi Jishi*《莊子集釋》, ed. Wang Xiaoyu (Beijing: Zhonghua Shuju Publisher, 1961), 731 & 441. Cao Feng makes similar note of the close relationship between "non-contemplation" and "non-action" in pre-Qin thought; see his "'*San De*' Shidu Shibaze"〈三德〉釋讀十八則, in his *Shangbo Chujian Sixiang Yanjiu* (see note 5), 193–95.

14. This is the case throughout most of the *Xunzi* anyway, but there are exceptions. Most notably, "*Jie Bi*〈解蔽〉" offers an image of ultimate sagacity that is described very much in *wuwei* terms: "The person of humanity, in practicing the Way, acts to no purpose; the sage, in practicing the Way, acts without forcing. The contemplation (*si*) of the person of humanity is unassuming; the contemplation of the sage is happy (/self-content)—such is the way of ordering the mind." Wang Xianqian, *Xunzi Jijie*, 403–4; cf. Knoblock, *Xunzi*, 108.

15. Wang Xianqian, *Xunzi Jijie*, 309–10. Cf. Knoblock, *Xunzi, v. III*, 16; Eno, *Confucian Creation*, 199; Machle, *Nature and Heaven*, 95–96. That the *tian* of "Tian Lun" simultaneously involves the seemingly contradictory notions of *tian* as the impersonal workings of nature and *tian* as the ultimate source and model of human ritual order has long been discussed and debated. Robert Eno stresses that the two notions—nonnormative Nature and normative natural force—while in one sense "fundamentally contradictory," remain consistent insofar as "both are designed to counter the devaluation of non-natural *li* (ritual) by contemporary naturalisms," the first notion denying "the possibility of finding value in the natural sphere," and the second positing "an essential continuity between normative nature and normative ritual behavior;" see his *Confucian Creation*, 165. Machle, on the other hand, attempts to deny any contradiction by understanding *tian* throughout the chapter as a kind of deity that is neither anthropomorphic nor "nonpersonal," but rather a morally resolute divinity that steadfastly plays its role at the apex of the cosmic hierarchy and normally "finds no occasion" to directly involve itself in human affairs; see his *Nature and Heaven*, esp. 165–78. While Machle's interpretation is not without explanatory value, it relies somewhat on a creative reinterpretation of key passages, one bent, it would seem, on demonstrating his central thesis that *tian* for Xun Zi meant nothing like our conception of "Nature." My own view is more in line with Eno's more historically minded analysis, although I seek here to broaden the conception somewhat of just which doctrines "*Tian Lun*" might have been taking on.

16. Wang Xianqian, *Xunzi Jijie*, 310. Cf. Knoblock, *Xunzi, v. III*, 16; Eno, *Confucian Creation*, 199; Machle, *Nature and Heaven*, 96.

17. Compare the *Xunzi*'s uses of such terms as *da yang* 大殃, *da zai* 大災, *da ji* 大吉, and *da shen* 大神; see Wang Xianqian, *Xunzi Jijie*, 65; 98; 143; 226; 278; & 162, respectively.

18. Wang Xianqian, *Xunzi Jijie*, 311. Cf. Knoblock, *Xunzi, v. III*, 17; Eno, *Confucian Creation*, 199; Machle, *Nature and Heaven*, 96.

19. Wang Xianqian, *Xunzi Jijie*, 311–12. Cf. Knoblock, *Xunzi, v. III*, 17–18; Eno, *Confucian Creation*, 200; Machle, *Nature and Heaven*, 108–9.

20. The second line here is particularly difficult to interpret; I tentatively treat *tian* 天 as a preposed topic. Alternatively, Fan Changxi sees 女 (=*ru* 如) as an error for *mu* 母, read *wu* 毋, thus "What Heaven detests, do not delight in." For「🈴」, Li Ling reads *ming* 明, in the sense of "daybreak"; *ming* 暝, "dusk," follows the interpretation of Fan Changxi. Another plausible interpretation of the graph is 晦, also "dusk" in this context, first suggested by Yan Changgui. All other readings here follow Li Ling.

21. Yan Changgui, "'*San De' Si Zha*《三德》四劄," http://www.bsm.org.cn/show_article.php?id=272.

22. Wang Liqi 王利器, *Yanshi Jiaxun Jijie (Zengbuben)*《顏氏家訓集解（增補本）》 (Beijing: Zhonghua Shuju Publisher, 1993), 96–97.

23. Specifically, as Yan Changgui notes, we have the following lines from the "Calendar Book A" 日書甲種 of the Qin Dynasty bamboo strips of Shuihudi 睡虎地秦簡 (back of strip 155): "On the final day of the month (*huiri* 墨（晦）日), it is advantageous to knock down walls, vacate rooms, or send forth deliveries; one must not sing. On the first day of the month (*shuori* 朔日), it is advantageous to begin occupancy of a room; one must not cry. On the day of the full moon (*wang* 望), it is advantageous to construct granaries." *Shuihudi Qinmu Zhujian*《睡虎地秦墓竹簡》, ed. Shuihudi Qinmu Zhujian Zhengli Xiaozu (Beijing: Wenwu Publisher, 1990), 115, 227.

24. The reading of *jin* 堇 as *qi* 期 follows the suggestion of Meng Pengsheng. As Cao Feng points out, the term *da huang* 大荒 also appears (in a somewhat different context) in a rhymed passage in the "*Liu Fen*" section of "*Jing Fa*" in the "Four Lost Texts:" "When the ruler is vicious and the ministers in turmoil, this is termed 'great dissipa-

tion'; arms employed both abroad and at home, Heaven will send down misfortune; such a state, no matter large or small, will meet with extermination; see Guojia Wenwuju Guwenxian Yanjiushi, *Mawangdui Hanmu Boshu* (*Yi*), 49; cf. Yates, *Five Lost Classics*, 69. The term also appears in the "Qiang Guo 〈彊國〉" chapter of the *Xunzi*: "Those who treasure each day become Kings; those who treasure each season become hegemons; those who [wait to] repair failings [after they occur] are in peril; those who indulge in great dissipation will perish;" Wang Xianqian, *Xunzi Jijie*, 304. The reading of *jing* 京 as *liang* 諒 follows Li Ling; here translated as "abide by," it might also be understood in the sense of "place trust in."

25. The readings here all follow those of Li Ling; *ji* 忌 may be understood in the sense of "treat as taboo." For the penultimate line, I had initially proposed a reading with *qi shen* 其身 as subject; I thank Terry Kleeman for pointing out to me what is certainly the preferable reading here.

26. Wang Xianqian, *Xunzi Jijie*, 313–14 & 316. Cf. Knoblock, *Xunzi, v. III*, 18; Eno, *Confucian Creation*, 201–2; Machle, *Nature and Heaven*, 111 & 119–20.

27. Wang Xianqian, *Xunzi Jijie*, 314. Cf. Knoblock, *Xunzi, v. III*, 18–19; Eno, *Confucian Creation*, 201; Machle, *Nature and Heaven*, 115–17.

28. Chen Jian would actually have strip 4 (beginning with *ru fan zhi* 如反之) follow strip 1 instead, but to my mind the double-rhyme of *kong ming* 孔明 with *xiong yang* 凶殃 and the overall natural flow of this stanza (despite the anomaly of a three-character third line) suggest that the original order of 3–4 is more likely the correct one.

29. While it might also be possible to interpret *tianli* 天豊 instead as *tianti* 天體, "Heaven's structure," it would amount to the same idea: a natural basis for such human ritual distinctions as internal (blood-line) versus external relations and appropriate separation between male and female. Given that such a notion is upheld in a text the likes of which Xun Zi may well have had in mind for criticism, it might be necessary to revise somewhat Eno's thesis—if still generally valid—that "*Tian Lun*" was framed primarily as a Confucian defense of ritual practices.

30. Wang Xianqian, *Xunzi Jijie*, 316–17; cf. Knoblock, *Xunzi, v. III*, 19–20; Eno, *Confucian Creation*, 202; Machle, *Nature and Heaven*, 116–17 & 120. The final phrase also appears in the "*Qiang Guo*" chapter; see *Xunzi Jijie*, 291.

31. Wang Xianqian, *Xunzi Jijie*, 317. Cf. Knoblock, *Xunzi, v. III*, 20–21; Eno, *Confucian Creation*, 202–3; Machle, *Nature and Heaven*, 125–26. Note that these lines are also rhymed, one rhyme per each pair.

32. The sense in which, for the *Xunzi*, human action is required to bring nature's works to completion has already been well discussed by Eno: "the forms of ritual and social order are the teleological culmination of the natural cosmos, and their transforming function establishes them as extensions of Nature and as ethical standards—that is, ritual order is the 'final cause' of the processes manifest in biological Nature, human action being the immediate agent of that culminating order." See his *Confucian Creation*, 138–39.

33. In the "*Shang Nong* 〈上農〉" chapter of the *Lüshi Chunqiu*, these two lines are placed in summation after the following three stanzas rather than before them, and are written 數奪民時，大飢乃來. As Fan Changxi—the first scholar to observe the parallels with "*Shang Nong*"—notes, *shu* 數 and *zou* 騶 (Li Ling's reading of *ju* 聚) are close in sound as well as meaning, and either *tian* 天 or *da* 大 could have resulted from graphic confusion. In place of these two lines, at the head of the passage, "*Shang Nong*" offers 時事不共，是謂大凶 ("If seasonal affairs are not attended to, this is called 'great misfortune'"). For the text of "*Shang Nong*" itself (from the "*Shirong Lun*" 〈士容論〉 section), see Chen Qiyou 陳奇猷, ed., *Lüshi Chunqiu Xinjiaoshi* 《呂氏春秋新校釋》 (Shanghai: Shanghai Guji Publisher, 2002), 1720.

34. For *youxu* 憂恤, "*Shang Nong*" has *youwei* 憂唯, which could be understood as "worrisome thoughts," but the "*San De*" reading seems superior in terms of both meaning and rhyme. For 怭, Li Ling reads *pi* 匹, but it is hard to make sense of that reading in this context; my interpretation instead follows the *bi* 粃 (秕) of the "*Shang Nong*" version, literally "empty grain (/rice) husks," that is, inferior grain, but here understood in the sense of crops more generally.

35. Only the first few graphs of the latter stanza remain—the strip that followed 16 presumably now missing—but the rest may be inferred from the "*Shang Nong*" parallels.

36. From *Mengzi* 1.3 (1A.3) and the "*Wang Ba*〈王霸〉" chapter of the *Xunzi*, respectively. See Jiao Xun 焦循, *Mengzi Zhengyi*《孟子正義》, ed. Shen Wenzhuo (Beijing: Zhonghua Shuju Publisher, 1987), 54–55; and Wang Xianqian, *Xunzi Jijie*, 229.

37. The readings of the first two lines follow those of Li Ling. Note that my readings for the last two are highly speculative and follow on the assumption that they, like the first two, address the issue of environmental manipulation. *Chong* 崇 for *zong* 宗 follows the reading of Liu Guosheng, although he does not take it in as literal as sense as I do here; *chuang* 牀 in the sense of "land-bed" is unattested in early Chinese, but its juxtaposition with *chong* here yields a quite natural opposition of lofty mounds and an underlying layer of terrestrial support. Alternatively, we may just read *zong* and *chuang* at face value and interpret the line in the unrelated sense of: "Don't wipe out your ancestral line, don't leave the bed empty!"

38. I tentatively read *ying* 縈 here as *ying* 攖 in the sense of "turmoil," "flux"; the reading of 㓪 as *nie* 孽 follows that of Ji Xusheng.

39. See Li Xiangfeng, *Guanzi Jiaozhu* (see note 8), 1533 & 1539; or Ma Feibai 馬非百, *Guanzi Qingzhong pian Xinquan*《管子輕重篇新詮》(Beijing: Zhonghua Shuju Publisher, 1979), 731, 733, 742–43, & 1017. Note that a number of scholars, beginning with Wang Guowei 王國維, consider the "*Qingzhong*" chapters to be works of the early Han. For similar parallels in the "*Jin Cang*" and "*Qi Chen Qi Zhu*〈七臣七主〉" chapters, see *Guanzi Jiaozhu*, 1017–18 & 995; further parallels may be found in the "*Kuang Shengma*"〈巨（匡）乘馬〉 and "*Xiao Kuang*〈小匡〉" chapters. Close parallels also occur in the "proscriptions of the Son of Heaven" ("*tianzi zhi jin* 天子之禁") quoted in an alliance oath sworn under the proclamation of Lord Huan of Qi 齊桓公 as recorded in the *Guliang Zhuan*《穀梁傳》; see Zhong Wenzheng 鍾文烝, *Chunqiu Guliang Jingzhuan Buzhu*《春秋穀梁經傳補注》, ed. Pian Yuqian and Hao Shuhui (Beijing: Zhonghua Shuju Publisher, 1996), 282–84.

40. Li Xiangfeng, *Guanzi Jiaozhu*, 1018. A similar parallel may be found in the "*Jun Zheng*"〈君正〉 section of "*Jing Fa*" in the *Four Lost Texts*; see Guojia Wenwuju Guwenxian Yanjiushi, *Mawangdui Hanmu Boshu* (*Yi*), 47. For further such parallels with the *Four Lost Texts*, see Cao Feng, "'*San De*' yu Huangdi Sijing Duibi Yanjiu" (see note 5).

41. Chen Qiyou, *Lüshi Chunqiu Xinjiaoshi*, 2. In the *Li Ji* version, 無 is written 毋.

42. These include the rare usage of *huangtian* 皇天 and *shangdi* 上帝 together, a feature peculiar to "*San De*" and otherwise limited to a few examples from the *Shang Shu*《尚書》. A particularly concise "summary" of the correspondences between the seasonal movements, prohibitions, and pitch standards may also be found in the "*Yin Lü*" 音律 chapter of the *Lüshi Chunqiu* ("*Jixia Ji*"〈季夏紀〉). Space here does not allow me to cite more fully the frequent and numerous parallels that occur between "*San De*" and the aforementioned *Guanzi* and *Lüshi Chunqiu* chapters; for details on all of these, see my "*Shangbo Wu 'San De' Pian Yu Zhuzi Duidu*," 314–23.

43. Li Xiangfeng, *Guanzi Jiaozhu*, 42.

44. He Youzu takes *yu* 芌 as a corruption of *hua* 華, although they can in fact be viewed as cognate graphs.

45. Li Xiangfeng, *Guanzi Jiaozhu*, 44.

46. Ibid., 1186.

47. For an overview of such precepts and taboos as seen in various Daoist texts from the fifth to seventh centuries AD, see Livia Kohn, "Living the Daoist Body," in *UBC Conference on Daoist Studies 2008: Academic Papers* (conference volume), 117–40, esp. 125–30. In these works, the subject of karmic concern is largely limited to the health and longevity of the individual.

48. In "*Fei Yue, Shang*," the quote is preceded by the words *nai yan yue* 乃言曰, "and subsequently said," making it appear to be the second of two quotes from the text attributed to King Tang. As Sun Yirang 孫詒讓 notes, however, a closely similar set of lines—likely a different stanza of the same text—is attributed in the "*Fei Ming, Xia*" 非命下 chapter to a section of the Zhou document "*Tai Shi*〈太誓〉"; Sun thus suspects

"*nai yan*" should read "*tai shi*" instead. See Sun Yirang, *Mozi Jiangu*《墨子閒詁》, ed. Sun Qizhi (Beijing: Zhonghua Shuju Publisher, 2001), 260–61 & 281–82. Note that the forger of the ostensibly Shang-period "*Yi Xun* 〈伊訓〉" and "*Xian You Yi De* 〈咸有一德〉" chapters of the inauthentic portions of the *Shang Shu* apparently took these lines as a continuation of the King Tang text, incorporating portions of them into those chapters on that basis.

49. Sun Yirang, *Mozi Jiangu*, 260–61. Following Guo Moruo 郭沫若, I read *huangyan* 黃言 as 簧言, in the sense of reeds and flutes. For *chang* 常, here translated "sanction," Wang Yinzhi 王引之 reads *shang* 尚, "uphold," "value"; following Sun Yirang, I read *jiu you* 九有 as equivalent to *jiu zhou* 九域. The graph for *yang* 殃 is actually written 歹+羊 in the text; one edition has *ri yang* 日殃 in place of *bai yang* 百(歹+)羊.

50. Strip 17. The graph 基 is unknown outside of this text, and my reading of it as *zhu* 著 is speculative and based largely on rhyme and context; for details, see my "*Shangbo Zhushu 'San De' Pian Zhuzhang Qianshi*," 283. The readings of *yu* 圓 and *ju* 矩 follow those of Chen Jian.

LISA RAPHALS

DIVINATION AND AUTONOMY: NEW PERSPECTIVES FROM EXCAVATED TEXTS

History is written by the victors. Much of the philosophical discussion of excavated texts has centered on the Guodian and Shanghai Museum texts, which augment or comment on the texts of the received tradition. This perspective omits the counterparts and competitors of the Warring States philosophers: the technical experts. The technical expertise traditions (medicine, the mantic arts, and astrocalendrics) were the counterparts and competitors of the philosophers, and far outnumber them in the perhaps narrow context of tomb texts.

Both the received tradition and excavated texts attest to contact and competition between mantic experts and the "schoolmen" associated with Masters texts. Both livelihoods relied on literacy and specialist expertise. Both claimed access to divine knowledge and authority. Their competition thus involved career choice, patronage, students, and the status of modes of knowledge.

In addition, it is now widely agreed that the bases of cosmological speculation first appeared in the ideas and methods of Warring States technical specialists, whose terms and techniques were later incorporated into the *yin-yang* 陰陽 and Five-phase theories of Han cosmology. This view was first argued by Angus Graham some twenty years ago, and third-century excavated texts on these technical arts have reinforced it by supplementing the sparser record in the received tradition.[1] In particular, technical experts were responsible for several developments that contributed to systematic thought and cosmology. These include (i) interest in symmetry, already visible in the oracle bone inscriptions; (ii) the articulation of a *yin-yang* polarity, abstracted as patterns of change, represented by numbers. These patterns were elaborated and nuanced in the hexagrams of the *Zhouyi* 《周易》; (iii) interest in astronomy and calendrics as systematic models of space and time; and (iv) systematic theories of physiognomy. All were based on observation of natural phenomena.

LISA RAPHALS, Professor, Department of Philosophy, National University of Singapore. Specialties: Chinese, comparative philosophy, history of science. E-mail: philar@nus.edu.sg

Journal of Chinese Philosophy, Supplement to Volume 37 (2010) 124–141
© *2010 Journal of Chinese Philosophy*

We see these interests reflected in the Numbers and Techniques (*shushu* 數術) category of the *Hanshu*《漢書》"*Yiwenzhi*〈藝文志〉," which is dominated by astronomy (*tianwen* 天文) and calendrics (*lipu* 歷譜), but also includes sections on prognostication by the Five Agents (*wuxing* 五行, including portents and omens), turtle and yarrow (*shigui* 蓍龜), diverse prognostications (*zazhan* 雜占, including oneiromancy, augury, and exorcism), and Morphomancy (*xingfa* 刑法, including physiognomy).[2] Historical narratives also provide many examples of the use of these methods in official and private contexts. Finally, when we turn to the tombs of actual government administrators and high officials, what they chose to have buried with them was technical works on the mantic arts and longevity.

Mantic texts offer important philosophical perspectives that receive little voice in the received tradition. I consider them under three headings: (i) their implications for questions of autonomy, fatalism, and freewill; (ii) naturalistic attitudes toward the cosmos, especially in astrocalendric texts; and (iii) notions of embodied virtue and self-cultivation, especially in texts on physiognomy.

I. AUTONOMY, FATALISM, AND FREEWILL

Mantic texts suggest a different discourse on fatalism and freewill than the arguments about *ming* and mantic practice within the received tradition.

1. Masters Texts

In the *Lunyu*《論語》, 6.22, Confucius famously recommends a respectful distance from "ghosts and spirits." A similar attitude appears in a text from Mawangdui 馬王堆 (Changsha, Hunan, 168), titled *Yao*《要》(Essentials) by modern editors. Here Confucius claims that cultivating virtue is superior to the mantic expertise of incantators and *wu* (*zhu wu bu shi* 祝巫卜筮). Yet in the same text, when asked whether he believes in prognostication by yarrow stalks, he replies that he has performed one hundred *Yi* divinations and seventy were correct.[3] The *Lunyu* never refers to Confucius personally prognosticating with the *Zhouyi*, but other texts in the received tradition do, for example, the *Lüshi Chunqiu*:

> Kongzi prognosticated and obtained Bi 賁; he said: "Inauspicious."
> Zigong said: "But Bi is also good, why do you call it inauspicious?"
> Confucius replied: "White should be white and black should be black; how can Bi be good?"[4]

Several Masters texts include a variety of claims for the superiority of Masters over mantic traditions. Several compare their eponymous Masters favorably with mantic specialists of various kinds. Both the *Mozi* and the *Lüshi chunqiu* include debates in which a Master gets the better of a *wu* 巫 (or someone with the name Wuma 巫馬, lit. *wu* horse).[5] The *Lüshi chunqiu* recounts a conversations between Confucius and two disciples, the political reformer Fu Zijian 宓子賤 and Wuma Qi 巫馬旗, both governors of Shanfu 單父 in *Lu*. When Fu tries to explain his philosophy of government, Wuma Qi cannot grasp it:

> I depend on people but you depend on force. Depending on force makes you labor; depending on people makes you relaxed.[6]

The passage continues that Fu Zijian was a *junzi*. Relaxed and perceptive, he cultivated his heart-mind and his *qi*, and as a result, governed without effort. Wuma Qi by contrast wore himself out, used up his energies and labored with his limbs. He maintained order in government, but was never equal to Fu Zijian. These passages emphasize the *wu's* incomprehension and inferior methods relative to those of the *junzi*.

In the *Zhuangzi* and *Guanzi* we find a stronger attack on mantic specialists: claims that the mantic arts are inferior to understanding of *dao*. In *Zhuangzi* 23, when someone asks Laozi about "the classic of life," he replies:

> Can you embrace the One? Can you not lose it?
>
> Can you understand good and ill auspice without turtle shell or yarrow?
>
> Can you stop? Can you let it go?[7]

The *Guanzi* describes this understanding in the chapter "Inward Training (*Nei Ye* 〈內業〉)." It tells us how: by concentrating *qi*:

> Concentrate your qi like a spirit, and the myriad things will be inside your hand.
>
> Can you concentrate; can you unify? Can you predict good and ill auspice without turtle shell or yarrow? Can you stop? Can you let it go? Can you not seek it in others but achieve it in yourself?[8]

The *Guanzi* chapter "Clarifying the Heartmind (*Bai Xin* 〈白心〉)" uses similar language to describe the conduct of a sage, who also eschews the mantic arts of astrology:

> He does not use sun and moon, but his affairs are accomplished by them.
>
> He does not prognosticate by turtle shell or yarrow, but skillfully predicts good and ill auspice.[9]

All these statements contrast the equanimity of the sage with the frenetic manipulations of the mantic specialist. Nonetheless, some Masters texts do recommend the mantic arts for practical purposes: the Moists for defensive strategy; the *Guanzi* to determine portents and to protect rulers.[10]

Despite these critiques, most Masters texts considered the mantic arts normal and acceptable, even if they sometimes chose to distance themselves its practitioners or directed claims to universal knowledge against the "limitations" of technical specialists. Masters texts also argued about *ming* 命 (fate or destiny), but these debates were distinct from critiques of divination. Masters texts debated the nature of *ming*, whether it was predetermined, predictable, moral, or mechanical in operation, and whether it was subject to human or divine intervention. For example, both Xunzi and Han Fei argue that prayer and divination do not cause good or bad fortune, but neither pursues the issues of determinism or causality beyond asserting their absence.[11]

2. *Fate and Freewill in Mantic Texts*

In contrast to the accounts of Masters texts, mantic texts provide concrete methods for the practical management of fate and imply a very different set of attitudes toward fatalism and freewill than the debates of the received tradition. Here we find the mantic arts reflecting tacit notions of personal and moral autonomy and individual agency. Excavated texts address issues of *individual* autonomy that fall below the radar of dominant Ru discussions of political agency and political autonomy. Some present methods to understand and control the future (personal and political) through prognostication. These traditions appear in several distinctly different kinds of text: (i) Mantic texts, including the *Zhouyi* and its predecessors (of which four versions have been excavated from tombs) and almanacs and other astrocalendric texts, especially Daybooks. (ii) Quasi-archival records of personal prognostication. We do not know the original sources of these records or why they were placed in tombs. They clearly were not intended for ongoing consultation by the living. Nonetheless we may be tempted to consider them archives insofar as they were deliberately assembled collections of mantic queries. (iii) Procedures and methods. Ritual texts such as the *Liji* and *Yili* give detailed accounts of mantic procedures and methods, but they have no equivalent in excavated texts. For example, prognostication records from Baoshan 包山 (Jingmen 荊門, Hubei, *c*. 316) give detailed directions for apotropaic sacrifices on behalf of the tomb's occupant. Legal texts from Zhangjiashan 張家山 (Jiangling, Hubei, 186) include instructions for the appointment of mantic personnel.[12] (iv) In addition, technical astrocalendric texts and instruments excavated from Qin and Han tombs are of increasing sophistication.

Of these four, records of personal prognostication are particularly interesting for purposes of the present discussion, insofar as they indicate attitudes toward the malleability of fate. Third-century records from Warring States tombs from Tianxingguan 天星觀 (Jiangling 江陵, Hubei, *c.* 340), Baoshan and Wangshan 望山 (Hubei, *c.* 309–278) contain records of prognostications performed on behalf of the tombs; occupants. The oldest are from Tianxingguan, the most extensive and well preserved from Baoshan.[13] They have no equivalent in the received textual tradition.

These records document attempt to predict success over a given period of time in what Chen Wei has described as Year (*sui* 歲) and Illness (*jibing* 疾病) divinations.[14] Year divinations sought to verify success over the ensuing year, for example in the Baoshan records:

> 自刑尸之月以庚刑尸之月，出入事王，盡卒歲，躬身尚母又(有)咎。
>
> From [this year's month] Xingyi to up to the next Xingyi, coming and going [lit. exiting and entering] in service to the king, for the entire year, may his [physical] person be without calamity.[15]

Year divination seems to have been a standard sequence, performed to ascertain (or establish) success in official service to the king. Illness divinations at Baoshan and other Warring States sites punctuate what seems to have been a normal sequence of Year divinations; and appear after the manifestation of a health problem.[16] For example, the Baoshan Illness divinations begin:

> 傍腹疾，以少氣，尚母又(有)咎。占之，貞吉，少未已，以其古(故)祝之。薦於野地主一羖，宮地主一羖，賽於行一白犬、酒食，占之曰：吉，刑尸且見王。
>
> There is an illness near the abdomen with shortness of breath; may there be no calamity. He prognosticated about it: the prognostication is auspicious; it is slight but it has not stopped; get rid of it according to its cause. He made offerings: one billy goat to the Lord of the Wild Lands, one billy goat to the Lord of the Grave. He performed *sai* [repayment] sacrifice to the Lord of the Path [Xing] with one white dog and wine oblations. He prognosticated about it: it is auspicious. In the month *xingyi* he [Shao Tuo] will have an audience with the king.[17]

Subsequent prognostications indicate a worsening condition, possibly (but not necessarily) deriving from the initial ailment. They end with the death of the tomb's occupant.

These records indicate attempts to manage personal fate through prayer and sacrifice. These attempts continue until very shortly before the death of the consultor. We do not know whether the occupant of the Baoshan tomb believed that his life span was fated at birth. We do know that he made every attempt to extend it through mantic procedures to address an illness or illnesses.

Such procedures are designed to prevent, or to redress, dangers and difficulties. In this sense they are negative. Their positive equivalent is questions about good auspice. We also find references to auspicious omens and auspicious days for particular activities in excavated text versions of the *Zhouyi*, in astrocalendric texts and in divination records, the latter also indicating prayers and sacrifices to specific gods. But if there are negotiations with gods and spirits to reach a desired result, there must be an active agent doing the negotiating, or even attempting to supplant divine powers through self-cultivation.[18] The assumption that humans could communicate with extra-human powers was part of a common Shang-Zhou religious heritage, based on the assumption of an inseparable connection between the human and extra-human worlds, visible in signs that could reveal information about the future and be used to enhance personal welfare, in sum, a belief in predictability and in the mutability of fate. Examples of what Poo Mu-chou 蒲慕州 has referred to as a *do ut des* (literally, "I give that you may give") interaction include records of divination and sacrifices to gods and ancestors.[19] In summary, excavated mantic texts and prognostication records show ongoing interest in the management of personal fate.

II. ASTROCALENDRICS AND NATURALISM

Astrocalendric texts present a quasi-mechanical and naturalistic view of the cosmos that differs from most philosophical treatments of Heaven. They also bespeak an early empirical interest in the systematic mapping and observation of the heavens. These methods depend on comprehensive and systematic representations of time (the sexagenary cycle) and space (correlative divisions of heaven and earth), often expressed in terms of *yin* and *yang* and the Five Agents. The use of these traditions is well represented in the technical treatises of the received tradition.[20] Excavated texts and instruments provide a different account of *yin-yang* and the Five Agents.

1. Abstraction in Mantic Texts

In both the early versions of the *Zhouyi* excavated from tombs and in other excavated texts and archaeological evidence, we see the early association of mantic statements with sequences of numbers. Both

Shang and Western Zhou metaphysics seem to have included the belief that aleatory procedures could reveal information about the good or ill auspice of an intended action.[21] Evidence from excavated texts on the origins of the *Zhouyi* indicates that omen statements were classified under the headings of the hexagrams. The availability and simplicity of these procedures (especially contrasted with bone and shell prognostication), and omen statements concerned with aspects of day-to-day life, suggest their use to optimize the effects of choices and life decisions.

Records of such number sequences first appear in Shang sites and become more prominent in Warring States prognostication records, where yarrow divinations are described as number sequences.[22] The linkage of number sequences and omens occurs in two of the four *Yi* texts (documents concerned with the *Zhouyi*) excavated from tombs, which provide evidence on the early evolution and variety of *Yi* traditions. The *Guicang Yi* text from Wangjiatai 王家台 (Jiangling, Hubei, 278–207) includes fifty-three hexagrams, each followed by the word *yue* 曰 and a statement of the form: [Hexagram Name] says: "In the past, X requested a prognostication about Y from Z; Z prognosticated and said: (in)auspicious." For example:

叁節曰，昔者武王卜伐殷而支占老考老考占曰吉

1-1-6-6-1-6 Jie says: In ancient times Wu Wang divined about attacking the Yin [Shang] and requested a divination from Lao Kao. Lao Kao prognosticated and said: Auspicious.[23]

These statements refer to legendary and historical events and are completely unlike the hexagram statements of the *Zhouyi*.

The Fuyang 阜陽 *Zhouyi* (Shuanggudui 雙古堆, Fuyang, Anhui, 165) consists of fragmentary bamboo slips of some fifty-two hexagrams and line statements. It uses numbers to represent hexagram lines and indicates the importance of line statements for particular topics, such as weather, punishment, warfare, illness, marriage, residence, pregnancy and birth, bureaucratic service, administration, travel, hunting, and fishing. For example, the hexagrams *Da You* 大有 and *Wu Wang* 無妄 both append the statement: "Prognosticating about rain: it will not rain" (*Bu yu bu yu* 卜雨不雨).[24] The hexagram *Sui* 隨 adds a reference to prognosticating about illness.[25]

The other two versions attest to the antiquity of the received text. The Shanghai Museum text, the oldest known *Yi* text, consists of bamboo slips or fragments of thirty-four hexagrams. It corresponds to the received text in many ways and indicates that a stable version of something like the received *Zhouyi* was in circulation by three hundred, but that its mantic interpretations were still flexible at this time.[26] The Mawangdui *Zhouyi*, the most complete of the excavated documents, includes the *Xici* commentary. It differs from the received text in the order of the hexagrams and their names and diagrams. There are also four previously unknown commentaries, which suggest the early existence of a Ru *Yi* tradition, professional *Yi* diviners, and ambivalent attitudes of Ru toward them.

This history suggests several roles of the *Yi* as a mantic text used for prediction and decision. First, it linked omen statements to cosmic patterns, expressed as sequences of numbers. Second, its was applicable to daily life. In particular, it could advise decisions about areas of potential risk or danger, such as bad weather, illness, warfare, travel, and so forth.[27]

2. *Daybooks*

Mantic statements on decisions in daily life also appear in daybooks (*rishu* 日書), where they are linked to the calendar and the sexagenary cycle. Daybooks and other almanac texts have been excavated from tombs, beginning with a calendric diagram known as the Chu Silk Manuscript (Changsha, Hunan, *c.* 300).[28] Some resemble the Monthly Ordinance texts of the received tradition. For example, the text titled Prohibitions (*Jin* 禁) from Yinqueshan 銀雀山 (Linyi, Shandong, 140–111) provides seasonal prohibitions linked to the calendar and four (of the five) phases. Most important for the present discussion are the daybooks excavated from some twenty tombs.[29] Daybooks are not almanacs in the strict sense because they do not cover the entire calendar systematically, but they do correlate the calendar to a regular set of transformations: in this case the Five Agents, rather than planetary movements.[30]

Daybooks were used to predict auspicious times for a wide range of activities such as marriage, childbirth, making clothes, building projects, travel, slaughtering farm animals, farming, and official audiences. Other topics included desertion, dreams, illness and leisure, and military activities. Their content reflects the interests of women as well as men (e.g., a prospective wife's wealth and character, a woman's chances of being abandoned). These concerns indicate perceived areas of risk and danger in daily life.[31]

Daybooks present a mechanical view of the workings of fate, for example in the sections on illness in the daybooks for Jiudian and Shuihudi. The Jiudian daybook is the oldest text known to use horary iatromancy. All illnesses that arise on the same day have the same etiology and prognosis: respite, recovery, or death. One section gives auspicious and inauspicious aspects of the Twelve Earth branches and associates each with the onset of a particular illness.

For example, if an illness begins on a *chen* 辰 day, respite occurs on a *you* 酉 day, recovery on a *xu* 戌 day, and death on a *zi* 子 day. If the onset is on a *wei* 未 day, respite occurs on a *zi* day, recovery on a *mao* 昴 day, and death on a *yin* 寅 day, and so on.[32] The two daybooks from Shuihudi are better preserved and include extensive sections on stem-branch iatromancy, with systematic correlation to the Five Agents. For example, Daybook A links the day of onset of an illness to a divine and a material cause:

> 甲乙有疾，父母為祟，得之於肉，從東方來，裹以桼（漆）器。戊己病，庚有閒，辛酢。若不酢，煩居東方，歲在東方，青色死。

> If there is illness on a *jia* or *yi* day, father and mother are the calamity, it is obtained from meat, and comes from the east, and is placed in a lacquer container. It manifests on a *wu* or *ji* day, there is a respite on a *geng* day and recovery on a *xin* day. If there is no recovery, Fever will be in the east quarter, Year will be in the east quarter, and the color of death will be azure.[33]

According to this formula, an illness manifests after four days, with a respite on the fifth or sixth day. Recovery occurs on the sixth or seventh day. If the illness does not resolve during this one-week period, it is attributed to Fever (*fan* 煩), associated with the star Year (Sui 歲), which transits over the four directions four times a year.[34] If both Fever and Year are in the quadrant associated with its origin, the illness is fatal. These hemerological methods contrast with the Illness prognostications from Baoshan and Wangshan. The daybooks are no longer apotropaic; they classify illnesses systematically into types to determine auspicious days for treatment.

3. Astrocalendric Texts and Instruments

Attempts to link predictions to cosmological cycles also appear in the use of diviner's boards and astrocalendric tables and instruments. Diviner's boards are models of the cosmos in which a round Heaven plate revolves within a square Earth plate. The earliest known is a Dipper board (*shi pan* 式盤) from Wangjiatai Tomb 15, used to orient the handle of the North Dipper among the Twenty-eight Lunar Lodges (*xiu* 宿).[35] An illustrated text from Zhoujiatai 周家台 discusses the use of the diviner's board. It shows the Ten Heaven Stems positioned in a cruciform figure at the center of the board.[36] The outer circle associates the four cardinal directions with the Twelve Earth Branches, the Five Agents, and the Lunar Lodges. There is an observation or prognostication for each Lunar Lodge, for example, "Sun emerges" (Room, East), "Sun at the center" (Seven Stars, South), and "Sun enters" (Pleiades, West). To obtain a prognostication, the

Heaven plate was keyed to the month and solar lodge associated with the time of the prognostication. Thus positioned, the dipper handle pointed to a Lunar Lodge and its associated prognostication.

Boards excavated from Fuyang were designed for the specific methods of Liuren 六壬 (Six Ren Days), Jiugong 九宮 (Nine Palaces), and Taiyi 太一 (Great One). These methods incorporate *yin-yang* and Five Agent theory.[37] They link the sexagenary cycle to a hierarchy of divinities, celestial phenomena, the four directions, and human activities and emotions. The effect was to subsume human action under cosmological change.

In summary, the evidence from excavated texts suggests a naturalistic world in which cosmic patterns can be observed and predicted. This evidence appears in the omen statements of *Yi* texts, in daybooks, and in astrocalendric texts and instruments. The hexagrams of the *Zhouyi* and the sexagenary cycle contributed to the systematic, and eventually cosmological orientation Han philosophy, as *yin-yang* and Five-phase theories were applied systematically (and perhaps arbitrarily) to a wide range of phenomena.[38]

III. Embodied Virtue, Self-Cultivation, and Physiognomy

Both Masters texts and excavated texts on physiognomy, health, and longevity describe physical practices for cultivating virtue through the transformation of *qi*. These practices overlap accounts of self-cultivation as originating in the will (*zhi* 志) in the received tradition. These texts have important ramifications for the understanding of early Chinese views of self-cultivation. They also describe its results as manifesting in the physical appearance of the body, visible through physiognomy. Excavated texts address two closely related issues: self-cultivation through the physical cultivation of *qi* within the body and physiognomic methods for reading the physical signs of these practices.

1. Embodied Virtue and Self-Cultivation

Mencius describes virtue as manifesting in the body. At 2A2 he famously describes *qi* as filling the body and moved by the will 志. He argues that its concentration is a function of morality, through accumulated righteousness (*ji yi* 集義). When asked about his own particular strengths, he replies that he understands language and is good at nurturing his flood-like *qi*. But if virtue is visible in the body it can be "read." At 7A21 Mencius describes the virtues of the *junzi* as visible in the body as a glossy color visible in the face and limbs. At 4A15 he recommends eye physiognomy on grounds that the eyes reveal a person's moral state by the clarity or cloudiness of the pupils. This argument is attacked by both Xunzi and Wang Chong, who argue that clarity or the pupils is determined at birth and does not depend on character. In "Against Physiognomy" (*Fei Xiang* 〈非相〉) Xunzi also argues that physiognomizing people's forms is inferior to speaking of their heart-minds. Poor physiognomy does not prevent correct values, and good physiognomy cannot take the place of incorrect values. What makes us human is the act of making distinctions, which does not depend on physiognomy.[39]

Mencius's views about *qi* conform to and probably draw on a culture of embodied self-cultivation practices, aptly described in a recent book by Mark Csikszentmihalyi.[40] These practices and the concepts behind them structured much of early Daoism, medical theory, and, more broadly, important areas of early Chinese ethics and metaphysics.[41] Such "material virtue" traditions held that the body-mind was constructed of *qi*, which could be transformed by embodied self-cultivation practices. These traditions appear both in the received tradition and in excavated texts.

In the received tradition, accounts of the cultivation of embodied *qi* appear in the *Daodejing* 《道德經》, *Zhuangzi* 《莊子》, the *Nei Ye* chapter of the *Guanzi* 《管子》, and parts of the *Huainanzi* 《淮南子》. For example, *Zhuangzi* 1 refers to a *shen ren* 神人 who has effectively transformed his physical body and its constituent *qi*. *Zhuangzi* 11 describes harmonizing the essences of the six *qi* in order to nurture life. According to *Zhuangzi* 22, human birth is caused by the gathering together of *qi*.[42] Fourth-century passages in the *Zuozhuan* and *Guanzi* also describe regulating *qi* to achieve emotional balance.[43] The *Nei ye* and *Lüshi Chunqiu* describe the cultivation of *qi* for wisdom and longevity.[44] Many other passages could be adduced. The point is that a sage or numinous person achieves that status through physical as well as metaphysical means, which are not distinguished. They are part of a "Nurturing Life" (*Yangsheng* 〈養生〉) tradition of physical self-cultivation and longevity techniques such as dietary practices, exercise regimens, breath meditation, and sexual cultivation techniques. These technical traditions were associated with *fangshu* in the received tradition and described in medical manuscripts excavated from tombs. Most do not survive in the received tradition beyond records of their titles in the last two sections of the *Hanshu Yiwenzhi*.

Excavated texts contribute significantly to an emergent view that individuals traditionally described as both Daoist and Ru shared a focus on the mental and physical cultivation of *qi*. This evidence includes medical manuscripts from Mawangdui, such as the "Draw-ings of Guiding and Pulling" (*Daoyin Tu* 〈導引圖〉), drawings of human figures performing exercises, some with captions.[45] Some are described in the "Pulling Book" (*Yinshu* 〈引書〉) from Zhangjiashan 張家山, which describes exercises based on imitation of animal move-ment (snakes, mantises, tigers, dragons, etc.) which may be the earliest known ancestors of contemporary martial arts or *wushu* 武術.[46] Both exemplify a tradition of exercise for both therapy and health known as *daoyin* (pulling and guiding). Other texts from Mawangdui describe dietetics and breath cultivation, for example, "Eliminating Grain and Eating Vapor" (*Quegu Shiqi* 〈卻穀食氣〉) and "Recipes for Nurturing Life" (*Yang Sheng Fang* 〈養生方〉).[47] "Harmonizing *Yin* and *Yang*" (*He Yin Yang* 〈合陰陽〉) and "Discussion of the Culminant Way of All Under Heaven" (*Tianxia Zhidao Tan* 〈天下至道談〉) use the movements and postures of animals to describe sexual techniques. All are part of a *yangsheng* culture, which construed self-cultivation as control over physiological processes of the body and mind, under-stood as transformations of *qi*. The result was moral excellence, health, and longevity.[48]

Two versions of a text titled *Wuxing* 五行 or "Five Kinds of Action" have been excavated from Mawangdui and Guodian 郭店 (Jingmen, Hubei, 310–300).[49] Csikszentmihaly has argued that the Ru defense against charges of hypocrisy was a moral psychology that provided an account of authentic practice.[50] The *Wuxing* texts provide this through descriptions of the process of how states of the inner mind are trans-formed by reflection to form virtuous action.[51] It thus presents an opportunity to significantly reread Mencius as part of an "embodied virtue" tradition that spans what have conventionally been classified as distinct "schools" and "genres" (Ru and Daoist, Classics and tech-nical works, etc.).

2. Physiognomy

Physiognomy is also part of the discourse on embodied virtue and potential. In traditional interpretations, Confucian schools empha-sized study and ritual and Daoist texts described meditative and longevity practices. In the light of the evidence of excavated texts, both can be viewed as part of a broader tradition of embodied self-cultivation practices. Material virtue traditions had important links with both Ru practices (possibly associated with Zisi 子思) and with Daoist traditions and southern schools, as well as potential links to the moralization of health in the traditions that culminated as the *Huangdi Neijing* 《黃帝內經》. Accounts of these practices appear in passing in the texts of the received tradition. Many more come from excavated texts.

In the received tradition, physiognomy titles appear in the *shushu* section of the *Hanshu Yiwenzhi*. All are lost, but their titles suggest a focus on practical physiognomy of persons and objects. If the transformed *qi* of a cultivated individual was visible in the body, a skilled individual should be able to "read" these transformations. But the subject matter of physiognomy texts included both physical characteristics that might result from self-cultivation and characteristics set at birth.

The earliest systematic exposition of the principles of physiognomy is in a manuscript from Dunhuang 敦煌 (Gansu, fifth to eleventh centuries CE) ascribed to the Han figure Xu Fu 許負.[52] Physiognomy (*Xiangshu* 《相書》) surveys the human body and explains the significance of each feature, especially (i) the form of the body and face and their proportions and appearance and fineness of shape of various parts of the body. In particular, brilliance and luminosity of the face, eyes, and hair portend good health but also good fortune, (ii) "color" of the face especially, but also the color of parts of the body, (iii) birthmarks, especially on the face, head, back, and genitals. Finally, (iv) lines and figures on the face, especially on the forehead, below the nose, on the tongue, hands, and feet. Like the early omen statements, the physiognomic prognostications in the *Xiangshu* are not systematic and are grouped under headings such as face, eyes, nose, and so on. Color attributes appear among the statements, but with no systematic significance. It is striking that some of these features might result from self-cultivation (luminosity, color, and facial lines), but others are set at birth (shape of the limbs, birthmarks, etc.).

In theory at least, the ability to physiognomize persons and things allowed a skilled reader to assess the merit and potential, not only of persons but of animals and plants used in agriculture, and even of materiel used in warfare. Physiognomy could be used to assess the economic worth of objects (clothing, equipment, swords), animals (domestic animal, silkworms), and people. It is not easy to reconstruct the methods used, because many of the passages that mention these arts do so for rhetorical purposes that have no interest in the techniques themselves.[53]

Excavated texts on physiognomy emphasize these practical contexts, for example, a text on physiognomizing dogs from Yinqueshan, a Han sword physiognomy text from *Juyan* 居延, and a text on the physiognomy of horses from Mawangdui.[54] These included animals and plants used in agriculture and even military materiel. All share the view that internal *qi* is reflected in appearance and makes it possible to judge character or potential. In economic and military contexts this meant judging the "character" of an animal or weapon.

IV. Concluding Remarks

In recent years, our understanding of early Chinese views of divination, fate, and agency has been transformed by new evidence from excavated texts that prominently include mantic and *qi* transformation techniques and texts, presumably used by the occupants of the tombs in which they were found. Such texts fall below the radar of specifically Ru discussions of political agency and political autonomy. Excavated texts clearly demonstrate the ongoing use of technical arts whose nature is suggested by the titles of the *Hanshu Yiwenzhi*. At the government level, mantic techniques were used to determine auspicious days for sacrifices, state ritual, and as part of military and political decision making. As used by private individuals (albeit within networks of relationships), these techniques demonstrate a tacit notion of autonomy, as they were (and are) used as an aid to formulating life plans and act on them by enhancing health, longevity, and efficacy in practical decisions.[55] The private use of these practices presupposes an active agent with desires and life plans. If the contents of high officials' tombs are a guide to what they chose to have buried with them, technical works on longevity and the mantic arts handily outnumber Classics or Masters texts.

In summary, recently excavated archaeological texts have greatly augmented our knowledge of these techniques and brought to light significant elements in Warring States philosophical and religious discourses on self-cultivation. Debates on divination, fate, agency, and responsibility had important implications for Chinese views of personal and moral autonomy. Some tacit notion of personal autonomy is a precondition for the aspiration to affect the future through mantic activity.

NATIONAL UNIVERSITY OF SINGAPORE
Singapore

Endnotes

Research for this article has been supported by a President's Research Fellowship in the Humanities from the University of California (2005–2006), and a grant from National Endowment for the Humanities and the American Council of Learned Societies for research in China (2006).

1. A. C. Graham, *Yin-Yang and the Nature of Correlative Thinking* (Singapore: Institute of East Asian Philosophies, 1986), 1–2 credited them with the development of

Five-phase cosmology. See also Angus C. Graham, *Disputers of the Tao: Philosophical Argument in Ancient China* (LaSalle: Open Court, 1991), especially 225–35; Ngo Van Xuyet, *Divination Magie et Politique dans la Chine Ancienne* (Paris: Presses Universitaires de France, 1976); and Li Ling 李零, *Zhongguo Fangshu Kao*《中國方術考》 (Beijing: Renmin Zhongguo Publisher, 1993) and *Zhongguo Fangshu Xukao* 《中國方術續考》(Beijing: Renmin Zhongguo, 2000).

2. *Hanshu*, 30 (Beijing: Zhonghua, 1962), 1701–84. It was compiled by Ban Gu (32–92 CE). The first four sections were based on Liu Xin's 劉歆 46 BCE–23 CE) description of the imperial library, but the two technical sections (*shushu* 數術 and *fangji* 方技, Recipes and Methods) were compiled by two technical experts: the Grand Astrologer Yin Xian 尹咸 and the imperial physician Li Zhuguo 李柱國. Dating: A. F. P. Hulsewé in Michael Loewe, ed., *Early Chinese Texts: A Bibliographical Guide* (Berkeley: Society for the Study of Early China and The Institute of East Asian Studies, University of California, Berkeley, 1993), 129–36. Discussion: Marc Kalinowski, "Technical Traditions in Ancient China and Shushu Culture in Chinese Religion," in *Volume 1: Ancient and Medieval, Religion and Chinese Society*, ed. John Lagerwey (Hong Kong: Chinese University Press, 2004), 223–48. For critical study of the *Yiwenzhi* see Wang Xianqian 王先謙, *Hanshu Buzhu*《漢書補注》(Changsha: Xushou Tang, 1900. Facs. repr. Beijing: Shumu Wenxian, 1995) and Gu Shi 顧實 (1875–1956), *Hanshu Yiwenzhi Jiang Shu*《漢書藝文志講疏》(Shanghai: Shangwu Publisher, 1924, rpt. Shanghai: Guji Publisher, 1987).

3. All dates are BCE unless otherwise indicated. Chen Songchang 陳松長 and Liao Mingchun 廖名春, "*Boshu 'Ersanzi Wen,' 'Yi zhi Yi,' 'Yao' Shiwen* 帛書二三子問易之義，要釋文," *Daojia Wenhua Yanjiu*《道家文化研究》3 (1993): 435.

4. *Lüshi Chunqiu Jiaoshi*《呂氏春秋校釋》, ed. Chen Qiyou 陳奇猷 (Shanghai: Xuelin Publisher, 1984), 1505 (*Yi Xing* 壹行 22.4). Richard Wilhelm translates *Bi* as "Grace," Richard John Lynn as "Elegance." See Richard Wilhelm, *The I Ching or Book of Changes*, trans. Cary F. Baynes (Princeton: Princeton University Press, 1950), 90 and Richard John Lynn, *The Classic of Changes: A New Translation of the I Ching as Interpreted by Wang Bi* (New York: Columbia University Press, 1994), 274.

5. This double-character name may refer to an office in the *Zhouli*. The *wuma* was in charge of the medical treatment of horses. See *Zhouli* (*Shisanjing zhushu* ed., comp. Ruan Yuan, 1815, facs. rpt. Taipei: Yiwen Jushu Publisher, 1980), 33.6b–8a.

6. *Lüshi Chunqiu*, 1441 ("*Chai Xian* 察賢," 21.2, cf. John Knoblock and Jeffrey Riegel, *The Annals of Lü Buwei: A Complete Translation and Study* [Palo Alto: Stanford University Press, 2000], 553). Fu Zijian 宓子賤 was the nickname of Fu Buqi 宓不齊 (b. 521). Wuma Qi was the style name of Wuma Shi 巫馬施, who succeeded Fu Buqi in Shanfu 單父 in Lu in southwest Shandong. Confucius also praises him in the *Analects*, 5.3. For another example, see for example, *Mozi Jiaozhu*《墨子校注》, *Xinbian Zhuzi Jicheng*《新編諸子集成》ed. (Beijing: Zhonghua Publisher, 1993), 46.656–61.

7. *Zhuangzi Jishi*《莊子集釋》, ed. Guo Qingfan 郭慶藩 (Beijing: Zhonghua Publisher, 1961) 23.785. An almost identical passage appears in *Daode Jing*, 44: "Therefore if you understand what is enough you will not be humiliated; If you know when to stop you will not be in danger and will be able to be long lasting." This passage also recommends simplicity, but does not mention divination.

8. *Guanzi* 管子 (*Sibu Beiyao* edition), 16.5a ("*Nei Ye*" 16.49), trans. modified from Rickett 2.50–51. The same question appears in *Guanzi* 13.6a ("*Xinshu Xia*〈心術下〉," 13.37; W. Allyn Rickett, trans., *Guanzi: Political, Economic and Philosophical Essays from Early China*, vol. 2 [Princeton: Princeton University Press, 1998], 60).

9. *Guanzi*, 13.10a ("*Bai Xin*," 13.38, cf. Rickett, *Guanzi* vol. 2, 89).

10. *Mozi*, 68.894–5; *Guanzi*, 12.20a ("*Yi Mi*〈侈靡〉," 12.35) and 22.4ab ("*Shan Quan*〈山權數〉," 22.75).

11. *Xunzi Jijie*《荀子集解》(Beijing: Zhonghua, 1988), 17.316 ("*Tian Lun*〈天論〉"). *Hanfeizi Jishi*《韓非子集釋》, ed. Chen Qiyou 陳奇猷 (Beijing: Zhonghua Publisher, 1958), 1102–3 ("*Xian Xue*〈顯學〉," 19.50).

12. *Zhangjiashan Hanmu Zhujian* (*Ersiqi Hao Mu*) 張家山漢墓竹簡 (二十七號墓)》 (Beijing: Wenwu Publisher, 2001), 203–4, slips 474–86. For context see Li Xueqin

李學勤 and Xing Wen 邢文, "New Light on the Early-Han Code: A Reappraisal of the *Zhangjiashan* Bamboo-Slip Legal Texts," *Asia Major* 14, no. 1 (2001): 125–46.

13. For Tianxingguan see *Wenwu*, 2001, no. 9: 4–21 and *Jingzhou Tianxingguan Erhao Chumu*《荊州天星觀二號楚墓》(Beijing: Wenwu Publisher, 2003). For Wangshan, see *Jiangling Wangshan Shazhong Chumu*《江陵望山沙塚楚墓》(Beijing: Wenwu Publisher, 1996).

14. Chen Wei 陳偉, *Baoshan Chu Jian Chutan*《包山楚簡初探》(Wuhan: Wuhan University Press, 1996).

15. *Baoshan Chujian*《包山楚簡》(Beijing: Wenwu Publisher, 1991), slips 197–98. This passage presents many complications and controversies. Translation follows Chen Wei, *Baoshan Chu Jian Chutan*《包山楚簡初探》, 231. He transcribes *geng* 庚 as *di* 帝 and reads it as *shi* 適, "to go." Transcription follows *Baoshan Chujian* as much as possible. I have used modern orthography to render what in the original were compound graphs (e.g., 之月，躬身) or have used later equivalents of Chu script characters (e.g., *xing* 刑 for a Chu graph consisting of *xing* 刑 with the element *tian* 田 under it and *shi* 尸 for the Chu graph consisting of *shi* 尸 with the element *shi* 示 under it). For another translation see and Constance Cook, *Death in Ancient China: The Tale of One Man's Journey* (Leiden: Brill, 2006), 154–55.

16. For this distinction see Chen Wei, *Baoshan Chu Jian Chutan*《包山楚簡初探》, 152–54. Of the twenty-seven entries, eleven are Year divinations; twelve concern illness and the others do not involve divination. Although the ritualists specialize in method and instrument, they do not specialize in Year or Illness divination. Eight perform Year divination, three exclusively; four perform Illness divination exclusively, and four perform both Year and Illness divination. See Lisa Raphals, "Divination and Medicine in China and Greece: A Comparative Perspective on the Baoshan Illness Divinations," *East Asian Science, Technology and Medicine* 24 (2005): 78–103.

17. *Baoshan*, slips 207–8, in Cook, *Death in Ancient China*, 168–69. This repeats in four entries dated to the eleventh month of the same year (slips 218 and 220).

18. Cf. Michael J. Puett, *To Become a God: Cosmology, Sacrifice and Self-Divinization in Early China* (Cambridge: Harvard University Press, 2002).

19. Mu-chou Poo, *In Search of Personal Welfare: A View of Ancient Chinese Religion* (New York: State University of New York Press, 1998), 27–29.

20. Astronomical treatises: *Huainanzi*, 3: *Tianwenxun*〈天文訓〉; "*Tianwenzhi*〈天文志〉," *Shiji*, 27; "*Tianwenzhi*〈天文志〉," *Hanshu*, 26. "The Pitch Pipes" (*Lü Shu*《律書》), *Shiji*, 25. The Five Agents: *Wuxingzhi*〈五行志〉, *Hanshu*, 27.

21. Major sites: Sipanmo 四盤磨 (Anyang, Anhui), Qishan 岐山 (Shaanxi, the Zhouyuan oracle bones), and Zhangjiapo 張家坡, near present-day Xian.

22. Zhang Zhenglang 張政烺, "*Shishi Zhou Chu Qingtongqi Mingwen Zhong de Yi Gua* 試釋周初青銅器銘文中的易卦," *Kaogu Xuebao*, 1980, no. 4: 403–15, trans. Horst R. Huber, Robin D. B. Yates et al., "An Interpretation of the Divinatory Inscriptions on Early Chou Bronzes," *Early China* 6 (1980): 80–96. Zhang Yachu 張亞初 and Liu Yu 劉雨, "*Cong Shang Zhou Bagua Shu Zi Fuhao Tan Shi Fa de Jige Wenti* 從商周八卦數字元號談筮法的幾個問題," *Kaogu*, 1981, no. 2: 155–63 and 154, trans. Edward Shaughnessy, "Some Observations about Milfoil Divination Based on Shang and Zhou Bagua Numerical Symbols," *Early China* 7 (1981–1982): 46–54.

23. Slip 198 as transcribed in *Wenwu*, 1995, no. 1: 41. This hexagram corresponds to Hexagram 60 (*Jie* 節 ["Articulation"]) in the transmitted tradition. Most "*Guicang* 〈歸藏〉" hexagram names correspond to the received *Yijing*; the exceptions resemble the Mawangdui *Zhou Yi*. The Wangjiatai *Guicang* also resembles extant portions of the *Guicang*. See Wang Mingqin 王明欽, "*Wangjiatai Qinmu Zhujian Gaishu* 王家台秦墓竹簡概述," in *Xinchu Jianbo Yanjiu*《新出簡帛研究》(Studies on Recently-Discovered Chinese Manuscripts), ed. Sarah Allan and Xing Wen (Beijing: Wenwu Publisher, 2004), 26–49 and 441–43.

24. Han Ziqiang 韓自強, *Fuyang Hanjian "Zhouyi" Yanjiu*《阜陽漢簡《周易》研究》(Shanghai: Guji Publisher, 2004), 53 slip 64; 59, slip 125.

25. Ibid., 54, slip 69.

26. Ma Chengyuan 馬承源 and Shanghai Bowuguan 上海博物館, *Shanghai Bowuguan Cang Zhanguo Chu Zhu Shu*《上海博物館藏戰國楚竹書》, vol. 3 (Shanghai: Guji

Publisher, 2003), 131–260. See also Liao Mingchun 廖名春, "*Cong Guodian Chu Jian Lun Xian Qin Ru Jia yu 'Zhouyi' de Guannian* 從郭店楚簡論先秦儒家與《周易》的關係," *Hanxue Yanjiu* 18, no. 1 (2000): 55–72; Liao Mingchun 廖名春 and Zhu Yuanqing 朱淵清 ed., *Shang Boguan Cang Zhanguo Chu Zhu Shu Yanjiu*《上博館藏戰國楚簡書研究》 (Shanghai: Shanghai Shudian Publisher, 2002); Pu Maozuo 濮茅左, *Chu Zhushu Zhou Yi Yanjiu: Jian Shu Xian Qin Liang Han Chutu yu Chuanshi Yi Xue Wenxian Ziliao* 《楚竹書周易研究: 兼述先秦兩漢出土與傳世易學文獻資料》, 2 vols. (Shanghai: Guji Publisher, 2006); Shaughnessy, "A First Reading of the Shanghai Museum Bamboo-Strip Manuscript of the *Zhou Yi*," *Early China* 30 (2005–2006): 1–24, especially 23–24.

27. For more on mantic activity and risk see Raphals, *Divination in Early China and Greece* (Cambridge: Cambridge University Press, forthcoming).

28. Strictly speaking, an almanac is an annual table or book of tables with a monthly calendar of days, that gives the locations of each planet in the zodiac throughout the year and other astronomical, astrological, and meteorological information. The term is more generally used for systems that combine cosmological and calendric principles, including *Yueling* 〈月令〉 (Monthly Ordinance) calendars in the *Guanzi, Lüshi Chunqiu, Huainanzi*, and *Liji*.

29. Especially Jiudian 九店 (Jiangling, Hubei, *c.* 330–270), Shuihudi 睡虎地 (Yunmeng 雲夢, Hubei, 217), Fangmatan 放馬灘 (Tianshui, Gansu, *c.* 230–220), Mawangdui, and Zhoujiatai 周家台 (Guanju 關沮, Hubei, 213–209), summarized in Kalinowski, "Divination and Astrology: Received Texts and Excavated Manuscripts," in *China's Early Empires: A Re-appraisal*, ed. Michael Nylan and Michael Loewe (Cambridge: Cambridge University Press, 2009), 339–66 and 353–59.

30. Different daybooks use different calendric principles, including the Stem-branch (*ganzhi* 干支) cycle, the *jianchu* 建除 (Establishment and Removal) series and cycles of Sanctions and Virtues (*xingde* 刑德).

31. Mu-chou Poo, *Search of Personal Welfare*, 72–89. For risk, see Raphals, *Divination in Early China and Greece*, chapter 8.

32. *Jiudian Chumu*《九店楚墓》, ed. Hubeisheng Wenwu Kaogu Yanjiusuo (Beijing: Wenwu, 1999), 52–53, slips 64 and 67, cf. Donald Harper, "Iatromancy, Prognosis, and Diagnosis in Early Chinese Medicine," in *Innovation in Chinese Medicine*, ed. Elisabeth Hsu, Needham Research Institute Studies 3 (Cambridge: Cambridge University Press, 2001), 99–120, especially 105–6.

33. *Shuihudi Qinmu Zhujian*《睡虎地秦墓竹簡》, 193, slips 68–69.

34. East (months 1, 5, and 9), south (months 2, 6, and 10), west (months 3, 7, and 11), and north (months 4, 8, and 12). See Kalinowski, *Cosmologie et Divination dans la Chine Ancienne: le Compendium des Cinq Agents* (Paris: École française d'Extrême Orient, 1991), 105; Liu Lexian 劉樂賢, *Shuihudi Qinjian Rishu Yanjiu*《睡虎地秦簡日書研究》 (Taipei: Wenjin Publisher, 1993), 116–22; Harper, "Iatromancy, Prognosis, and Diagnosis," especially 105–13.

35. See Jingzhou Diqu Bowuguan, ed., "Jiangling Wanjiatai 15 hao Qin Mu" 江陵王家15台号秦墓, *Wenwu*, 1995, no. 1: 42.

36. *Guanju Qin Hanmu Jiandu*《關沮秦漢墓簡牘》 (Beijing: Zhonghua Shuju Publisher, 2001), 107.

37. The definitive study of Han *Liuren* boards is Kalinowski, "Les instruments astro-calendériques des Han et la methode *liu ren*," *Bulletin de l'Ecole Française d'Extrême-Orient* 72 (1983): 309–419. Recent archaeology: Yan Dunjie 嚴敦傑, "Guanyu Xi-Han Chuqi de Shipan he Zhanpan 關於西漢初期的式盤和占盤," *Kaogu Xuebao*, 1978, no. 5: 334–37 and Kalinowski, "Les Traités de Shuihudi et l'Hémérologie Chinoise à la Fin des Royaumes-Combattants," *Toung-pao* 72, no. 4/5 (1986): 175–228, especially 62–72.

38. For detailed discussion, see Raphals, *Divination in Early China and Greece*, chapter 10.

39. *Xunzi*, 5.72–73 78 ("*Fei Xiang* 〈非相〉"); *Lunheng Jiaoshi*《論衡校釋》 (Beijing: Zhonghua Shuju Publisher, 1990) 13.135 ("*Ben Xing* 本性").

40. Mark Csikszentmihaly, *Material Virtue: Ethics and the Body in Early China* (Leiden: Brill, 2004).

41. For an excellent summary, see Vivienne Lo, "Self-cultivation and the Popular Medical Traditions," in *Medieval Chinese Medicine: The Dunhuang Medical Manuscripts*, ed. Lo and Christopher Cullen (London: Routledge Curzon, 2005), 207–25.

42. *Zhuangzi Jishi*《莊子集釋》, ed. Guo Qingfan 郭慶藩 (Beijing: Zhonghua Shuju Publisher, 1961), 1:28, 11:386, 22:733.

43. *Zuozhuan*, ed. Yang Bojun 楊伯峻 (Gaoxiong: Fuwen Tushu Publisher, 1981), 1458 (*Zhao*, 25.3); *Guanzi* X 26:2a.

44. *Guanzi*, 16.4ab ("Nei Ye," 16.49); *Lüshi Chunqiu*, 136–44 ("*Jin Shu*〈盡數〉," 3.2).

45. *Mawangdui Hanmu Boshu*《馬王堆漢墓帛庭》, ed. Mawangdui Hanmu Boshu Zhengli Xiaozu, vols. 1/2, 3, and 4 (Beijing: Wenwu Publisher, 1980, 1983, and 1985).

46. Zhangjiashan Hanjian Zhengli Xiaozu, ed., "*Zhangjiashan Hanjian yinshu shiwen* 江陵張家山漢簡引書釋文," *Wenwu*, 1990, no. 10: 82–86; Peng Hao 彭浩, "*Zhangjiashan Hanjian Yinshu Chutan*《張家山漢簡引書初探》," *Wenwu*, 1990, no. 10: 87–91.

47. Harper, *Early Chinese Medical Literature* (London and New York: Kegan Paul International, 1998), especially 25–30.

48. See Lo, "The Influence of Nurturing Life Culture," in *Innovation in Chinese Medicine*, ed. Elisabeth Hsu, Needham Research Institute Studies (Cambridge: Cambridge University Press, 2001).

49. *Mawangdui Hanmu Boshu* vol. 1 (1980), 17–27; *Guodian Chumu Zhujian* 《郭店楚墓竹簡》, ed. Jingmenshi Bowuguan (Beijing: Wenwu Publisher, 1998), 147–54 (both translated in two appendices in Csikszentmihalyi, *Material Virtue*). For structural analysis, see Xing Wen 邢文, "*Chujian Wuxing Shilun* 楚簡五行試論," *Wenwu*, 1998, no. 10: 57–61.

50. Most telling is Robber Zhi's critique in *Zhuangzi Jishi*《莊子集釋》, 9. 991–2.

51. Csikszentmihalyi, *Material Virtue*, especially 7, 59, and chapter 5.

52. It survives in three manuscript versions (2572, 2797, 3589). These texts can be accessed at the International Dunhuang Project: http://idp.bl.uk. See Catherine Despeux, "Physiognomie," in *Divination et Société dans la Chine Médiévale: Étude des Manuscrits de Dunhuang de la Bibliothèque Nationale de France et de la British Library*, ed. Kalinowski (Paris: Bibliothèque Nationale de France, 2003), especially 521–23.

53. Raphals, *Divination in Early China and Greece*, chapter 10.

54. Li Ling, *Zhongguo Fangshu kao*, 84–87. The Yinqueshan text includes Recipes for Physiognomizing Dogs (*Xiang Gou Fang*《相狗方》). See Wu Jiulong 吳九龍, *Yinqueshan Hanjian Shiwen*《銀雀山漢簡釋文》(Beijing: Wenwu Publisher, 1985: 243) and slips 208, 213, 221, 242, 261, 271, 302, 315, 374, 889, 899, 1937, 2570, 3788, and 4047. For transcription of the Juyan slips, see *Juyan Xin Jian: Jiaqu Houguan yu Di Si Sui* 《居延新簡: 甲渠候官與第四燧》, ed. Gansu Sheng Wenwu Kaogu Yanjiusuo (Beijing: Wenwu Publisher, 1990), 98. For Mawangdui, see "*Mawangdui Hanmu Boshu Xiangma Jing Shiwen* 馬王堆漢暮帛書相馬經釋文," *Wenwu*, 1977, no. 8: 17–22.

55. Here I follow Charles Taylor's discussion of moral status as requiring a sense of self, a point of view, and the capacity to hold values, make choices, and adopt life plans. See Taylor, "The Concept of a Person," in *Human Agency and Language: Philosophical Papers, volume 1* (Cambridge: Cambridge University Press, 1985), 97–105. This topic is also pursued in Raphals, "Thirteen Ways of Looking at the Self in Early China," *History of Philosophy Quarterly* 26, no. 4 (2009): 315–36.

CHUNG-YING CHENG

ON INTERNAL ONTO-GENESIS OF VIRTUOUS ACTIONS IN THE *WU XING PIAN**

In any theory of the development of the concept of human self we must recognize that the human self has to have an inner content that enables itself to know and respond to the world in such a way that we may find eventually an autonomy of will that can make moral choice and adopt a norm to follow in action. This does not mean that human person may not act without an inner consciousness or a will that makes normative decisions. He could for example simply pursue an end but not worry about the way of pursuing. But as a human being qua human being it seems clear that an understanding of inner self as a source or its interaction with the world is important for the assertion of the meaning and purpose of moral life. In the Western tradition we can see that the belief in human soul was assumed when the Greek came to speak of the human self. But as to how this inner self is composed, we have to wait for Plato to give its logical articulation and distinction. What we have is an ontology of the human self whose genesis is metaphysical and mysterious.

In the case of the Chinese philosophy, a human being has to recognize the outer world and then respond to and reflect on his knowledge of the world so that he may recognize his own identity as a human self. This human self is seen as having a mind capable of questioning what one wants and seeking what one pursues and thus making distinction between what is good and bad relative to his needs and conception of what he wishes to achieve in the end. The formation of this concept of self is not transcendent nor transcendental but ascertained on experiential grounds of observation and reflection on feeling and perception. What we have witnessed is an onto-genesis of various feelings and dispositions under a fundamental conception of self, which presents itself in the practice and performance of virtues. I shall call this Chinese metaphysics "onto-generative metaphysics of human self" (*ziwo benti xingshangxue* 自我本体形上学)[1] in distinction from the ontological metaphysics or simply ontology of the Greek kind.

CHUNG-YING CHENG, Professor, Department of Philosophy, University of Hawaii at Manoa. Specialties: Confucianism and Neo-Confucianism, hermeneutics/onto-hermeneutics, philosophy of language. E-mail: ccheng@hawaii.edu

Journal of Chinese Philosophy, Supplement to Volume 37 (2010) 142–158
© 2010 Journal of Chinese Philosophy

In this article I shall describe how Confucianism has formed an important notion of the onto-generative self in terms of reflective internalization of virtues into the nature of the human person. It will be suggested that it is through the interplay of the function of mind as cognitive ability and heart as affective ability in response to the outside world. It is on the basis of this interplay that the classical Confucian philosophy gradually comes to a full exploration of mind in a deep experiential understanding of the mind in the human person or human self. We could see such a process in the received texts of the writings of Confucius and his school up to Mencius and even to Xunzi, but how this process took place and found its way has only become evident with the possession of recently excavated texts.

I. SELF AND VIRTUE IN THE *ANALECTS*

If there is one word which can characterizes the essence of Confucius's teaching, it must be the word "*ren* 仁." For Confucius, *ren* must be a force both presenting and defining *dao* in the world and an ability and vision arising from oneself and therefore a virtue conceived as acquired or inherited from the *dao*. There are several occasions that Confucius comes to creatively define *ren* either directly or indirectly. In almost all the statements Confucius speaks of a person or a superior man as having *ren* in reference to his behavior or conduct with other people, but there are three statements that address the activities of *ren* by addressing the subject "self" (*ji* 己) and the subject "myself" (*wo* 我) which is the self that anyone can experience. This amounts to defining *ren* in terms of powerful internal activities that are exhibited in feelings or attitudes in the self.

Thus Confucius twice speaks of "己所不欲勿施與人。(For anything any self does not wish for his self [or herself] he or she will not wish for others.)"[2] Next, he speaks of a benevolent person as "己欲立而立人，己欲達而達人。(In wishing to establish oneself any self would wish others to establish themselves, in wishing to reach for an end oneself any self would wish others to reach for an end.)"[3] The reference to a self is also manifest in speaking of "克己復禮為仁。一日克己復禮，天下歸仁焉。為仁由己，而由人乎哉。(To subdue one's self and return to propriety, is perfect virtue. If a man can for one day subdue himself and return to propriety, all under heaven will ascribe perfect virtue to him. Is the practice of perfect virtue from a man himself, or is it from others?)"[4] In these three statements Confucius refers to a human self who is a subject of desiring, wishing, and willing and who is capable of controlling himself to do or not do something, in this case not to impose on others what he does not wish or desire for himself. Being capable of restraining himself makes it possible to practice and perform rituals (*li* 禮) in relating to others, and this is necessary for a society to function harmoniously.

Finally, we come to the most significant statement "子曰：仁遠乎哉？我欲仁，斯仁至矣。(The Master said, "Is virtue a thing remote? I wish to be virtuous, and lo! Virtue is at hand.")[5] Here we see that *ren* is not only an object and goal of one's will and desire, but it is this desire and will that we can call *ren*. The statement identifies the human self in such a way that anyone can call forth and experience *ren* at will. We can see that the language conveys the meaning of the I (*wo* 我) as an active force that can bring out what is felt inside oneself because it is its own hidden or deep identity. With this said we may say that for Confucius, humanity is individualized in human persons but all individual persons have in themselves an identity that wishes to relate and identify with others. This is expressed in the negative wish and will of a person to not harm others as well as the positive wish to help others, as *ren* can be experienced and willed by any human self reflectively. It is in his insight and insistence on this wish and will to relate to others that he sees the rise of virtues from *ren*.

For what is a virtue if it is not what is already rooted in the human self or humanity of the self? In this connection we must point out the relevance of *zhong* 忠 and *shu* 恕. As an intuitive understanding we can see that *zhong* is a matter of integrity and loyalty to oneself, and thus the capacity to think of others as myself. On the other hand we can see *shu* as a matter of sympathy and empathy with others so that one can think of myself as others or in others' place. These two constitute what we may call the reciprocity between the self and others so that we can derive rules of no harm (the Silver Principle) and the rules of benefit (the Golden Principle) the conjunction of, which constitutes the concretization of the *ren* as a feeling and will. It is only when the virtue becomes concretized in rules of action that the internal source of *ren* becomes externalized in action. In fact, as Confucius sees it, *ren* must be the root and source of all virtues or any virtues that have to arise in humans dealing with others. The practice of *ren* leads to many different virtues addressing various circumstances and this process of implementing *ren* makes it possible to say and project *ren* as a perfect virtue

(This grounding in the human self) could be eventually identified with the mind and nature of the human person. (While an examination of these topics is beyond scope of this article, we can note one example) where important aspects of *xin* 心 (heart-mind) are revealed, when Confucius says, "At seventy I let my heart pursue what it likes (*cong xin suoyu* 從心所欲) and it would not trespass any rules of right (而不逾矩)."[6] Zhu Xi sees this statement as indicating that one lets go one's heart-mind and yet one still will naturally attain a state of virtue.[7] It is obvious that *xin* has the status of feeling which may respond to anything within or without the human self, and yet it has the function of desiring and liking on its own strength which may have to do what one decides to do or what not to do. Here we can see that *xin* can be in a state of freedom or free action which may be at the same time result from education and self-discipline.

In light of what Confucius has said about the process of moral growth, this state of freedom of heart-mind is better seen as a result of self-discipline, reflective experience, and deep knowledge embodying emergent awareness of the *tianming* 天命 (mandate of heaven) in one's life. Based on this observation, one can see how this freedom of *xin* is also an exhibition of the regulation (*ming*) of heaven and that is also the reason why it cannot trespass any rule of right. From grasping this single statement in the Analects, we have come to grasp a deep understanding of *xin*, namely *xin* as a feeling which is capable of grasping the law of heaven. But *xin* is still basically our ability to feel and respond to the world and a capacity to know the world in terms of both unity and multiplicity of things. *Xin* can be also seen as embodying the principle of active realization of the human self in the context and process of interaction with other things and people who have an internal structure of heart-mind. It is also significant to see that we can feel what we know and we can also come to know what we feel so that we may decide to act more efficiently and more consistently and this is hidden function of heart-and-mind as *yu* 欲 as *zhi* 志 or desire-will. Confucius thus speaks of "*boxue duozhi* 博學篤志 to learn wide and to be sincere in one's will"[8] and "*bu jiang qi zhi* 不降其志 not to surrender one's will.[9]

II. Distinction between Internal and External in the *Wu Xing Pian*

The discovery of silk and bamboo manuscripts such as the *Wu Xing Pian*〈五行〉(WXP henceforth) and the *Xing Zi Ming Chu*〈性自命出〉(XZMC henceforth)[10] provide us a clue as to how the theory of self-cultivation develops after Confucius. But no texts simply speak for themselves without a coherent preunderstanding and a coherent post-understanding. Without deep reflective understanding of Confucius, we cannot come to see how these texts are to be properly interpreted, nor how they could have given rise to received Confucian

texts such as the *Da Xue*《大學》and the *Zhong Yong*《中庸》. Thus the
above analysis of Confucian concepts of self provides a framework for
raising questions and orienting responses and answers in the silk and
bamboo texts we are to consider. Given the Confucian reflection and
expression in the Analects, it is clear that Confucius left unanswered
a few essential questions regarding nature and virtue, the source and
origin of nature and mind, how virtues must be rooted in one's nature,
and whether human nature can be regarded as good or bad.

In the 1973 Silk Manuscripts later titled *Wu Xing* or *Wu Xing Pian*
〈五行篇〉we find that some attempts have been made by early Confucians, possibly the first generation disciples of Confucius, to answer
the question of how virtues could be said to arise from internality and
activity of the human self. The main tone of the text is to stress the
function and process of how virtues arise internally in a person so that
he could be said to be genuinely virtuous.[11] In light of this tone, these
texts may have been developed by the first generation of Confucian
disciples and continued by their own disciples or disciples of their
disciples. In the following I shall use the *Boshu Wu Xing*《帛書五行》
(Silk Text of the *Wu Xing*) text as the main reference although I also
consult the *zhushu* 竹書 (bamboo texts) in a few places.

As regarding the merits and demerits of the two texts, I have
generally agreed with Pang Pu and Liang Tao in taking the *Boshu* text
as more primary and treating the *Zhushu* text as an attempt to reno-
vate some parts of the *Boshu*.[12]

This difference of time is shown, in my view, in the *Boshu* order of
virtues as *ren zhi yi li sheng* 仁智義禮聖, in contradistinction from the
Zhushu order of virtues as *ren yi li zhi sheng* 仁義禮智聖, which
obviously is a more recent ordering. Philosophically, *ren* and *zhi* are a
more primary polarity than *ren* and *yi*. The former forms a primary
polarity in the sense that if one has no *ren* or no *zhi* then we would
not have a whole virtue. This idea has not been fully worked out
but is clearly indicated in Confucius's idea of "*zhi ji ren shou*
知及仁守" (The knowledge has reached an end and takes benevolence
to preserve it).[13] But the contrast between *ren* and *yi* is matter of
realization of virtue in action in concrete circumstances. All other
virtues are determinates of the determinable *ren*. *Zhi* in the primary
sense is the condition of *ren* as a whole virtue just as *ren* in the primary
sense is the condition of *zhi* (in *zhi* 智) as a whole virtue. Here we have
a primary sense of unity of *ren* and *zhi* as two aspects of the whole
virtue which we may call *renzhi* 仁智 or *zhiren* 智仁.

There is no denial that one could be virtuous in action without such
internal motivation because one's virtuous action could be simply
explained as a matter of following the rules of propriety. The distinction between these two sorts of virtuous action is obviously important

because we can see that in Confucius there are two grounds and reasons for the performance of virtues. One ground and reason is that there is *li* 禮 (rules of propriety) and we could follow the *li* in showing our virtue. Li is the external restraint which has been institutionally established to create orderly behavior of people in a society. The practice of *li* can be traced to Xia 夏 people who worshipped ghosts and spirits with sacrificial rites which became the source of *li*. In this sense one could speak of "*yue zhi yi li* 約之以禮 (restrained by *li*)" or "齊之以禮 (uniformed by *li*)."[14] However, although *li* is established as an external restraint, for Confucius it is only a partial requirement for virtuous action of *ren* 仁, which consists in an internal action of the human self in overcoming one's desires or prejudices called *keji* 克己 (disciplining oneself). This no doubt leads to a contrast between the externality of *li* and the internality of *ren*.

In speaking of *ren* as "*keji fuli* 克己復禮" as we have seen earlier, Confucius stresses the fact that the virtue of *ren* is from oneself (*ji* 己), not from others, and that *ren* must result from overcoming one's desires and prejudices, leading to the practice of *li*. As to how an individual overcomes his desires and prejudices Confucius did not elaborate but one can see that for a person to practice the restraining of self one has to remove from one's mind and heart those desires and prejudices which prevent the performance of *li*. One could be forced to do so, but it can be a matter of voluntary choice and even a decision of the individual's will to discipline oneself for the purpose of performing *li*. Whether passive or active, the internal action of self-discipline and self-restraint is required and thus the virtue of acting out *ren* and even the virtue of following the *li* must involve an internal action of the human self or the human mind. But this explanation of *ren* does not vitiate the fact that one can still perform the virtuous action of *li* without the conjunction of an action from one's mind. In that case one can see that the performance of *li* has the merit of performing a virtue from external cause but does not have the merit of performing it from both the external and internal sources.

Because of this distinction it was natural for the Confucian disciples to make a distinction between performance of a virtue from a source in oneself and performance of a virtue from an external cause. As the author of the WXP calls the virtue formed from inside oneself action of virtue (*de zhi xing* 德之行), and he calls a virtue not performed from inside a person just performance or action (*xing* 行), we can see that he has affirmed the virtue formed from inside a self to be a genuine virtue without denying that the virtue not so formed could be also a virtue. Thus it is an open question whether an action of *li* is an action of virtue or not.

Consider the following inceptive content of the Wu Xing Pian:

仁形於內謂之德之行，不形於內謂之行。義形於內謂之德之行，不形
於內謂之行。禮形於內謂之德之行，不形於內謂之行。智形於內謂之
德之行，不形於內謂之行。聖形於內謂之德之行，不形於內謂之德之
行。

德之行五，和謂之德，四行和謂之善。善，人道也。德，天道也。君
子亡中心之憂則亡中心之智，亡中心之智則亡中心之悅，無中心之悅
則不安，不安則不樂，不樂則亡德。

五行皆形於內而時行之，謂之君子。士有志于君子之道謂之志士。
善，弗為無近；德。弗之不成；智，弗思不得；思，不清不識。思
不長不形，不形不安，不安不樂，不樂亡德。

"When the *ren* is formed from within [a person], it is called the action
of virtue; if it is not formed from within, it is called action. When the
yi is formed from within, it is called the action of virtue; if it is not
formed from within, it is called action. When the *li* is formed from
within, it is called the action of virtue; if it is not formed from within,
it is called action. When the *zhi* is formed from within, it is called the
action of virtue; if it is not formed from within, it is called action.
When the *sheng* is formed from within, it is called the action of virtue;
if it is not formed from within, it is called action." (My translation)

"There are five types of action of virtue, when they form a harmony,
[together they] are called the virtue. If four types of action form a
harmony, [together they] are called good (*shan*). Good is the way of
man. Virtue (*de*) is the way of heaven. When a *junzi* (cultivated man)
does not have worry in his mind, he would also not have wisdom in
his mind. Once he does not have wisdom in his mind, he would not
have joy in his heart. Without joy in his heart, he would become
uneasy. Once uneasy, he would be unhappy. If unhappy, then there is
no virtue." (My translation)

"When five actions are formed from within [a person] and they are
practiced from time to time, this type of person is called *junzi* (a
cultivated man). If a *shi* (a man of position) is devoted to the *dao* of
the *junzi*, he is called a *zhishi* (man of position with moral aspiration). Good is such that if one does not act on it one would not get
close to it; virtue is such that if one does not reach for it, one would
not accomplish it; wisdom is such that if one does not think on it, one
would not attain it. Thinking (*si*) is such that if one is not clear about
it, one would not recognize it. Thinking is such that if one does not
concentrate on it long, one will not form it. If one does not form a
thinking (a settled an idea of a value), one will feel uneasy. Once
uneasy, one would be unhappy. If unhappy, there is no virtue." (My
translation)[15]

The author has here introduced the distinction between internal and
noninternal for all five virtues, namely *ren*, *yi*, *li*, *zhi*, and *sheng*. The
first puzzle is how *ren* could be formed not from inside oneself. To
solve this, one has to see action of *ren* as an action which can be
described as *ren* but which may lack the internal motivation or

sourcing. Thus a person may act as if thinking not to impose on others what he does not want others to impose on him, but in reality he is acting not according to such a golden principle, but out of a conspiracy for his future gain. In other words, how we recognize the moral meaning of an action has to depend on the presence of a moral intention or a moral rule as motivating force for the action.

A second puzzle is how other virtues are related to *ren* so that they can be considered genuine actions of virtue. The answer is to be found in Confucius, who takes *ren* as the root and foundational virtue and sees other virtues as grounded in and grow out of *ren*. For example, he says that a *ren* person must have courage but not vice versa. *Yi* is to do things right and righteous and it certainly requires a concern for fairness or justice in treating a person in relation to society. Hence it involves an internal consideration of mind as to how to act right and righteous. For *li*, it has been shown above regarding how *li* could be performed with willingness and positive affirmation from the mind heart of a person, instead of just blindly following a taboo. As to *zhi*, it is clear that we have to distinguish genuine action of wisdom and knowledge of the right versus wrong from just hitting the right path by luck.

When we come to the virtue of *sheng*, we see that Confucius treats *sheng* as even larger or higher virtue than *ren*. For he replies to Zigong's question on the moral value of the action of "博施於民，而能濟眾，。。。。。。何事於仁，必也聖乎？ (Widely give benefits to people, and thus can help people . . . It is not just a matter of *ren*, but must it be also a matter of being a sage?)"[16] A person has the virtue of *ren* if he treats everyone with *ren*, but if he is capable of treating all the people with *ren* and making *ren* effect the actual result of preserving life and helping all the people, his *ren* would qualify for being *sheng*, a person who is perfect in *ren* and who benefits all people. There then arises a more difficult puzzle: if a person can do this without any moral motivation in him, can we still withhold the title of virtue from him? Or perhaps there is no person who can achieve such a result without have intention and motivation to benefit others? Perhaps it is for this reason the author of the *Wu Xing Pian* Chapter speaks of five internal virtues in harmony and only four external actions in harmony which have the effect of virtues. *Sheng* itself cannot be imagined to be an unmotivated virtue as many results have to be demanded from *sheng*.

It is also interesting to see that the author of the *Wu Xing Pian* has proposed an analysis of the internal process of moral motivation for a genuine virtue. He says: 君子亡中心之憂則亡中心之智，亡中心之智則亡中心之悅，無中心之悅則不安，不安則不樂，不樂則亡德。 (When a *junzi* (cultivated

man) does not have worry in his mind, he would also not have wisdom
in his mind. Once he does not have wisdom in his mind, he would not
have joy in his heart. Without joy in his heart, he would become
uneasy. Once uneasy, he would be unhappy. If unhappy, then there is
no virtue.)[17] What he sees is that the moral agent must do his action
from an intrinsic joy (*yue* 悦) of doing this, for without this intrinsic
joy he cannot feel easy and well and thus may not achieve and
perform his virtue. For the *junzi* 君子, this intrinsic joy is to be actually
derived from his concern and care *you* 憂 for people so that he has to
deliberate *zhi* 智 as to what to do, and hence in doing his virtuous
action, he can be said well motivated.

That a person can come to take people and others as his concern
and care is what makes him a *junzi*. This concern and care for
people would then stir the heart-and-mind of the person to find a
way of action which would relieve his concern and care. This is then
his disposition to act according to *ren* and he would act with intrinsic joy because he would find that it befits his nature and heart-and-
mind. One may ask what initial power could make a person actually
concerned with and care for people. Again the answer is subtly suggested in the text: it is based on nature or heaven and from this
point of view we can call these five virtues internally motivated the
virtues the ways of heaven (*tian dao* 天道). This sense of the virtue
de 德 is distinguished from actions of *shan* 善 (good) which are not
internally formed actions. This means that actions of *shan* must be
judged as results of action or as actions conforming to an outer rule
of *li* 禮.

We can also consider the difference between *de* and *shan* from
the meaning of the word *de* also understood as *de* 得 (gained). We
may say that the five internally formed virtues are what a *junzi*
has gained or derived from *tiandao* or *tian* 天, whereas the four
actions of good can be so considered. But how a *junzi* has gained
and been derived virtues from heaven remains unanswered in the
text. However, it we take consideration of *Zhong Yong*, it is clear
that the virtues must derive from our nature *xing* 性 because our
nature is endowed with roots of virtue by heaven. This shows that
the text could play a role of leading Zisi to the development of
Zhong Yong as answer to the question of the relation of virtues
between the human person and heaven. It is in *Zhong Yong* that we
find the notion of nature brought out explicitly and defined by reference to the order of heaven. In other words, *Zhong Yong* has
answered the question of *de* in distinction from *shan* by pointing to
the endowment from heaven in the nature of man. Because we do
not have any indication of this sort in the WXP text, it might contain
earlier discussions before a final understanding is achieved. This in a

way justifies my suspicion that *Wu Xing Pian* could be an earlier work than *Zhong Yong*.

On the other hand, the externally followed actions that may be regarded as virtuous in so far as they do produce a result of good, we may simply call them actions of *shan*, which reflect the way of man, on the condition that they harmonize with each other. The way of man refers to institutional regulations of *li* which are invented by sage-kings and observed by convention. But there is some reason to think that those actions of good may not be harmonious. Thus this wording "*sixing he* 四行和" from the second paragraph of the *Wu Xing Pian* text of the above actually suggests the harmony of the four actions of good as a whole. Similarly when the *Wu Xing Pian* speaks of the five internally formed virtues as *he* 和, the author is addressing the totality and harmony of the five virtues as a whole. This distinction between *de* and *shan* here also suggests a distinction between motivation and consequence of moral action.

This distinction also appears in how the WXP author defines a virtuous man (*junzi*) in distinction from a *zhishi* 志士. He says "五行皆形於內而時行之， 謂之君子。 ("When five actions are formed from within [a person] and they are practiced from time to time, this type of person is called *junzi* (a cultivated man).")" This of course summarizes what Confucius has said about *junzi* in the Analects. A *junzi* is therefore a virtuous person who is motivated to cultivate the way of *junzi* from his heart-mind or his self. But a person who has the will to reach for virtue *de* so that the *de* can be actualized is called a *zhishi*. The difference for the *zhishi* is that he has yet to do good from his heart even though he has practiced good. As we can see, in either case thinking and feeling (including feeling of joy) have to be present in mind. This again indicates that the human mind has to be actively involved for generating a willingness and disposition to act in a virtuous way, that is, developing a motivation rooted inside oneself for performing the virtue. It is interesting that the notion of human nature *xing* 性 is not suggested or proposed. This may indicate an early origin of this text when the discussion of human nature was not yet focused, even though the need for a concept of nature is deeply felt.

As to how virtues are to be actually formed in the *xin* 心 of a person, we have seen how the author of the text refers to misgiving (*you* 憂) as the beginning of the process of formation of virtue. With *you* one comes to *zhi* which reflects on the *you* for some possible solution (hence I like to explain the term *zhi* 智 not only as broadly wisdom but specifically as insightfulness) and this gives rise to an intrinsic joy (*yue*) of heart so that one may say that one has gained and developed virtue *de* as a potential power. This process is certainly

vividly true of our reflective experience for resolving an anxious
problem of life. Once we have such a problem we have to look in our
mind for a way-out and when we get a way-out, we not only come to
know what to do but we experience a certain joy at the same time. This
means that we can carry out an imaginary experiment or recall our
own experience on making decisions on some life problem and therefore come to understand experientially what the author has in mind in
making his point. He points out that if we do not have insight we shall
have no joy and remain unsettled or anxious in front of our problem
and this will make us unhappy (*bule* 不樂). This again suggests that *de*
is living experience of what we have gained and knowing what to do.
It involves *zhi* 智 as a component or even as a predetermining force of
the *de*. We may of course consider a well-formed habit of this sort as
a settled *zhi* and hence a disposition to act accordingly. Hence the
meaning of *de* need not be innate but acquired.

The author of the text then speaks of a more concrete process for
the formation of the virtues.[18] He refers to the process of thinking
(*si* 思) in mind as a differentiating factor for various different virtues.
Thus he speaks of the *si* of *ren* as pure (*qing* 清), of the *si* of *zhi* as
lengthy, of the *si* of *sheng* as light. The question is whether we already
have the stuff of those basic virtues for us to think through. We know
from Confucius that *ren* arises in us as a spontaneous sense of care
and concern. It can be identified with our feeling for others even in
spite of myself.[19] It can even be conceived as based on our experience
of our filial love for our parents and natural regard for our siblings.
Other virtues may arise in some forms of feelings of concern, sometimes with a strong awareness of an objective situation. Hence we
would have the basic concerns for the five virtues in its inceptive form
of concerns (*you*). As to the most outstanding virtue of *sheng* (all
salient and all caring) it may be said to be a state of mind which is
devoted to searching for ways of solving all problems for all the
people. The thinking process for formation of a virtue of *sheng* is
described as "*qing* 清."

Why is so described is not clear, but one may conjecture that the
qing could be like in the case of *ren*, or it may implicitly refer to a light
type of *qi* which moves to become sky. The paragraph then moves on
to a deeper sense of understanding and subtle openness toward all the
people. It is still *ren* but *ren* as perfected.

In moving from chapters of 7 and 8 to 10, 11, and 12 of the *Zhujian*
《竹簡》 we see an attempt of describing the feeling process in forming
other virtues such as *yi* and *li*, the obscurities of which seem to incur
Xunzi's criticism as "*piyuan er wulei* 僻遠而無類 marginal, remote
and not belonging to any proper category."[20] I believe that this is an
experimental way of thinking in order to give a psychological internal

basis for understating the formation of different qualities of different virtues. They may not tell us anything conceptually significant but the process of searching is indicative of active thinking toward finding a theory of explaining the internality and internal-origins of the virtues.

We may indeed call these internal virtues as *ren*-oriented in order to contrast the *li*-oriented virtues which are externally shaped. The reason that the internal virtues are *ren*-oriented is that *ren* is what Confucius takes to be rooted and springing from himself on his own desire as explained in earlier part. Any virtue which is to be seen as formed inside must come up like *ren* whenever one desires to do so. On the other hand, to experience *ren* may not necessarily be determined by will. If so it would be Kantianism, namely to address something called free will which would act on a motto of morality or which must legislate for any action to be taken by the agent. It seems clear that for Confucius *ren* is a feeling or sentiment of one's regard and care for others. It is said that "When a root is established, the way will be a generated. Are filial piety and fraternal respect basis for the *ren*?"[21] This observation is correct in so far as once we find a natural relation founded on a natural feeling, it is natural to extend this feeling or to call up this feeling with regard to similar cases. In this sense *ren* can be seen as a feeling one may naturally have for people in general or for any one who is not one's family.

There is therefore an element of feeling which arises from a natural situation, and there is also an element of will which requires determination and devotion to extend it and make it applicable to a similar and enlarged case. In this sense we can see all and each of virtues as being rooted in something called human nature or humanity which become specialized and differentiated in responses to different situations and with regard to different relationships. In this sense we can see how *ren* can be the base, motive, and ground for arising of other virtues as feelings differentiated by objective circumstances. In this fashion we can speak of *yi* (righteousness), *zhi* (wisdom), *li* (propriety) and *xin* (trustworthiness) or *sheng* (sageliness, or perfect benevolence and care for people) as *ren*-based and oriented virtues. The *Wu Xing Pian* article may find other occasions and chain reactions for the arising of these end virtues. But there does not seem to have any pattern or order on how feeling of a virtue is to be aroused. However, when we speak of these virtues, a definitive content from our understanding has arisen from our experience of an occasion and a feeling.

On the other hand, we have to examine how *li*-oriented virtues are to be conceived without reference to any internal feelings for the author of the *Wu Xing Pian* chapter. It is clear that they can arise as obedience and observation of a *li* rule or a law which are external to a person in a community. We may call those *li* rules basis for creating the virtuous actions of a person and the person may follow these rules as a habit or as a command. Thus we may have rules of *li* which command actions of *ren, yi, li,* and *zhi*. We must notice that there is no rule of *li* which could command the action of a *shengren* 聖人 as it is by understanding that a *shengren* is a person who can do all actions virtuously from inside himself but not from outside. There is in fact another reason for *sheng* being not ruled by *li* as simply rule of action. The system of *li* is supposed to be instituted by *shengren* as argued by Xunzi. In instituting *li* system for regulating and harmonizing a society of people the *shengren* has to deeply think through and feel through all occasions of humanity. If we want our *li* rules to be effectively applicable, it must be based on our knowledge of things in the world so that we can tell how people normally function so that we could find ways to govern them for their ends as well as for the ends of governance. In order to devise *li* the sage has to inquire and know inclinations and temperaments and emotions of people by observation and comparison. Knowing this way or that way is to reach for the *li* 理 or order/principle of things[22] and this may eventually becomes a matter of achieving a unity among all collected cases and items for understanding. In this regard, it is also obvious that Neo-Moists and Xunzi's doctrine of learning and knowing from experiences and examples are heeded. Specifically we have to know people by seeing them ("*mu er zhizhi* 目而知之").[23]

The next question is how people come to follow them. The *Wu Xing Pian* Chapter has a paragraph describing how the external *li* could become internalized because they could be appreciated, liked and enjoyed by the people who follow them:

聞君子道，聰也。聞而知之，聖也。聖人知天道也。知而行之，義也。行之而時，德也。見賢人，明也。見而知之，智也。知而安之，仁也。安而敬之，禮也。聖，知禮樂之所由生也，五行之和也。和則樂，樂則有德，有德則邦家舉。[24]

"To hear about the *dao* of the *junzi* is a matter of acuity. To come to know from hearing is a matter of sageliness. The sage knows about the way of heaven. He knows and also practice it, that is righteousness. To practice it timely, it is a matter of the virtue. To see those who are worthy of seeing is clarity. To meet the worthy and come to recognize him is a matter of wisdom. To know and feel settled is a matter of *ren*. To feel settled and harbor a feeling of respect is a matter of *li* Sage is one who knows origins for *li* and *le* (rites and music) and this amounts to the harmony of the five powers. Being harmonious, music ensues. Once there being the music, there is virtue. Once there being virtue, family and state will flourish." (My translation)[25]

The sage is keen to know the *li* rule by knowing the way of heaven and therefore to practice and make it a matter of natural response.

In this sense the sage can be said to internalize the *li* and in fact it is due to an internalization of his knowledge of the way of heaven that he could design the *li* rules for people to follow. Thus it is said that the sage knows how *li* and *yue* are generated. He knows this because he embodies these and experiences their harmony (*wu xing he* 五行和) and respect them. He further enjoyed them because of their harmony and takes this to his heart and makes this a virtue from him. He has thus reached his *de* from his knowledge. With his virtue he would be able to uphold his family and his state. Of course we may also presume that an average person could learn the *li* rules created and experienced by the sage and practice it and feel it in his practice and enjoyed the communicated feelings of joy from the practice. In time *li* could also become a part of himself and therefore we may come to see how an average person could also acquired the virtue *de*.

We may now review what the *Wu Xing Pian* article has proposed in its theory of distinction between two types of virtues: the internally generated and the externally generated (noninternally generated). The former has to go through a process of thinking or reflection and the latter must be derived from observation of things. What is not clearly stated in the former in such an account is what sort of objects are to be reflected on in order that they may become internalized dispositions of actions which we will call the actions of virtue *de zhi xing* 德之行. What is missing in the latter account is how knowledge from observation could become basis for formulating rules of *li* which prescribe virtuous action. It is clear that the former account has to assume that something called feelings (*qing* 情) is the object given to be reflected on (*si* 思) so that one can come to see how it arises and what it means to the human self. One will have to see that certain feelings are basic to humanity and be liked and enjoyed by all human beings. In the text the concern and care or misgiving for people (*you* 憂) is singled out as a basic example of feelings and shown how it leads to the formation of virtue or a willingness to act out in certain way. The *ren* in Confucius can be obviously shown to be a good example of such feeling-based and oriented virtues.

As to the account of *li*-based virtues they are virtues because they are actions of following the *li*. But *li* has to come from some source so that it can be so followed. The text assumes that it is the sage who has learned the *tiandao* to formulate the *li*. But this is again not explicitly stated. *Li* is considered a virtue capable of internally generated but it cannot be generated without knowledge of things and people in the world. Hence we must recognize the source of *li* (rules governing our moral or ought-behavior) from knowledge deliberation a sage has achieved and developed from the world.

The sage may come to know human feelings and needs, and therefore, devise *li* in order to regulate and order their desires and feelings so that they will not result in conflict and chaos. Therefore there is a normalization process of transforming knowledge of people into the *li* rules of action in light of the goal or end of a harmonized and ordered society. This process may also require feeling and insight on the part of the sage so that the sage may be creative of the *li* rules. In fact, the sage being concerned with humanity will see his concern as cause for his seeking a solution in terms of the formation of the *li*. Thus for the sage it should be both internally and externally formulated, but for the common people *li* rules will be first learned and implemented and therefore could become bases and incentives for virtues noninternally formed. However the text seems also to suggest that common people could internalize the rules and thus transforming them into virtues. They may experience feelings and come to see how to act according to *li* is the best solution to a worry and problem of action in a community.

III. APPRAISAL FROM THE PERSPECTIVE OF THE *ANALECTS*

Based on the above conceptual analysis of the WXP, we can see how WXP may have answered some of the difficult questions around the formation of virtues in the Analects, often embodying a reflective and analytic approach in which what is implicit in Confucius's sayings are made clear and explicit. Thus the main issue of distinction made in the WXP between internally formed virtues and externally formed goodness is actually a reflection of the distinction between *ren* and *li* in the Analects. The question therefore is how we may integrate both so that those who have *li* would have *ren* and those who have *ren* would act in accordance with *li*. This may become the motivating issue for the WXP authors, but in order to do this they have to account for how there could be two types of moral action, one as internally formed virtues and the other as externally formed good action. They produce the criteria of internal formation starting with a concern with people and concluding with intrinsic joy of finding a solution.

This distinction is insightful and innovative, and thus contributes to our understanding of the generative internality of virtues. But on the one hand, they ignored the Confucian experience of the explicit subject and self which initiates *ren* and is explicit in the Analects, as we have shown. They failed to see the self-reflexivity of the self. They also failed to analyze the statements of the golden and silver rules of moral action as presupposing an internal generative process of identification of oneself with others and of others with oneself through self-reflexivity, which is a characteristic of mind. While they ultimately come to speak of a mind which has the five senses and feet as its servants, there is yet no recognition of emotions or feelings as natural channels for the expression of mind or nature as we find in Zisi's *Zhong Yong*. However, the efforts of WXP to account for the rise of various virtues such as *sheng*, *ren*, *yi*, and *li* in connection with certain forms of thinking and certain types of feelings are significant. Of course, the idea of human nature is not developed either, and yet it is something that one has to be aware of in order to ascertain the internality of virtues.

As to how *ren* and *li* are integrated, Confucius himself has provided the best answer in the Analects, that is to discipline one's private desires and to perform the *li*, and this, I believe, is his most powerful definition of *ren*. This suggests that virtue has an internal genesis in disciplined desires and yet it reaches for an externality in *li* or ritual form. This also means that there are no genuine virtues apart from such an internal genetic process. But this does not seem to be the conclusion of the WXP, for the authors of WXP, distinction between virtuous actions and actions of good would be acceptable. This, however, needs not to be the position of Confucius who would take *ren* and *li* as necessarily requiring union with each other.

UNIVERSITY OF HAWAII AT MANOA
Honolulu, Hawaii

ENDNOTES

* This article was formed from some selected sections of my lengthy manuscript on Confucian theory of internality and internal onto-genesis of virtues. I wish to warmly thank Professor Franklin Perkins for giving his generous time to reading and reforming the early writing. I also wish to thank Linyu Gu for her detailed copy-editing. down to punctuation. Without their helpful hands, the present appearance would not be possible.

1. I shall not discuss this concept of "*benti xingshangxue*" here as I have addressed this notion in many other places, including my article on *benti* "On the Metaphysical Significance of *Ti* (Body-Embodiment) in Chinese Philosophy: *Benti* (Origin-Substance) and *Ti-Yong* (Substance and Function)" in *Journal of Chinese Philosophy*, 29, no. 2 (2002): 145–161. My purpose is merely to indicate the germination of a *benti* notion of human self in the Confucian philosophy from the very beginning.

2. See *Lunyu*《論語》, 5.12, 12.2, and 15.24. In each there is a descriptive state of one's negative feeling self-state, then it follows a negative normative rule of action. This is a great insight and a rejection of Hume's dictum that one cannot derive ought from is or ought-not from is-not by broad implication.

3. See *Lunyu* (Analects) 6.30.

4. Ibid., 12.1.

5. See *Lunyu* 7.30.

6. Ibid., 2.4.

7. See Zhu Xi's *Si Shu Ji Zhu*《四書集注》in corresponding chapter and section.

8. Ibid., 19.6.

9. Ibid., 18.8.

10. The bamboo manuscript known as Xing Zi Ming Chu is contained in the excavated texts of Kuodian in 1993 and the bought excavated texts of Shanghai Metropolitan Museum 1997. I shall not deal with issues of XZMC in this article but will treat those issues in a sequel to this article.

11. Here I do not wish to explore into the issues of the dating and authenticity or even the authorship of this article, as this text is well established as an authentic text dated before 350 BCE. Historians of Chinese thought such as Pang Pu has first called attention to the importance of this text in connection with the Xunzi's critique of Zisi and Mengzi on this doctrine of the *Wu Xing Pian*. By discovering this text, now we know what Xunzi refers to when he condemns this doctrine in his famous article *Fei Shier Zi* (Refutation of the 12 Schools of Thought)〈非是二子〉We come to generally accept that this text could result from writings of disciples of Zisi if not Zisi himself. For all these I take no issue as I see that Pang Pu's explanation is well reasoned and perhaps remains the best explanation we have had. In fact the title of the text *Wu Xing Pian* is given by Pang Pu, in his well-known article. See his article "*Boshu Wu Xing Pian Jiaozhu* 帛書五行篇校注," in *Zhuhua Wenshi Luncong* 《中華文史論叢》," Vol. 4 (Shanghai: Shanghai Guji Publisher, 1979).

12. For Pang Pu, see reference in endnote 15. For Liang Tao, see Chapter 4 Section 2 of his book in Chinese titled《郭店竹简与思孟学派》(Bamboo Manuscripts in Guodian and Si-Meng School) (Beijing: Renmin University Press, 2008), 208–218.

13. *Lunyu*, 15.33.

14. See *Lunyu* 6.27 and *Lunyu* 2.3, respectively.

15. See Mawangdui Silk Manuscripts *Wu Xing Pian* 《五行篇》 as emended and annotated by Pang Pu's "*Zhubo Wuxing Pain Jiaozhu ji Yanjiu* 竹帛五行篇校注及研究" in *Pan Pu Wenji* 《庞朴文集》(Collected Papers of Pang Pu), Vol. 2 (Taipei: 万卷楼图书有限公司, 2000), 117–151.

16. Ibid., 6.30.

17. This is from the second paragraph of the Wu Xing Pian as quoted and translated on page 22.

18. I refer primarily to the next four strips of WXP after the first three of the Guodian Zhujian where notions of qualities of thinking *qing* 清 (purity), *zhang* 長 (duration), and *qing* 轻 (lightness) are introduced for characterizing degrees of virtuousness of virtues of *ren* 仁 \ *zhi* 智 \ *sheng* 聖.

19. This is what Mencius would call "the heart of unbearable feeling toward people (or even animals) in suffering" (*bur en ren zhi xin* 不忍人之心).

20. See Book of Xunzi essay 6 "Fei Shi-er Zi" (Refutation of the 12 Schools of Thought), as seen in texts of Xunzi Reader 荀子读本 (Taipei: Sanmin Publishers, 1977), 105. One must also note the other two further criticisms of Zisi and Mencius: "幽隐而无说" (obscure, hidden, and having no argument) and "闭约而无解" (closed, shortcut, and bearing no explanation).

21. *Lunyu*, 1.1.

22. Chapter 21 of the *Zhujian* text.

23. Chapter 23 of the *Zhujian* text. Pang Pu takes this word as a loan from *mou* 侔. See Pang Pu, "*Boshu Wu Xing Pian Jiaozhu*," 85. But I doubt and want to keep it as 目, because 目 as a verb of seeing makes better sense. In the *Zhujian* it reads as "*jian er zhi zhi* 見而知之." This says we have to know things directly by viewing them and by comparative analogies (*yu* 喻 and *pi* 譬) and by micro-inspection; this also is "*ji er zhi zhi* 幾而知之 (to see small beginnings of things)" that also requires viewing while other ways of knowing are by analogy and examples.

24. Chapter 18 of the *Zhujian*.

25. Notice here the pun or ambiguity of the term *le* 乐 which refers to music and the feeling state of happiness which gives rise to music. It could be the music which, when performed, invoke happiness in the heart of people. But my translation of "*bule* 不乐" in an early portion of the Wu Xing Pian on page 22 is "unhappy," for it cannot be *wule* 无乐. This implies that there is an unhappy feeling state of people from which no happy and harmonious music would arise.

JOURNAL OF CHINESE PHILOSOPHY

The *Journal of Chinese Philosophy* is an anonymous peer-reviewed philosophical journal devoted to the study of Chinese philosophy and Chinese thought in all their phases and stages of development and articulation.

In our view there are three main efforts among recent studies of Chinese philosophy which merit specific mention. First, there is an attempt to make available important philosophical materials (in careful translation) from the history of Chinese philosophy, which constitute a contribution to the scholarly understanding of Chinese philosophy in its original form. Second, there is an attempt to make appropriate interpretations and expositions in Chinese philosophy, which constitute a contribution to the theoretical understanding of Chinese philosophy in its truth claims. Third, there is an attempt to make comparative studies within a Chinese philosophical framework or in relation to schools of thought in the Western tradition, which constitutes a contribution to the critical understanding of Chinese philosophy and its values. All three efforts will be recognized and incorporated in this journal as fundamental ingredients. To better articulate these efforts, we wish to emphasize in this journal employment of critical and rigorous methodology of analysis, organization, and synthesis, for we believe that Chinese philosophy, including those parts which have been labeled mystical, can be intelligently examined, discussed, and communicated. We will thus aim at clear and cogent presentation of ideas, arguments, and conclusions. We will honor creative work in Chinese philosophy—for we ask imagination as well as scholarship in our approach to various aspects and dimensions of Chinese philosophy.

As a summary statement of the intended comprehensive scope of this Journal, we shall mention four major historical periods and five major fields of discipline in Chinese philosophy. The four major historical periods are Classical Chinese Philosophy in Pre-Qin and Han Eras, Neo-Daoism and Chinese Buddhism, Chinese Neo-Confucianism, and Modern and Contemporary Chinese Philosophy since the nineteenth century. The five major fields of discipline are Chinese Logic and Scientific Thinking, Chinese Metaphysical Theories, Chinese Moral Philosophy and Philosophy of Religion, Chinese Art Theories and Aesthetics, and Chinese Social and Political Philosophies. We hope that a cross fertilization of these periods and fields will yield a still greater wealth of insight and ideas on nature, life, society, government, and human destiny.

Contributions are now invited in the above fields and from those who take a serious interest in Chinese philosophy and Chinese thought regardless of their orientation. Short and critical reviews are welcome. Special attention will be given to articles dealing with narrow topics with broad significance. In the future, plans will be made for organizing issues on specifically prescribed topics of contemporary interest.

Submissions are to be compatible with the exact format style as shown in our most recent publications, and please particularly note that a regular article should be limited within 8,000 words, a review essay 5,000 words, and a book review 2,500 words. All submissions are to be sent via e-mail unless advised differently. Please contact Dr. Linyu Gu, Managing Editor of the *Journal*, at linyu@hawaii.edu to obtain detailed guidelines and general policies. Before meeting these primary requirements, a submission may not be available to process.

All submissions and editorial correspondence should be addressed to the editor:

Professor CHUNG-YING CHENG
Editor-in-Chief
Journal of Chinese Philosophy
Department of Philosophy, University of Hawaii
2530 Dole Street, Honolulu, Hawaii 96822, U.S.A.
Tel.: (808) 956-6081
Fax: (808) 956-9228
E-mail: ccheng@hawaii.edu

For books to review and book reviews, please address to:

Professor ON-CHO NG
Associate Editor and Book Review Editor
Journal of Chinese Philosophy
History and Religious Studies, Pennsylvania State University
108 Weaver Building, University Park, Pennsylvania 16802, U.S.A.
Tel.: (814) 863-7703
Fax: (814) 863-7840
E-mail: oxn1@psu.edu

JOURNAL OF CHINESE PHILOSOPHY

EDITOR-IN-CHIEF: CHUNG-YING CHENG, University of Hawaii, *Honolulu*
ASSOCIATE EDITORS: LAUREN PFISTER, Hong Kong Baptist University, *Hong Kong*
ON-CHO NG, Pennsylvania State University, *University Park*
MANAGING EDITOR: LINYU GU, *Journal of Chinese Philosophy, Honolulu*
REVIEW EDITORS: LAUREN PFISTER, Hong Kong Baptist University, *Hong Kong*
ON-CHO NG, Pennsylvania State University, *University Park*
LINYU GU, *Journal of Chinese Philosophy, Honolulu*
FRANKLIN PERKINS, DePaul University, *Chicago*
EUROPEAN REVIEW EDITOR: HANS VAN ESS, University of Munich, *Munich*
ASSISTANT EDITOR: JOHN L. TROWBRIDGE, *Journal of Chinese Philosophy, Honolulu*

EXECUTIVE EDITORIAL COMMITTEE:
CHUNG-YING CHENG (Chairman), University of Hawaii at Manoa, *Honolulu*
LAUREN PFISTER, Hong Kong Baptist University, *Hong Kong*
ON-CHO NG, Pennsylvania State University, *University Park*
JOSEPH GRANGE, University of Southern Maine, *Portland*

LINYU GU, *Journal of Chinese Philosophy, Honolulu*
NICHOLAS BUNNIN, Oxford University, *Oxford*
VINCENT SHEN, University of Toronto, *Toronto*
SHUN KWONG-LOI, Chinese University of Hong Kong, *Hong Kong*
MANYUL IM, Fairfield University, *Fairfield*

EDITORIAL BOARD:
GUENTER ABEL, Berlin Technical University, *Berlin*
ROBERT ALLINSON, Chinese University of Hong Kong, *Hong Kong*
ROGER T. AMES, University of Hawaii, *Honolulu*
STEPHEN C. ANGLE, Wesleyan University, *Middletown*
KARL-OTTO APEL, Frankfurt University, *Frankfurt*
FRIEDERIKE ASSANDRI, University of Heidelberg, *Heidelberg*
RICHARD J. BERNSTEIN, New School for Social Science Research, *New York*
TONGDONG BAI, Fudan University, *Shanghai*
CHEN LAI, Peking University, *Beijing*
ARTHUR DANTO, Columbia University, *New York*
ELIOT DEUTSCH, University of Hawaii, *Honolulu*
WM THEODORE DE BARY, Columbia University, *New York*
FENG JUN, People's University of China, *Beijing*
HERBERT FINGARETTE, University of California at Santa Barbara, *Santa Barbara*
THOMAS FRÖHLICH, University of Erlangen-Nuernberg, *Erlangen*
TOMOHISA IKEDA, Tokyo University, *Tokyo*
XINYAN JIANG, University of Redlands, *Redlands*
WOLFGANG KUBIN, Bonn University, *Bonn*
D. C. LAU, Chinese University of Hong Kong, *Hong Kong*
CHENYANG LI, Central Washington University, *Ellensburg*

SHU-HSIEN LIU, Academia Sinica, *Taipei*
TORNJOERN LODEN, University of Stockholm, *Stockholm*
ALASDAIR MACINTYRE, University of Notre Dame, *Notre Dame*
JOSEPH MARGOLIS, Temple University, *Philadelphia*
ACHIM MITTAG, University of Tuebingen, *Tuebingen*
DONALD MUNRO, University of Michigan, *Ann Arbor*
ROBERT C. NEVILLE, Boston University, *Boston*
DAVID NIVISON, Stanford University, *Stanford*
HEINER ROETZ, Bochum University, *Bochum*
JOHN SMITH, Yale University, *New Haven*
TANG YIJIE, Peking University, *Beijing*
MIKHAIL TITARENKO, Russian Academy of Sciences, *Moscow*
TU WEI-MING, Harvard University, *Cambridge*
SANDRA A. WAWRYTKO, San Diego State University, *San Diego*
HELLMUT WILHELM, University of Washington, *Seattle*
GUENTER WOHLFART, Wuppertal University, *Wuppertal*
DAVID WONG, Duke University, *Durham*
XINZHONG YAO, King's College, *London*
JIYUAN YU, State University of New York at Buffalo, *Buffalo*
YU YING-SHIH, Princeton University, *Princeton*
QIANFAN ZHANG, Peking University, *Beijing*
BROOK ZIPORYN, Northwestern University

JOURNAL OF CHINESE PHILOSOPHY (ISSN 0301-8121 [print], ISSN 1540-6253 [online]) is published quarterly by Wiley Subscription Services, Inc., a Wiley Company, 111 River St., Hoboken, NJ 07030-5774.

Information for Subscribers: For new orders, renewals, sample copy requests, claims, change of address, and all Information on subscribers should appear on a new line. Other subscription correspondence, please contact the Journals Department at your nearest Wiley-Blackwell office.

Subscription Rates for Volume 37, 2010:
Subscription prices for 2010 are: Institutional Print & Online Rate: US$802 (the Americas), US$1,132 (Rest of World), €734 (Europe), £578 (UK). Personal Rate: US$96 (the Americas), £79 (Rest of World), €117 (Europe), £79 (UK).

Prices are exclusive of tax. Australian GST, Canadian GST and European VAT will be applied at the appropriate rates. For more information on current tax rates, please go to www.wiley.com, click on Help and follow the link through to Journal subscriptions. The Premium institutional price includes online access to the current and all online back files to January 1st 1997, where available. For other pricing options, including access information and terms and conditions, please visit www.interscience.wiley.com/journals

Journal Customer Services: For ordering information, claims and any enquiry concerning your journal subscription please go to interscience.wiley.com/support or contact your nearest office:
Americas: E-mail: cs-journals@wiley.com; Tel: +1 781 388 8598 or 1 800 835 6770 (Toll free in the USA & Canada).
Europe, Middle East and Africa: E-mail: cs-journals@wiley.com; Tel: +44 (0) 1865 778315
Asia Pacific: E-mail: cs-journals@wiley.com; Tel: +65 6511 8000
Japan: For Japanese speaking support, Email: cs-japan@wiley.com; Tel: +65 6511 8010 or Tel (toll-free): 005 316 50 480. Further Japanese customer support is also available at http://www.interscience.wiley.com/support
Visit our Online Customer Self-Help available in 6 languages at http://www.interscience.wiley.com/support

Delivery Terms and Legal Title: Prices include delivery of print journal to the recipient's address. Delivery terms are Delivered Duty Unpaid (DDU); the recipient is responsible for paying any import duty or taxes. Legal title passes to the customer on despatch by our distributors.

Back Issues: Back issues are available from cs-journals@wiley.com at the current single issue rate. Earlier issues may be obtained from Periodical Services Company, 11 Main Street, Germantown, NY 12526, USA. Tel +1-518-537-4700, Fax: +1-518-537-5899, E-mail: psc@periodicals.com. **Microform:** The journal is available on microfilm. For microfilm service, address inquiries to University Microfilms International, 300 North Zeeb Road, Ann Arbor, MI 48106-1346, USA.

Mailing: Journal is mailed Standard Rate. Mailing to rest of world by Singapore Post. Postmaster: Send all address changes to *Journal of Chinese Philosophy*, Journal Customer Services, John Wiley & Sons Inc., 350 Main Street, Malden, MA 02148-5020.

Advertising: For information and rates, please visit the journal's website at www.blackwellpublishing.com/jocp, or contact the Academic and Science Advertising Sales Coordinator at corporatesalesusa@wiley.com; 350 Main Street, Malden, MA 02148; Phone: (781) 388-8532; Fax: (781) 338-8532.

Production Editor: Michelle McCauley (email: JOCP@wiley.com). This journal is available online at Wiley InterScience. Visit www3.interscience.wiley.com to search the articles and register for table of contents and e-mail alerts.

Access to this journal is available free online within institutions in the developing world through the AGORA initiative with the FAO, the HINARI initiative with the WHO and the OARE initiative with UNEP. For information, visit www.aginternetwork.org, www.healthinternetwork.org, www.oarescience.org

© 2010 *Journal of Chinese Philosophy*. All rights reserved. With the exception of fair dealing for the purposes of research or private study, or criticism or review, no part of this publication may be reproduced, stored, or transmitted in any form or by any means without prior permission in writing from the copyright holder. Authorization to photocopy items for internal and personal use is granted by the copyright holder for libraries and other users of the Copyright Clearance Center (CCC), 222 Rosewood Drive, Danvers, MA 01923, USA (www.copyright.com), provided the appropriate fee is paid directly to the CCC. This consent does not extend to other kinds of copying for general distribution for advertising or promotional purposes, or for creating new collective works for resale. Special requests should be sent to jrights@wiley.com.

Abstracting and Indexing: Arts & Humanities Citation Index, Current Contents, I B Z-Internationale Bibliographie der Geistes- und Sozialwissenschaftlichen Zeitschriftenliteratur, International Bibliography of the Social Sciences, Internationale Bibliographie der Rezensionen Geistes- und Sozialwissenschaftlicher Literatur, M L A International Bibliography of Books and Articles on the Modern Languages and Literatures, Philosopher's Index, Repertoire Bibliographique de la Philosophie, Russian Academy of Sciences Bibliographies, Personal Alert.

Wiley's Corporate Citizenship initiative seeks to address the environmental, social, economic, and ethical challenges faced in our business and which are important to our diverse stakeholder groups. We have made a long-term commitment to standardize and improve our efforts around the world to reduce our carbon footprint. Follow our progress at http://www.wiley.com/go/citizenship

Disclaimer: The Publisher and Editors cannot be held responsible for errors or any consequences arising from the use of information contained in this journal; the views and opinions expressed do not necessarily reflect those of the Publisher and Editors, neither does the publication of advertisements constitute any endorsement by the Publisher and Editors of the products advertised.

Printed and bound by CPI Group (UK) Ltd, Croydon, CR0 4YY

09/06/2025

14685997-0004